VITAL
CHRISTIANITY

VITAL
CHRISTIANITY

SPIRITUALITY, JUSTICE, AND CHRISTIAN PRACTICE

EDITED BY

David L. Weaver-Zercher
& William H. Willimon

t&t clark

NEW YORK • LONDON

T & T Clark International
Madison Square Park, 15 East 26th Street, New York, NY 10010

T & T Clark International
The Tower Building, 11 York Road, London SE1 7NX

T & T Clark International is a Continuum imprint.

Unless otherwise indicated, biblical quotations are from the New Revised Standard Version of
the Bible, copyright 1989, Division of Christian Education of the National Council of the
Churches of Christ in the United States of America. Used by permission. All rights reserved.

Cover and interior design: Corey Kent

Library of Congress Cataloging-in-Publication Data

Vital Christianity : spirituality, justice, and Christian practice / edited by David L. Weaver-
Zercher and William H. Willimon.
    p. cm.
  Includes bibliographical references and index.
  ISBN 0-567-02551-9 (pbk.)
  1. Christian life. 2. Social justice. 3. Church and social problems. 4. Christian sociology. I.
Weaver-Zercher, David, 1960- II. Willimon, William H.
  BV4501.3.V58 2005
  261.8—dc22
                                          2005006784

Printed in the United States of America
05 06 07 08 09 10   10 9 8 7 6 5 4 3 2 1

CONTENTS

Preface vii
David L. Weaver-Zercher and William H. Willimon

Introduction 1
David L. Weaver-Zercher

PART I: SPIRITUALITY AND SOCIAL JUSTICE CONCEPTUALIZED

1. The Strangeness of Spirit, the Oddness of Justice 13
   William H. Willimon

2. Spirit and Spirituality: Reclaiming Biblical Transcendence 23
   C. Norman Kraus

3. The Love of God as the Source of Spirituality and Social Justice 36
   David Rensberger

PART II: THEOLOGICAL RESOURCES FOR CONNECTING SPIRITUALITY AND SOCIAL JUSTICE

4. Justice, Spirituality, and the Church: The Atonement Connection 49
   J. Denny Weaver

5. Ecclesial Discipleship and the Unity of Spirituality and Social Justice 59
   Richard D. Crane

6. Holistic Spirituality as Witness 72
   Brad J. Kallenberg

PART III: HISTORICAL RESOURCES FOR CONNECTING SPIRITUALITY AND SOCIAL JUSTICE

7. Living Out the Peace of God: The Apostle Paul's Theology
   and Practice of Peace 91
   Raymond H. Reimer

8. The Fulfillment of Human Nature in Eastern Patristic Christianity 102
Lisa D. Maugans Driver

9. The Hiddenness of God and the Justice of God:
Negative Theology as Social Ethical Resource 115
J. Alexander Sider

10. Deconstruction, Messianic Hope, and Just Action 126
Gerald J. Biesecker-Mast

PART IV: CONNECTING SPIRITUALITY AND SOCIAL JUSTICE IN PRACTICE

11. *Prayer:* Just Praying, Acting Justly: Contemplation and Manifestation 141
Kent Ira Groff

12. *Iconography:* Learning to See: The Sacralized Vision of
Byzantine Iconography 154
Randi Sider-Rose

13. *Singing:* Luke's Songs as Melodies of the Marginalized 167
Rick L. Williamson

14. *The Lord's Supper:* Food for the Journey:
Wesleyan Eucharistic Piety and the Integrated Christian Life 177
Aaron Kerr

15. *Table Fellowship:* The Spirituality of Eating Together 188
Reta Halteman Finger

16. *Sabbath-Keeping:* Christian Sabbath-Keeping and the Desire
for Justice 201
L. Roger Owens

17. *Service:* Challenging Legacies of Economic Oppression and Religious
Neglect: Habitat for Humanity in the Mississippi Delta 212
William R. Sutton

18. *Education: Cura Personalis:* The Matrix for Social Justice in
Jesuit Secondary Education 225
*Dominic P. Scibilia (with excurses by Roberto Concepcion Jr.,
Michael Monteleone, Drew Sheeran, Robert Simone, Stephen Spiewak,
and Kapil Verma)*

Contributors 239

Index 241

PREFACE

"*Spirituality* is a tricky word," writes Rodney Clapp in his recent exploration of the topic, *Tortured Wonders: Christian Spirituality for People, Not Angels*. Clapp summarizes well what other students of American religion have so often observed: Americans like to think of themselves as "spiritual" (as opposed to "religious"), but just what they mean by "spiritual" is often amorphous, if not entirely vacuous. Then again, sometimes the word is not at all hard to decipher. It is simply code for rejecting disciplined, sometimes painful, participation in a religious community in favor of self-defined quests for the Divine.

This book rejects that individualistic, God-and-me view of spirituality from cover to cover. At the same time, it does not discard the term. Although we as editors confess a healthy skepticism toward the way "spirituality" is bandied about, we would rather see the term rehabilitated than abandoned. This volume seeks to advance that rehabilitation, both conceptually and practically, by noting the embodied character of Christian spirituality, as well as the connections that exist—or at least *should* exist—between Christian spirituality and endeavors for social justice.

Our choice to focus on one particular aspect of Christian work and witness—the quest for social justice—is no accident. It is an intentional effort to overcome one of the more pernicious bifurcations in contemporary Christianity (especially in North America), a divide that reveals itself in the following question: Should Christians devote their time, their energy, and their money to social concerns, or to spiritual concerns? This easy and unfortunate dualism finds numerous sources of sustenance in the contemporary Church, particularly in the ways Christians are encouraged to think about the work of the Holy Spirit, the practice of Christian spirituality, and the relative importance of the spirit and the body. We are not so naïve to think that one small volume will entirely undercut that long-standing dualism; the roots run too deep for that to happen quickly or easily. Still, we hope the essays that comprise this volume will provide preachers, teachers, and activists with resources to counter the forces, both historical and theological, that contribute to the practice of an attenuated gospel.

The genesis of this volume was a conference called "Reconnecting Spirituality and Social Justice" held at Messiah College in June 2002. Sponsored by the college's Sider Institute for Anabaptist, Pietist, and Wesleyan Studies, and funded by the Lilly Endowment and the Mennonite Central Committee, the conference brought together two hundred fifty scholars, pastors, and activists from a variety of theological traditions to discuss the theology and practice of living integrated Christian lives. Many of the conference presentations came from persons who identify with the Anabaptist and Wesleyan traditions; correspondingly, a number of the essays in this volume espouse or otherwise manifest those theological perspectives. At the same time, this volume gives voice to multiple theological traditions and disparate emphases within those traditions. The result is less a unified argument than it is a coordinated conversation, with the voices in turn offering resources for imagining the scope and contours of vital Christian living. We believe that Christians from a range of theological traditions will benefit from the ideas set forth in the following pages.

As editors, we are grateful for the many people and institutions that enabled this conversation. At Messiah College, Kim Phipps and Jon Stuckey wrote and oversaw the college's Lilly Endowment grant on Christian vocation, which provided funding for both the conference and this resultant volume. A host of people at Messiah assisted with the conference, which was capably coordinated by Mike Baker and his conference services staff. Later, Carol Steffy helped with various administrative details related to producing this book. Mark Fretz read the book proposal in its early stages, and Richard Crane, Douglas Jacobsen, and Jay McDermond offered insightful feedback on the volume's introduction.

Of course, our biggest debt of gratitude goes to those who contributed essays to this volume, a process that involved writing and rewriting, and in many cases, rewriting again. All of the contributors responded graciously to our suggestions (which is not to say that they liked everything we suggested!), and all did their work with care. They should not be held responsible for the whole of this volume. We do hope, however, that they are pleased to be associated with the final product, even as we are pleased to be associated with them.

David L. Weaver-Zercher   William H. Willimon
Grantham, Pennsylvania   Birmingham, Alabama

INTRODUCTION

— David L. Weaver-Zercher —

Christians have long been proponents of both spirituality and social justice. Informed by Jesus' example and compelled by his rendering of the greatest commandments—to love God with all one's heart, soul, and mind, and to love one's neighbor as oneself (Matt 22:37–39)—believers from the first century forward have recognized that a life of Christian faithfulness entails loving commitments to beings both seen and unseen, to realms both material and immaterial. This vision to pursue both works of justice and things of the Spirit long anticipated Jesus' life and the gospel writers who narrated it. Centuries earlier, Hebrew prophets such as Amos and Micah proclaimed that God discounted, and even despised, Israel's spiritual practices—worship, burnt offerings, and the like—unless those who practiced them exhibited accompanying commitments to mercy and justice (see Amos 5:21–24 and Mic 6:6–8).

Christian history is replete with persons who, in both word and deed, fulfilled God's requirements in these regards.[1] But it is nevertheless easier to find examples in the Church's life, particularly in North America, in which spirituality and social justice have been severed from one another or, worse yet, set at odds. At the very least, many North American Christians have tended to champion one of these facets of faithfulness over the other as being the essence of the Christian life. For many, spirituality has comprised that essence, with social justice work reduced to an optional activity for those so inclined. Conversely, other believers have been so concerned with effecting social justice that they have reduced spirituality to a prelude to the *real* work of building the kingdom of God, or perhaps abandoned it altogether. All too rarely, it seems, have Christians been able to live the full-orbed, integrated faith the prophets imagined and Jesus commanded.

1

This book seeks to redress that problem by exploring the numerous threads that can and should connect these spheres of corporate and individual faithfulness. The contributors to this volume do not wish to conflate spirituality and social justice, invoking them as simple synonyms for one another. Nor do we wish to subsume one into the other, reducing social justice work, for example, to merely one among many expressions or components of Christian spirituality.[2] Rather, we wish to focus on the connections, both conceptual and practical, between these two crucial but nonetheless distinguishable aspects of a robust Christian faith. By providing theological and practical resources for reconnecting spirituality and social justice, we hope to counter some disjunctive forces that track a long history in the Christian Church, forces that appear to have as much energy today as ever. More fundamentally, we hope to enable contemporary North American Christians to answer more fully and faithfully Micah's clarion call to do justice, love kindness, and walk humbly with God (Mic 6:8).

Spirituality and Social Justice Defined

For a concept-driven volume like this one, definitions are important. Although such work can be difficult, even laborious, defining terms such as "spirituality" and "social justice" is not just an academic exercise devoid of practical significance. On the positive side, a careful delineation of these terms reveals integral connections between the two even from the start.[3] Conversely, definitions of these terms that too sharply divide one from the other—definitions that we believe are quite common in contemporary North American churches—contribute to a debilitated Christian faith or, as some contributors to this volume would contend, a faith that is not truly Christian.

A few examples of these dichotomized definitions help to illustrate the problem. Some Christians believe spirituality refers to the "inner life" whereas social justice refers to the "outer life," definitions that are often further elaborated by associating spirituality with passive, individual practices and social justice with active, communally oriented practices. This stark distinction between the inner and outer life is probably more common in popular parlance than it is in scholarly discourse. Still, the preface to an influential series on the history of Christian spirituality displays this very assumption, defining spirituality as the "inner dimension of the person . . . , the deepest center of the person [where] the person experiences ultimate reality."[4] In a similar vein, some Christian writers have defined spirituality as the development of one's "vertical" relationship with God, contrasting it to the notion of nurturing compassionate "horizontal" relationships with other people.[5] As with most less than adequate definitions, some useful elements can surely be found in these. But the reliance upon such starkly contrasting notions—"inner" versus "outer," "passive" versus "active," "contemplative" versus "bodily," "vertical" versus "horizontal"—has unwittingly paved the way for separating spirituality from social justice and, in some cases at least, has placed the component activities of the Christian life in an unhealthy hierarchy.[6]

The history of Christianity provides numerous examples of this division and its less than happy consequences. In some eras, for instance, such dichotomized thinking has resulted in the denigration of the body in hopes of nurturing the soul; consider, for example, the medieval and early modern saints who bloodied themselves with whips and starved themselves into a state of "holy anorexia."[7] Or consider the witness of eighteenth and nineteenth-century Christian slaveholders who, in their estimation, could treat their slaves as they wished throughout the week as long as they attended to their slaves' souls on Sundays.[8] Particularly in this latter case, it is easy to see how the strict separation of the "spiritual" from the "material," the "vertical" from the "horizontal," "spirituality" from "social justice," has succeeded in making ethics a secondary, even trivial, concern. And while we do not anticipate chattel slavery making a comeback in America anytime soon, many North American Christians do in fact reduce their faith to privatized relationships with God. Similarly, the claim that a person's heart is "in the right place" seems, in many contemporary churches, to trump all concerns about whether that person is living rightly and treating his or her neighbors appropriately.[9]

While the foregoing examples reveal how "spiritual" concerns have often been given precedence over "worldly" concerns, a stark division can also contribute to the opposite effect: the deprecation of the spiritual in favor of worldly relevance. This, of course, was the route that Marx and many of his followers chose to take, rejecting religion as a clear and intractable detriment to social change. Given the world-denigrating examples of the previous paragraph, it is not difficult to see how Marx and others arrived at the conclusion that religion, Christianity in particular, was more an emotional opiate than it was a force for social change, particularly with respect to remedying economic injustices. Moreover, given the prevalence of injustice throughout the world, it is understandable when self-consciously Christian social activists perceive spirituality as an unnecessary diversion or, perhaps more commonly, as little more than the fuel they need to get through the week. But even if these moves are understandable, they are ultimately counterproductive to establishing the sort of justice that God desires. If nothing else, the deprecation of spirituality runs the risk of producing activist agendas captive to ideologies far removed from the gospel of Jesus Christ, of producing programs for establishing justice that run counter to the reign of God as exemplified in Jesus' life and ministry.

It is easy, of course, to criticize those who have sacrificed spirituality on the altar of social justice, or vice versa, and easier still to complain about definitions that fail to get it right. How then shall we think of spirituality and social justice? Again, it is not our goal in this volume to conflate the two concepts, abolishing all distinctions between them or subsuming one into the other. Rather, we hope to help people think carefully about what spirituality and social justice are, allowing conceptual distinctions between the two, but also envisioning the many ways they can and should connect in fundamentally integral ways.

Toward that end, I offer some provisional definitions of these two terms.[10] *Spirituality is practiced attentiveness to the spirit of God, a posture that helps to attune its practitioners to God's purposes and activities in the world.* Central to this definition is the word "posture," a term that is often used to describe the way a person positions his or her body in the world. Spirituality, then, is a set of *bodily* practices, enacted both by embodied individuals and by "the body of Christ" (see 1 Cor 12), that enable Christians to orient themselves to God. Although the practice of Christian spirituality assumes some theological content, it is more than mere belief, for it also assumes a *commitment* to the triune God who was revealed in Jesus Christ and who continues to make himself known through the work of the Holy Spirit. Even more than that, it entails a careful, even vigilant, attentiveness to the Holy Spirit's ways. Christian spirituality is not haphazardly experiential or miraculously attained. While open to surprises and corrections, it is a practiced, disciplined approach to the Christian life that enables one, or many, to sense God's presence and activity in the world.[11] This posture might be assumed by an individual in his or her prayer closet, though it should never be reduced to a privatized pursuit, disconnected from the body of Christ. To the contrary, the corporate body assumes this posture as well, providing some of the discipline (in the form of guidance and correction) and multiplying the attentiveness, thereby helping the individuals who comprise the Church to see more clearly God's desires for and activity in the world.[12]

Bodies not only posture themselves, however; they also move in ways that make and remake the environment around them. If spirituality is a posture of attentiveness, social justice work is *human activity that seeks to further God's reign through the way the world's resources are shared and the way people and the structures they create treat other people.* This particular definition seeks to delineate the contours of *Christian* social justice work by linking that activity to the New Testament concept of God's reign.[13] According to New Testament scholar James D. G. Dunn, this concept comprised the essence of Jesus' teaching, and it meant at least two things to the first-century listeners who heard and embraced it: "a readiness to acknowledge the importance of the rule of God as a factor in daily living and . . . the recognition that Jesus' ministry provided a window into that rule."[14] Dunn continues by pointing out that this concept now provides the marrow for contemporary Christian discipleship. "Jesus' own teaching and life-style," writes Dunn, "show what living in the light and in the power of the Kingdom should mean" for Christians today.[15] Dunn concludes his exegetical analysis of this phrase by identifying more specifically the contours of living "in the light of the Kingdom," pointing first to a shared responsibility for the poor, then to the need for Christians to reach across social boundaries, and finally to Jesus' command that all this be done according to the principle of love.[16] In sum, the notion of working to further God's reign not only provides the *grounds* for Christians to work for social justice, it also determines the *goals* and the *methods* of that work.[17]

The work of establishing God's reign in the world is a complex and multi-faceted endeavor, to be sure. It is certainly not our intention in this volume to imply that social justice work is the only activity that Christians are called to perform. Neither do we wish to imply that all Christians should abandon their day jobs, whatever they might be, and become full-time social activists. We do believe, however, that *all* Christians should strive to *recognize* the ways in which they and others develop, participate in, and perpetuate social structures that harm others, particularly the poor and vulnerable people of the world. Moreover, we believe that *all* Christians should seek to *counter* and *correct* those structures that are incompatible with God's reign on earth. What form that work will take in a particular Christian's life or a particular Christian community we do not claim to know. At the same time, we reject the notion that only a select few Christians are called to be active in fighting injustice. Doing justice, like walking humbly with God, is part and parcel of the Christian life.[18]

This returns us to the primary purpose of this volume: to limn the connections between (to reconnect, if necessary) spirituality and social justice. Again, the posture of Christian spirituality should not be confused with the goal-oriented work of social justice. But even as they should not be confused, neither should they be set at odds with one another, by definition or in practice. An approach to social justice that dismisses spirituality as trivial cannot help but diminish an attentiveness to God's desires that is absolutely crucial for justice work to be truly *Christian*. Conversely, an approach to spirituality that fails to recognize God's desire for justice does not, in our estimation, deserve to be called *Christian* spirituality. In sum, this volume seeks to help those who claim the name of Christ to assume the right sort of posture as they pursue a particular endeavor that God requires of them.

Spirituality and Social Justice Connected

The first half of this volume is largely an expansion upon this introduction, offering critiques of some prevalent views of spirituality and social justice and, on the constructive side, providing biblical and theological resources for reconceiving and reconnecting these concepts. But even as we hope to develop the theological foundations for reconnecting spirituality and social justice, the contributors to this volume wish to offer more than just theoretical/theological insights to those who find this book's arguments convincing. Therefore, the last and longest section of this volume features essays on "practices," providing readers with some concrete, practical suggestions for recognizing, and perhaps securing, the connectedness of spirituality and social justice.

What exactly do we mean by practices? In their introduction to *Practicing Our Faith: A Way of Life for a Searching People*, Craig Dykstra and Dorothy C. Bass define practices as "things Christian people do together over time in response to and in the light of God's active presence for the life of the world."[19] These practices, which for Dykstra and Bass include things such as providing hospitality, keeping the Sabbath, sharing testimonies, joining in discernment, offering forgiveness, and singing, all have very practical purposes: to feed guests, to experience rest, and to shape communities.[20] But they are not, write Dykstra and Bass, "treasured only for their outcomes." Rather, they are good in and of themselves, providing a sort of "satisfaction" for those who practice them and, taken together, nurturing a way of life that possesses meaning, purpose, and integrity.[21] In sum, practices are the repeated and repeatable expressions of Christian spirituality. They are the day-to-day or otherwise regularly practiced gestures and rituals that comprise and sustain the posture I have called Christian spirituality.

Catholic Christians have long demonstrated a greater affinity for spiritual practices than have their Protestant counterparts, a reality that is not insignificant for a volume like this. From the Protestant Reformation forward, the deep-seated Protestant suspicion of "works righteousness" has resulted in the widespread deprecation of many Christian practices—prayer and Bible reading being the obvious exceptions—and a subsequent disinclination to reflect upon the potentially productive role of disciplined spiritual practices.[22] Roman Catholics have been far less reticent in this regard, thereby producing a much richer and more extensive corpus of literature on the practice of Christian spirituality. Given one of the theses of this book—that a disciplined, practiced attentiveness to God's desires nurtures a concern for social justice—it is no coincidence that the Catholic Church can also claim a more thoroughgoing social justice tradition than Protestant churches, taken as a whole, can rightfully claim.[23] Indeed, the twentieth century alone reveals a remarkable list of Catholic faithful who incarnated the dual concerns of this book—Dorothy Day, Thomas Merton, Oscar Romero, Gustavo Gutiérrez, Henri Nouwen, and Joan Chittister, to mention just a few.[24] And while these aforementioned persons may not be entirely comfortable with the following pedagogic metaphor, Protestants would surely be wise to sit at their Catholic sisters' and brothers' feet as they ponder the connections between spirituality and social justice.[25]

That said, this particular volume is a largely Protestant volume, written by Protestants with Protestant readers in mind.[26] The editors of this volume do not intend this theological orientation to suggest that Protestants cannot learn from Catholics (or from Orthodox Christians, for that matter) or that Protestants are now upstaging Catholics in their attention to spirituality and social justice. Rather, we believe that Protestants, who have their own theological resources to bring to bear on the issue of connecting spirituality and social justice but who have nonetheless been relatively silent on that topic, need to find their own voices. This volume provides a forum for that to happen. And while such an endeavor is not entirely unique in contemporary Protestantism, it is, unfortunately, all too rare.[27]

We begin, then, with some careful definitional work. The first section, titled "Spirituality and Social Justice Conceptualized," features three essays that deal in foundational ways with terms such as "spirit," "spirituality," and "justice." With an eye toward both Christian history and the contemporary Church, the authors of these essays are constructive critics, challenging some theologically flimsy views of spirituality and social justice and offering language for thinking more responsibly about the concepts this volume wishes to connect. And, in some provisional ways, they begin to make those connections.

The second section, titled "Theological Resources for Connecting Spirituality and Social Justice," continues the volume's conceptual work by identifying more explicitly some theological frameworks for connecting spirituality and social justice. While each of the essays in this section pursues a unique theological track, the notion of *the Church* as the primary locus for connecting spirituality and social justice emerges prominently in all three. In other words, the authors who have contributed to this section, while directing their readers' attention to different theological concepts and considerations, all agree on two points: first, that Christian spirituality is not a privatized, individualistic pursuit, and second, that social justice work is the work of the entire Church, not that of a few select individuals.

The third section, "Historical Resources for Connecting Spirituality and Social Justice," complements the second section by addressing some important issues in narrower, more historically focused ways. Each of the four essays in this section examines the witness of a historical figure or figures, bringing to bear these figures' insights on this discussion. Some of these historical subjects are venerated Christian theologians (the Apostle Paul, the Cappadocian fathers, and the sixth-century Syrian monk known as Pseudo-Dionysius), and some are contemporary social critics (Jacques Derrida and Slavoj Žižek). The contexts, concerns, and even the commitments of these persons vary dramatically; Derrida and Žižek, for example, would not even profess to be Christians. In each case, however, these persons offer insights for connecting the posture of one's life to the establishment of God's reign on earth, a reign characterized by peace, justice, and care for all creation.

The volume's fourth and final section, titled "Connecting Spirituality and Social Justice in Practice," returns us to the idea of Christian practices. Each of the eight practices considered in this section—prayer, meditation/iconography, singing, the Lord's Supper, table fellowship, Sabbath-keeping, service, and education—constitutes a bodily gesture that orients those who participate in the practice. It is quite conceivable that these practices could be performed in such a way as to ignore the work of social justice. To choose just one example, most North American churches exhibit very little regard for social justice in their congregational singing practices. According to our authors, however, social justice can and should be part and parcel of all these practices. And although the authors do not pretend to provide approaches that can be casually applied to all Christian communities in cookie-cutter fashion, they do provide illustrations and/or theological rationales for connecting these spiritual practices to the work of social justice.

We recognize this volume is only an introduction. Not only could other spiritual practices be usefully considered, a companion volume could very well be organized around particular justice issues (racism, economic oppression, and others) and their connections to spiritual practices. Indeed, we recognize that Christians working on these specific social issues will not find much in our volume regarding the way *particular* justice issues might be approached in spiritually sensitive and integrated ways. Still, we hope that our conceptual efforts from the standpoint of Christian theology and practice will provide serviceable resources to all justice-seeking Christians as they ponder, and seek to incarnate, the connections between Christian spirituality and the work of social justice.

Notes

1. For some recent examples, see Gary Commins, *Spiritual People, Radical Lives: Spirituality and Justice in Four 20th Century American Lives* (San Francisco: International Scholars Publications, 1996). Commins probes the lives of A. J. Muste, Dorothy Day, Martin Luther King Jr., and Thomas Merton.

2. The tendency to use the word "spirituality" as a synonym for the whole of the Christian life, thus subsuming everything into it, is quite common. Anne Carr calls spirituality "the whole of our deepest religious beliefs, convictions, and patterns of thought, emotion, and behavior in respect to what is ultimate, to God." Similarly, Alister McGrath defines Christian spirituality as "the quest for a fulfilled and authentic Christian existence, involving the bringing together of the fundamental ideas of Christianity and the whole experience of living . . . the Christian faith." This volume assumes a narrower definition of spirituality, a definition that will be specified in the following section. See Anne Carr, "On Feminist Spirituality," in *Exploring Christian Spirituality: An Ecumenical Reader* (ed. Kenneth J. Collins; Grand Rapids: Baker, 2000), 37; and Alister E. McGrath, *Christian Spirituality* (Oxford: Blackwell, 1999), 2.

3. One contributor to this volume finds the notion of *reconnecting* spirituality and social justice flawed, since it assumes separation or detachment. According to J. Denny Weaver, the notion of reconnecting mistakenly assumes that spirituality is something that exists independently from other facets of the Christian life, including justice work. From a theological standpoint, Weaver's warning is a good

one, and this volume affirms his contention that an authentic Christian faith is an integrated faith, the components of which cannot be detached from one another. From an analytical standpoint, however, this volume assumes that spirituality and social justice are not precisely the same thing and can thus be examined in turn. Moreover, sociological analysis reveals that many self-professing Christians do in fact bifurcate spiritual practices from concerns about social justice. In that sense, at least, it is valid to advocate for *reconnecting* spirituality and social justice.

4. Ewert Cousins, "Preface to the Series," in *Christian Spirituality: Post-Reformation and Modern* (ed. Louis Dupré and Don E. Saliers; New York: Crossroad, 1989), xii.

5. Klaus Issler, *Wasting Time with God: A Christian Spirituality of Friendship with God* (Downers Grove, Ill.: InterVarsity Press, 2001), tends in this direction. In addition to defining spirituality as an "experientially dynamic relationship with our trinitarian God" (25–26), Issler characterizes the pursuit of "loving relationships" with other people as a means to an end, performed "*in order to* continue growing in our loving relationship with God" (39–40; emphasis added).

6. For a similar critique, see Rodney Clapp, *Tortured Wonders: Christian Spirituality for People, Not Angels* (Grand Rapids: Brazos, 2004). Clapp writes that too many Christians assume that spirituality is something "inward and invisible, a hidden affair of the private heart" (15). Clapp argues, as this volume does, that Christian spirituality must account for the fact that Christians are embodied beings (people), not bodiless spirits (angels).

7. See Rudolph M. Bell, *Holy Anorexia* (Chicago: University of Chicago Press, 1985). Bell writes that, in addition to starving herself, Saint Veronica (1660–1727) used a dozen different "sharply studded flagellating instruments" to beat her body, wore a heavy wooden yoke on her shoulders, and pressed her tongue with a large rock (79).

8. See H. Shelton Smith, *In His Image, But . . . : Racism in Southern Religion, 1780–1910* (Durham, N.C.: Duke University Press, 1972).

9. For evidence of this, see Robert Wuthnow, *After Heaven: Spirituality in America since the 1950s* (Berkeley: University of California Press, 1998); Wade Clark Roof, *A Generation of Seekers: The Spiritual Journeys of the Baby Boom Generation* (San Francisco: HarperSanFrancisco, 1993); and Harold Bloom, *The American Religion: The Emergence of the Post-Christian Nation* (New York: Simon & Schuster, 1992).

10. Please note that these are *my* definitions, not ones adopted by all the contributors to this volume. That said, many of the contributors to this volume operate according to these definitions or very similar ones. Moreover, these definitions provide the underpinnings for the organization of this volume.

11. I will return to the idea of practices later in this introduction. See also Brad J. Kallenberg's essay, "Holistic Spirituality as Witness" (ch. 6).

12. For similar definitional emphases, see Fred Kammer, *Salted with Fire: Spirituality for the Faithjustice Journey* (New York: Paulist Press, 1995), 8 ("Spirituality is essentially about seeing God's presence and activity in the midst of human reality"); and Clapp, *Tortured Wonders*, 15 ("Christian spirituality is participation and formation in the life of the church that is created and sustained by the Holy Spirit").

13. Needless to say, numerous definitions of "justice" circulate today, as do many grounds for doing justice work. See Alasdair MacIntyre, *Whose Justice? Which Rationality?* (Notre Dame, Ind.: University of Notre Dame Press, 1988), who writes in his introduction: "Some conceptions [of justice] appeal to inalienable human rights, others to some notion of social contract, and others again to a standard of utility. Moreover, the rival theories of justice which embody these rival conceptions also give expression to disagreements about the relationship of justice to other human goods" (1).

14. James D. G. Dunn, *Jesus' Call to Discipleship* (Cambridge: Cambridge University Press, 1992), 13.

15. Ibid., 31.

16. After outlining Jesus' theology of poverty, Dunn concludes, "If Jesus is right, a discipleship of the non-poor which lacks a sense of oneness with the poor, and so of shared responsibility for the poor, is in danger of forfeiting the blessing reserved for the poor, the blessing of the Kingdom" (ibid., 61).

17. Walter Wink and others have interpreted Jesus' teaching about the reign of God to mean the rejection of violence, arguing that violent acts, even in the pursuit of a particular vision of justice, participate in a "domination system" that is antithetical to "God's domination-free order" (the reign of God). Many contributors to this volume agree with Wink's assessment, and thereby link social justice work to nonviolence. Not all the contributors to this volume are pacifists, however. See Walter Wink,

Engaging the Powers: Discernment and Resistance in a World of Domination (Minneapolis: Fortress, 1992), especially the section titled "Engaging the Powers Nonviolently" (175–257).

18. This reference, of course, is to Mic 6:8, which contains a metaphor ("walk humbly with your God") that further punctuates the embodied nature of spirituality.

19. Craig Dykstra and Dorothy C. Bass, "Times of Yearning, Practices of Faith," in *Practicing Our Faith: A Way of Life for a Searching People* (ed. Dorothy C. Bass; San Francisco: Jossey-Bass, 1997), 5. Dykstra and Bass credit moral philosopher Alasdair MacIntyre, specifically his work *After Virtue: A Study in Moral Theory* (2nd ed.; Notre Dame, Ind.: University of Notre Dame Press, 1984), for providing the philosophical foundation to their book's argument.

20. My list of practices, outlined below, overlaps with but also departs from the twelve practices discussed by Dykstra, Bass, and their assembled authors in *Practicing Our Faith*.

21. Dykstra and Bass, "Times of Yearning," 7.

22. The work of the evangelical Quaker Richard J. Foster, especially his book *Celebration of Discipline: The Path to Spiritual Growth* (San Francisco: Harper & Row, 1978), is the exception that proves the rule. Despite his book's Protestant-oriented defense of spiritual practices, Foster was roundly criticized in some Protestant circles for supposedly advocating a works-oriented theology.

23. The caveat "taken as a whole" is important here, for the African-American church, to take a notable example, which in the United States is largely Protestant, can also boast an impressive history in this regard. While the historical record is no doubt mixed, C. Eric Lincoln and Lawrence H. Mamiya conclude that "the Black Church heritage has contributed to both the survival and liberation traditions that have shaped black attitudes toward politics" by fostering "the motivation, discipline, and courage needed for this-worldly political action." C. Eric Lincoln and Lawrence H. Mamiya, *The Black Church in the African American Experience* (Durham, N.C.: Duke University Press, 1990), 234.

24. For representative works, see Dorothy Day, *The Long Loneliness: The Autobiography of Dorothy Day* (New York: Harper, 1952); Thomas Merton, *The Hidden Ground of Love: The Letters of Thomas Merton on Religious Experience and Social Concerns* (ed. William H. Shannon; San Diego: Harcourt Brace Jovanovich, 1993); Oscar A. Romero, *The Violence of Love* (ed. James R. Brockman; San Francisco: Harper & Row, 1988); Gustavo Gutiérrez, *A Theology of Liberation: History, Politics, and Salvation* (trans. and ed. Sister Caridad Inda and John Eagleson; Maryknoll, N.Y.: Orbis, 1973); Henri Nouwen, *The Road to Peace: Writings on Peace and Justice* (ed. John Dear; Maryknoll, N.Y.: Orbis, 1998); and Joan Chittister, *The Fire in These Ashes: A Spirituality of Contemporary Religious Life* (Kansas City, Mo.: Sheed & Ward, 1995).

25. Other less celebrated Catholics have written extensively on the topic of connecting spirituality and social justice. For a start, see Donal Dorr, *Spirituality and Justice* (Maryknoll, N.Y.: Orbis, 1984); James McGinnis, *Journey into Compassion: A Spirituality for the Long Haul* (Maryknoll, N.Y.: Orbis, 1989); and Wilkie Au, *By Way of the Heart: Toward a Holistic Christian Spirituality* (New York: Paulist Press, 1989).

26. The one authorial exception is ch. 18, which was written by a Catholic school teacher and his students at St. Peter's Preparatory School in Jersey City, N.J. Of course, other contributors to this volume draw heavily on Roman Catholic thinkers, and still others point to the theology and practices of Eastern Christianity as helpful resources for connecting spirituality and social justice.

27. Two relatively recent books written by Protestants on this topic are Arthur Paul Boers, *On Earth as in Heaven: Justice Rooted in Spirituality* (Scottdale, Pa.: Herald Press, 1991); and Maria Harris, *Proclaim Jubilee: A Spirituality for the Twenty-First Century* (Louisville, Ky.: Westminster John Knox, 1996).

PART I

SPIRITUALITY AND SOCIAL JUSTICE CONCEPTUALIZED

1

THE STRANGENESS OF SPIRIT, THE ODDNESS OF JUSTICE

— *William H. Willimon* —

Jesus makes the world strange. He loves to defamiliarize. We think we know the "real world" until Jesus enters and revalues the world. How often did he begin his stories with, "The kingdom of God is like . . ."? He seems interested first in getting us to see what is going on—what God is up to—before bothering us with what we ought to do.

"Jesus, say something ethical."

"*A man was going down the road from Jerusalem to Jericho when he fell among thieves who stripped him, beat him, and left him half dead. By chance, down the road came a Samaritan [or was it a Mafioso? or a member of the PLO?] who stopped, ripped his suit into bandages, put the man on the leather seat of his Porsche, took him to the hospital, and spent every dime he had on the man's recovery. In this kingdom, sometimes your saviors will be your enemies. Now, go and do likewise.*"

When we talk ethics, we usually think with Immanuel Kant, who sought to detach ethics from subservience to any story other than the story that we had freely selected on our own.[1] More specifically, Kant sought to free ethics from the narratives of religion, basing them instead upon anthropological generalizations such as "reason." This led to particular Christian convictions and narration being suppressed in order to develop an ethic that would apply to everyone in general and no one in particular. Kant did this in order to make ethics as universal as possible—right behavior done by anyone anywhere. Never mind that we have learned in recent years how provincial and limited were the Enlightenment ethics of Kant. He remains the basis for most of our thought about ethics.

Karl Barth, on the other hand, launched his *Church Dogmatics* with the doctrine of the Trinity, for it is there that "we actually gather who the God is who reveals Himself."[2] For Barth, ethics began not where modern thought placed it, in human self-consciousness, but in divine being and action. It is only because of a God who reveals what he is up to that we know what we are to be doing. In sum, Barth sought to make ethics as particularly *theological* as possible.

This is but one reason why it is difficult to speak of spirituality and social justice. The problem is not only in the words "spiritual" and "justice" but also in the word "and." To state the matter in this way is already to assume that we are dealing with two separate realms—spirituality and something that we know as justice. Stanley Hauerwas has criticized this conjunctive theology.[3] Christians cannot know justice without knowing spirituality. Or as Barth might say, we must try to think about these matters in such a way as to avoid escaping from the reality of God.[4]

Spirituality, American Style

"Spirituality," says the humorist qua theologian George Carlin, has become "the last refuge of a failed human." It is "just another way of distracting yourself from who you really are."[5] "Spirituality" is Christianity rendered so insubstantial and innocuous that no one could get hurt being religious. According to Marva Dawn, it exchanges the faith once delivered for a spiritual high instantly delivered.[6] Spirituality thus conceived is part of our continuing attempt to make Christianity intelligible and useful to the dominant economic order without attachment to that set of cultural habits called the Church.[7]

How did we get to spirituality from such a decidedly materialistic faith? When philosopher William James, father of all truly American theology, said, "God is the natural appellation, for us Christians at least, for the supreme reality, so I will call this higher part of the universe by the name God," we began down a road from theology to anthropology.[8] James led to Reinhold Niebuhr's severely attenuated God, who was too weak to offer resistance to the American belief that America was the future of the world. Niebuhr's theological move was made for political reasons; sentimental theism, emptied of cross and resurrection, gave Americans the minimalist theology that Niebuhr thought was demanded by America's pluralist environment. In America, the only way to maintain a pluralistic religious society was to render religion personal and private, subservient to the prior claims of a liberal, democratic political order. This, we were told, is "freedom of religion." By this arrangement, theological claims lost their public status. American Christians jettisoned public claims such as "Jesus Christ is Lord" for the privilege of being able to participate in the public discussion of issues such as justice. American Christians were now content to contribute insights derived from their relationship with the "higher part of the universe."

Ironically, such an arrangement not only robbed Christians of anything interesting to say in discussions about the public good, but it also rendered them unable to analyze or to resist those American practices upon which so much injustice thrives. Spirituality is no worthy competitor for capitalism. Instead, one suspects spirituality is but the latest product of the consumer economy.

Whose Social Justice?

If there is anything that Christians can agree on these days, it is on the need to do justice.[9] A Christian advocate for justice is about as interesting as a Christian advocate for love; in fact, it is even *less* interesting, for as Reinhold Niebuhr convinced us, Christian love is far too individualistic, too specific to the demands of Jesus, to be relevant in the curing of social ills.[10] "If You Want Peace, Work for Justice" is how the bumper sticker puts it. The only way out of a world at war is by reshaping society through the eradication of structural injustice.

Aristotle taught that justice was giving each his or her due. This notion of justice appeals to most Americans. We are a society of rights, and justice is no more than giving someone rightful due. On the other hand, love tends toward charity—demeaning, if well-intentioned, gifts to the poor. Justice gives us something to do, something that we ought to do, and is thus a supremely ethical concept. Though we are a bit unnerved by Niebuhr's warning that "no society ever achieved peace without incorporating injustice into its harmony," still, justice is as close as we will get in this world to something approximating the kingdom of God.[11] If we want peace we ought to work for justice—even though, as Niebuhr warns, it is precisely our desire for peace, our lust for harmony in a most disharmonious world, that leads to injustice.

In defining justice as giving each his or her due, Aristotle does so from a prior assumption that he knows who we truly are and are meant to be. He does not talk ethically about justice until he talks philosophically about who we are (ontology) and for what we were made (teleology). So we cannot tally justice, giving each of us our due, until we have first inquired, "Who are we?" If our answer to that question is different from Aristotle's, then our account of justice will be different. Or perhaps more to the point, we ought first to ask, "Where are we? Is this world, with some astute social tinkering, our home?" Aristotle avoids dreamy Platonic visions of what ought to be, preferring the more secure footing of what is. But what if Christianity is, in great part, a quarrel with the world over what is?

Unlike Aristotle, Christian reflection on justice begins not with reflection on the nature of the magnanimous man of the resonant voice and the slow gait, not in a general conception of the good or an analysis of those excellencies of character required to be virtuous people, but rather in being obedient to the one who said, "Follow me." Jesus Christ is the embodiment, the enactment, of the righteousness of God. Discipleship is his call to ordinary folk like us to come and be part of that kingdom that makes us odd, not because the world is normal and Jesus is strange, but because Jesus is the truth in a world that likes to live by lies.

Following this Jesus will unavoidably set Christians at odds with the most prominent American conceptions of justice. Liberalism hoped to create just societies through the design of just procedures, just legislation, and just rules. Aristotle taught that there is no way to have justice without the creation of wise people who have cultivated the virtues necessary for just behavior. Christians agree; there is no way to have justice without just people. But Christians should fear any attempt to secure justice through an agreed-upon set of universal principles among people who share no common goods or virtues. Indeed, wise Christians surmise a connection between liberal democracy's attempt to do justice *without God* and the creation of peculiarly violent cultures such as ours, which must incarcerate nearly a million and a half of its citizens in order to make society work. Only a crucified God who convicts us of our sin and who forgives us, only a God who calls people like us to be part of the revolution called the kingdom of God, only a God who places us within a new family called Church—a place where ordinary folk like us are given the gifts we need to live just lives—only this God enables justice.

We ought therefore to be cautious in our talk of justice. Augustine warned us that pagan virtues (including justice?) require Christian love before they can be radical enough for Christian edification. Luther warned that even the noblest pagan virtue, if not embraced under the cross, is just another scheme for self-salvation.[12] If we assume with the Westminster Confession that we were created "to glorify God and to enjoy him forever," then this peculiar sort of spirituality will make a major difference in our understanding of justice. "What ought I to do?" is necessarily subservient to "Who am I created to be?"

Too often, however, even Christians' conceptions of justice are predominantly formed by the larger culture in which they live. For example, I assume that poverty is bad and ought to be eradicated. Yet I do so mainly from the standpoint of an American society that assumes, in contradiction to the Westminster Confession, that the "chief end of man" is to accumulate as much stuff as possible, that there is no way to live a good life apart from having a great deal of material possessions. The United States is willing to tolerate great economic disparities in the interest of great political freedom for the individual to acquire as much as possible. We are even told by our political leaders that this is why so much of the world hates us: They envy our freedom. Quite predictably, in the aftermath of the September 11 attacks, we were duly informed that the most patriotic thing we could do was to shop, thus exposing the notion that the primary purpose of our national polity is unrestrained accumulation. Then along comes Jesus, who not only blessed the poor, promising them a place at the center of his coming kingdom, but who also calls *me* to become poor. It is then that I realize that some of my concern for the poor is a defense against the Christian question, "If I am following Jesus, then why am I so rich?"

Aristotelian appeals to the principle of distributive justice do not seem to work in all circumstances of inequality. Some poverty may not be due to injustice—the failure by a society to give each person his or her due—but to bad luck. I recently returned from a mission trip to Haiti, the poorest place in the Western Hemisphere. Haitians are suffering from a history of bad government and poor land use, as well as American mismanagement. Still, I do not see how they can be empowered to improve their material situation appreciably. Haiti thus presents a wonderful opportunity, not just for economic development but also for charity. It is also an opportunity for me to repent of how superficial I am in comparison with many of the Haitians I met. Haiti is just the sort of place where only love would go. But that, I suspect, is a prejudiced Christian statement that has been conditioned by hearing stories like we find in Luke 16, where the poor end up in the bosom of Abraham and the rich go to hell.

I am making here the point made better by philosopher Alasdair MacIntyre in his contention that, when talking about justice, the important question is not how much, or how little, by what means, or which strategy, but rather "whose justice?"[13] There is no such thing as freestanding, self-evident, nonconflicted justice. There are only different stories of what justice would look like if we ever saw it. Justice is dependent upon and linked to social practices and configurations that make justice meaningful. In fact, MacIntyre shows that Aristotle, in criticizing *pleonexia*, which some translate as "greed," was criticizing more than self-seeking gotten out of hand. Rather, Aristotle considered *pleonexia* to be the disposition of character that deludes us into thinking that life can be enhanced through acquisition of a higher standard of material well-being.[14] Aristotle would thus be unhappy not simply with our poor distribution of economic goods but also with our nation's assumption (so well indoctrinated through advertising) that the freedom and the means to acquire more things is enough reason to have politics in the first place.

All accounts of justice, even Kant's, are tradition dependent, symbiotic with some prior story of what is going on in the world and why we are here. Appeals to justice do not save us from debates about what sort of world we have and who we are meant to be. Rather, they drive us into such debates if appeals to justice are to be more than mere sentimentality.

Jesus on Justice

"Jesus, say something about justice."

"For to all those who have, more will be given, and they will have an abundance; but from those who have nothing, even what they have will be taken away" (Matt 25:29).

Or, *"When evening came, the owner of the vineyard said to his manager, 'Call the laborers and give them their pay, beginning with the last and then going to the first.' When those hired about five o'clock came, each of them received the usual daily wage. Now when the first came, they thought they would receive more; but each of them also received the usual daily wage. And when they received it, they grumbled against the landowner. . . . But he replied to one of them, 'Friend, . . . are you envious because I am generous?' So the last will be first, and the first will be last"* (Matt 20:8–16).

In light of these two statements of Jesus on justice, we should assume that if and when we Christians have anything to contribute to discussions about justice, our contribution will be considered odd. It will be considered odd because it is inextricably linked to Jesus as the embodiment of a strange announcement of what is going on in the world. Any account of justice that is peculiarly Christian will necessarily build on the answer to a prior question, "What sort of God have we got?" or, perhaps, "What sort of God has got us?"

It is curious that contemporary Christians attempt to talk politics by talking justice, an infrequent biblical word. In the New Testament, *dikaiosunē* is translated in the NRSV as "righteousness" seventy-four times and as "justice" only three times (e.g., in a discussion justifying the wrath of God against our sin, Paul writes in Rom 3:5 that "our injustice serves to confirm the justice of God"). Furthermore, there is no place in the Christian Scriptures where there is any interest in justice as a freestanding, independent concept. All references to justice, few though they are, are in the context of the righteousness of God. To be sure, it is much easier for us to talk about matters of right and wrong as issues of justice than it is to discern and honor the righteousness of God. Still, I suspect that talk about justice increases in a world without God. This helps to explain why much of our justice talk provides ideological justification for the growth of state power that provides the political structure for our godlessness. Justice becomes that means of action whereby our actions are unaccountable to Christian presuppositions.[15]

I further suspect that the main reason American Christians are reluctant to speak of the righteousness of God is that we fear doing so would relegate us to the fringes of political debate. We would thereby lose any possibility of power. True, the power we want is the power to do good, and while there is nothing wrong with people like us wanting power, again we must raise the prior questions: To what end? For what purpose? With what world in mind?

Indeed, what world do American Christians have in mind? Many people in the Middle East believe, not without reason, that our drive to liberate Muslims from the Qur'an in order to increase democracy has much to do with the domination of, and our enslavement to, Hollywood, Wall Street, the Pentagon, and Microsoft. These Middle Eastern observers are perceptive enough to be unimpressed by what we call "freedom," and they are consequently unmoved by our accusations of their "injustice." In a related vein, we can only launch a "just war" against Middle Eastern countries if we first distinguish between "good" and "bad" Muslims, the latter of which are also called "Muslim fanatics" or "Muslim fundamentalists." As best I can tell, a "Muslim fanatic" is anyone running around for whom "Muslim" is a more important qualifier than "American." In most Americans' minds, it is a "just war" if we kill to right the wrongs perpetrated against the United States; it is "insanity" if others kill to right the wrongs done against Allah.

Christians ought to be the sort of people who serve America by questioning the justice of such thinking. We do not question such thinking because we believe that it is just for some Muslims to kill in the name of God, but rather because we are trying to worship a God for whom killing to preserve the honor of a government or a political-economic system is no better than killing for God. We hold that strange notion not necessarily because we have a higher notion of justice than our Muslim brothers and sisters, but because we have been met by a God who refuses to let us defend him.

During Islamic Awareness Week at Duke University a few years ago, I was on a panel discussing religious conflict. The visiting imam said, "Islam is very tolerant of other faiths. In fact, the Prophet Muhammad says that if your religion is attacked by an unbeliever, then I am under obligation to defend you. I must punish the one who persecutes you." I responded, "I wish Jesus had said that! There are people out there that need to be punished! Unfortunately, Jesus wouldn't allow his disciples to use the sword to defend him."

For notions of this sort our God was crucified, not by Muslim fanatics, but rather by the state. Christians, informed by the story of a savior who was murdered by people (Pilate and Caiaphas) who wanted "peace with justice," should therefore always be suspicious of peace-with-justice claims. Stanley Hauerwas provides a poignant warning:

> In the interest of working for justice, Christians [too often] allow their imaginations to be captured by concepts of justice determined by the presuppositions of liberal societies, and as a result, contribute to the development of societies that make substantive accounts of justice less likely. Out of an understandable desire to be politically and socially relevant, we lose the critical ability to stand against the limits of our social

orders. We forget that the first thing as Christians we have to hold before any society is not justice but God.[16]

In sum, ethics begins in imagination, with some vision of where the world is moving and what is going on. Christians believe that what is going on is gospel, good news, the cross and resurrection of Jesus. If we have our imaginations captured by sub-Christian accounts of justice, we will forfeit our ability to say anything the world is dying to hear.

Jesus Justice, Christian Spirituality

A Duke University student who refuses to hear me preach (because I'm "soft on Scripture," he says) was telling me that his fundamentalist church has just purchased an apartment in Durham's worst public housing project. A family from the church lives in the apartment and uses it as a center for ministry within the projects. Families in the church are matched with families within the projects. They bring their families to church activities, including worship, and share at least three meals a week together as families. The church runs evening classes in the projects on how to get a job and how to use a computer. "Jesus is using us to rescue one family at a time by becoming their best friends," said the student.

This is Jesus justice and Christian spirituality. The Church is often defended by Christians (and tolerated by unbelievers) as a helpful means of being "spiritual" and/or as an agent for "social justice." For us, Church becomes the *content* of spirituality, or at least a fundamental, bodily challenge to the notion that Christianity is about anything "spiritual." Church is also the only means we have of knowing what justice looks like. When Christians think justice, we must think Church, for the Church is not only where we learn the true story of what is going on in the world, it is also the culture that Christian practices produce. For Christians, the truth of an idea like justice must reside in its practical force, in the way it is embedded in, or absent from, the habits and practices of those who claim to follow Jesus.[17]

I recently spent a few days at a Florida retirement center filled with retired missionaries and church workers. I learned that fifty people there speak Arabic, mostly due to their earlier work for the Church. These people have a very interesting read on America's "war on terrorism." Most of them, because of Jesus, have spent their lives in predominately Islamic countries. They proudly described to me their project whereby they produce self-propelled vehicles, which they then donate to missionaries around the world to give to otherwise immobile land mine victims. They have built and donated nearly a thousand of these vehicles over the years, putting a new face on how one should spend the golden years of retirement in Florida. Once again, Jesus justice and Christian spirituality.

One evening in a dormitory at Duke, I was leading a group of students through Matt 20, which begins with Jesus' parable of the laborers in the vineyard. A farmer had some grapes to be harvested. He went out in the early morning, found some workers, and assured them that he would pay them "what's right." They went to work. That ought to be the end of the story. Yet as is so typical of Jesus' stories, it is not. At midmorning, the farmer is back downtown. He hires more workers. At noon, in the afternoon, and finally *one hour before quitting time,* he is back downtown hiring more workers. At the end of the day he pays everyone the same wage.

I asked the students, "What interests you about this story?" One student replied, "He's never at the farm!" And she was right. Here is a farmer who seems to be more interested in employment than grape harvesting. Most of the action in this parable is expended in these repeated forays back and forth into town. Remember that the farmer told his employees that he would pay them "what's right." It raises the issue of "what's right?" What is justice? For most Americans, justice is a blindfolded woman with scales in the one hand and a sword in the other—blind, dispassionate, bureaucratic judgment. For Jesus, justice appears to be a matter of relentless reaching, seeking, intrusion, and invitation.

Anyone who hears such stories and dares to do them will have some strange notions about both spirituality and justice.

Notes

1. "Enlightenment is man's release from his self-incurred tutelage. Tutelage is man's inability to make use of his understanding without direction from another. Self-incurred is this tutelage when its cause lies not in lack of reason but in lack of resolution and courage to use it without direction from another." Immanuel Kant, *Foundations of the Metaphysics of Morals, and What Is Enlightenment?* (trans. Lewis White Beck; New York: Liberal Arts Press, 1959), 85.

2. Karl Barth, *Church Dogmatics*, I/1 (trans. G. W. Bromiley et al.; Edinburgh: T&T Clark, 1957), 358.

3. Stanley M. Hauerwas, *Sanctify Them in the Truth: Holiness Exemplified* (Nashville: Abingdon, 1998), 35.

4. This is a paraphrase of Barth who, after equating a "general conception of ethics" with "sin," wrote, "There can be no more trying to escape the grace of God." Barth, *Church Dogmatics*, II/2, 518.

5. George Carlin, *Napalm and Silly Putty* (New York: Hyperion, 2001), 29.

6. See Marva J. Dawn, *Reaching Out without Dumbing Down: A Theology of Worship for the Turn-of-the-Century Culture* (Grand Rapids: Eerdmans, 1995).

7. See Hauerwas, *Sanctify Them in the Truth*, 157–73.

8. As quoted in Stanley M. Hauerwas, *A Better Hope: Resources for a Church Confronting Capitalism, Democracy, and Postmodernity* (Grand Rapids: Brazos, 2000), 34.

9. In the following discussion I draw on Stanley Hauerwas, "The Politics of Justice," in *After Christendom: How the Church Is to Behave if Freedom, Justice, and a Christian Nation are Bad Ideas* (Nashville: Abingdon, 1991), 45–68. I would like not to be so indebted to Hauerwas on these ideas; however, I cannot get beyond his analysis of the matters before us. Failing at being an "original thinker," all I can do is be a rather flaccid Hauerwasian.

10. According to Niebuhr, love was a fine (if rather impossible) ideal for one-on-one relationships but not for groups or nations. Justice, something less specifically demanding than love, was what was needed in a "realistic" assessment of social problems. Niebuhr's effort to win a place for Christians in

discussions of these issues within the wider society through appeals to "justice" is itself a curious commentary on his rather vague, undemanding, and also unchristian notions of justice.

11. Reinhold Niebuhr, *Moral Man and Immoral Society: A Study in Ethics and Politics* (New York: Charles Scribner's Sons, 1932), 129.

12. See Stanley M. Hauerwas and Charles Pinches, *Christians among the Virtues: Theological Conversations with Ancient and Modern Ethics* (Notre Dame, Ind.: University of Notre Dame Press, 1997), 27–28.

13. See Alasdair C. MacIntyre, *Whose Justice? Which Rationality?* (Notre Dame, Ind.: University of Notre Dame Press, 1988).

14. Ibid., 112.

15. In this regard we should recall that George W. Bush's first name for the war against the Taliban was "Operation Infinite Justice." He backed down only after some Muslims reminded our Methodist president that even the U.S. Army cannot give us that much justice.

16. Hauerwas, "Politics of Justice," 68.

17. Christian discipleship requires discipline, that is, it requires a community that sustains and enables, through Christian practices, the discipline of discipleship.

SPIRIT AND SPIRITUALITY: RECLAIMING BIBLICAL TRANSCENDENCE

— C. Norman Kraus —

In the 1960s and 1970s, words such as "parachurch" and "pre-evangelism" became common parlance in evangelical circles. In addition to being popularly disseminated and widely embraced, these terms manifested a concept of the Church and its mission that was based upon a clear division between the spiritual realm, which implied a supernatural reality, and the natural realm, which included the physical, psychological, and social dimensions of life. Most evangelical leaders in these years still championed dualistic supernaturalism, which Princeton theologian B. B. Warfield had decades earlier dubbed the life breath of orthodox Christianity.[1] In this rendering of the faith, *the gospel* was a strictly "spiritual" message that called for "supernatural" rebirth. Correspondingly, *salvation* was defined as a spiritual and theological transaction apart from which *social service* was humanistic busy work. For these evangelicals, the true mission of the Church was evangelism, which they understood as calling people to belief. Attempts to express New Testament *agape* in social terms could only be justified as "*pre*-evangelism."[2]

Although the evangelical movement, broadly defined, has moved beyond this point, the issue remains a source of tension. For example, Franklin Graham's careful distinction between the "spiritual" and the "social" activities of his relief organization, Samaritan's Purse, and his insistence upon verbal apologetics against Islam, highlight the tension. Even popular magazines have honed in on

this dilemma, particularly as it pertains to the presence of Christian missionaries in societies that have made proselytizing illegal.[3] What does it mean to
evangelize Muslims? How is the "secular humanitarian team" of an evangelical
missions organization related to its goal of evangelism? Is "nonproselytizing
material aid" a sufficient Christian witness? Or must it be "aid plus gospel"?
How is "relationship evangelism" related to "saving souls"? Clearly the theological definitions underlying the Church's missional philosophy need careful
evaluation and, in some cases, considerable rethinking.

Spirit and Flesh

Conceptualizing the relationship between the spiritual and the physical/material
has been a persistent problem in Western thought. The problem is already
reflected in the New Testament, which adopts the language of the Greek ethos
in order to continue the salvation story of the Hebrew Scriptures. With the
continuing shift in the Church's early centuries from implicit Hebraic assumptions to Neoplatonic dualism, the spirit-flesh question became especially
focused in Christian theological discussions.

In the Hebrew tradition, the spiritual realm did not infinitely transcend the
earthly realm. God the invisible sovereign Spirit (*ruach*) ruled both the invisible and visible realms, which were part of one total reality or universe.
Humanity was created in God's image and made to partake in God's *ruach*. In
other words, God was transcendent Creator, the *independent* Sovereign of the
universe, who granted humanity *dependent* creaturely life to serve as coregents
over the earth. The heavens, which were beyond human control, were God's
domain—the bridge between the visible and invisible, as it were. God dwelt
beyond the outermost reaches of the visible realm, but nevertheless in the universe. God dwelt in eternity, but eternity was nonetheless conceived as the
extension of time.

The implications of this paradigm for understanding the relationship
between spirit and flesh should be obvious. While acknowledging two dimensions of reality—transcendent and earthly, invisible and visible, independent
and dependent, spirit and flesh—the Hebrew framework represented an organic
continuum of being. Humanity in all of its sentient aspects—physical, psychological, social, political, intellectual, and emotional—was resonant with spiritual being. Flesh was considered an embodiment of the vital spirit that was
manifest in both creaturely being (*nephesh*) and the Creator.

This Hebrew paradigm stood in sharp contrast to the philosophical dualism that, in various ways, influenced early Christian conceptions of flesh and
spirit. Greek dualism conceptualized the spirit and the flesh as infinitely discrete substances. According to a view that we might call infinite transcendence,
the ultimate source of being was beyond being. According to Neoplatonic
thought, a series of theoretical emanations was needed to bridge the infinite

divide between the Ultimate Spiritual Unity (*to on*, the One) and a divine being called the Demiurge, who created the flawed world of matter that humans actually experience.

Therefore, when the Neoplatonists thought of spirit with respect to humanity, they pictured it as a spark of the divine on loan from the creative spirit. They conceived spirit not as a gestalt or image in which human beings had been created, but rather as a spirit or soul that was trapped in a physical body. They thus reified spirit as a highly refined substance that intermingled with the flesh, and they deemed the flesh (animal body) to be evil, or at least a lesser, corruptible good—the source of temptation to the spirit that should be ignored, destructively indulged, or vigorously disciplined. In sum, the Neoplatonists associated the spiritual life with the mind (*nous*) and its refined intellectual activity, and they devalued physical and societal activity as an unavoidable consequence of the fleshly body and its needs. Salvation, in this view, was reduced to an escape of the spirit from its fleshly entrapment.

Already in the second century some Christians had adopted this dualistic paradigm and had consequently defined true spirituality as detachment from the material-social world. The goal of gnostic Christian spirituality, writes Robert Grant, was escaping to "the world infinitely remote and infinitely close because [it was] attainable within oneself."[4] Thus, according to the gnostics, the truly spiritual person lived a life of detachment from the material-physical and social aspects of life. Under the influence of Neoplatonism, Christian leaders such as Origen defined spirituality in intellectual and mystical terms, and they championed asceticism and martyrdom as the purist type of spirituality.

Given this philosophical framework, it is hardly surprising that early Christian theologians considered virginity—that is, a life of sexual continence—to be the epitome of Christian spirituality. What we often miss, however, are the broader social implications of virginity being the highest expression of spirituality. Virginity was not primarily a moral rejection of sexuality, but rather the renunciation of the fleshly, human society based on marriage and family ties. According to Peter Brown, sexual intercourse constituted "the necessary act on which the solidarity and perpetuity of the human race depended." The monasteries and convents were seen as alternative spiritual societies bonded in "angelic" solidarity, not flesh and blood. They were, Brown observes, "an exact imitation on earth of the 'life of the angels.'"[5]

Furthermore, many early Christians understood virginity as a form of mediation between God and humanity. Extrapolating from Christ's virgin birth and Mary's exaltation to divinity, Gregory of Nyssa wrote that "virginity has become the linking force that assures the intimacy of human beings with God."[6] It was both a condition and expression of ultimate spirituality. Celibate life in monastic community was thus considered the highest form of Christian spirituality. This model of spirituality, so dominant in the Church for fifteen hundred years, identified spirituality with renunciation of

temporal vocations and natural social relationships. And with the secularization of the temporal and natural, the gap between the spiritual and the secular became even more pronounced.

This dualism played itself out in many ways in the Church's history. For
instance, the governance of Christendom was soon divided between the spiritual and temporal realms, with "temporal" in this case meaning "social-political."
Within this dualistic framework, "religious" was understood as the sphere of
spiritual vocation and "secular" was understood as the sphere of natural giftedness. The clergy thus assumed sacramental spiritual power, and the secular
laity did little but receive their spiritual services. In the Church's ethical reflection, numerous Christian thinkers drew a qualitative line between the spiritual
virtue of *agape* love and the secular virtue of social justice. More recently,
many Christians have drawn a stark distinction between spiritual ministry and
the humanitarian professions, and between evangelism and social service. And
in the personal lives of Christians, popular theologians have distinguished
between sanctification and self-discipline, between Spirit-inspired "gifts" and
natural human compassion.

North American Developments

A brief look at some twentieth-century theological developments confirms the
lingering effects of theological dualism in North American evangelical theology. These years, historians tell us, exhibited a strong and sustained conservative reaction to the threat of rational empiricism, often referred to as
liberalism. While many conservative theologians participated in this battle, few
were as widely read or as influential as Lewis Sperry Chafer, who founded
Dallas Theological Seminary in 1924 and taught there until his death in 1952.
Chafer is perhaps best known for organizing the work of the Plymouth
Brethren and C. I. Scofield into an eight-volume theological work.[7] But in
addition to his systematic theology, Chafer published numerous other books,
one of which—*He That Is Spiritual* (1918)—is particularly relevant for our
purposes, for it quickly became a definitive text for conservative dispensation-
alists, who dominated America's fundamentalist movement for most of the
twentieth century.

Dispensationalism itself was not Chafer's invention, but rather had its
origins in Great Britain's Darbyite (Plymouth Brethren) movement. An eschatological scheme that divided Christian history into seven distinct eras (dis-
pensations), dispensationalism significantly impacted theology in the United
States through the teaching of the Plymouth Brethren following the Civil War.[8]
Men such as D. L. Moody and A. T. Pierson, who played significant roles in the
promotion of Protestant missions, were greatly influenced by the Brethren.
More recently, Billy Graham has commented appreciatively that evangelicals
have all milked the Plymouth Brethren cow.

Although dispensationalism is best known for its eschatological claims, it is most significant for our purposes to note that the Plymouth Brethren made an ontological distinction between the spiritual world and the empirical, material world, and thus operated with a sharply dualistic understanding of the created order. Human beings, they believed, were made up of distinct entities: body, soul, and spirit. The Brethren made a similarly sharp distinction between the Church as spiritual body and the Church as a social organization (denomination), and between the spiritual life and social life of the individual. They understood the Bible to be the inerrant (supernatural) words of God, thus identifying spirituality with a strict biblical literalism, and they defined salvation as a supernatural spiritual rebirth (regeneration) that was distinct from any renewal of the soul (rational faculty) or healing of the body. According to the Brethren, the single vocation of the Church was to rescue souls from hellfire—in their words, to "snatch them from the burning"—and call them to a higher spirituality.

Working within these parameters, Chafer sought to define spirituality. In contrast to liberal concepts of the spiritual as "human potential"[9] and, at the other pole, the Pentecostals' concept of the spiritual as an ecstatic empirical experience, Chafer defined spirituality as a strictly theological virtue.[10] He insisted that Christian spirituality was a supernatural gift of the Holy Spirit received by faith alone, something quite distinct from human aptitudes or abilities. The most he would grant Pentecostals by way of feeling was "celestial heart-ecstasy," that is, an inner assurance that God gave spiritual people according to their faith.[11]

Chafer begins his argument in *He That Is Spiritual* by drawing an impenetrable line of distinction between the Holy Spirit of God and the human spirit and, from that, between Christian love and human love. The human spirit, says Chafer, is not only creaturely but also depraved. Correspondingly, Christian love, which is inspired by the Spirit of God, "may be manifested in a human life" but should never be confused with human love.[12] Supernaturally gifted love is the only basis for Christian virtue; human love, on the other hand, is the source of humanitarianism and humanism.

Building on this particular understanding of love, Chafer was able to define true spirituality as the "direct manifestation of the Spirit" and to claim further that each true Christian had a "foreordained" spiritual service that could only be known by those yielded to the Spirit.[13] Chafer's distinction between spiritual and unspiritual Christians is particularly clear in the following claim: "Any Christian may enter into his own 'good works,' since the enabling Spirit is already indwelling him; but only those do enter in who are yielded to God; for it is service according to *His* will."[14] In sum, the secret of genuine spirituality is "total yieldedness" to the Spirit. For Chafer, then, spirituality is virtually equated to what Andrew Murray called "absolute surrender."[15] Apart from this yieldedness, service and ministry are "fleshly undertakings."

This brand of spirituality, it must be noted, is a purely inward virtue. Its only empirical sign is "true Christian character," not "works." Authentic spiritual "works" are "gifts of the Spirit," not the result of "natural ability," and there is no one kind of work that can be used as a test of spirituality (though "intercessory prayer" is the greatest ministry a spirit-filled Christian can engage in).[16] When we consider these claims, and add to them the fundamentalists' suspicion of any kind of "social work," we can easily see how spirituality and social justice work became disconnected in fundamentalism by their very definition!

This pattern of spirituality—epitomized by Chafer and still predominant in much of contemporary conservative North American Christianity—begins with the concept of spirit as one discrete part of the human being: spirit, soul, and body. It defines spirituality as giving priority to the spiritual in contrast to the rational (soul) or fleshly (body). Identifying the spirit with the interior aspects of life, it emphasizes inwardness, subjectivity, and the inner life. And it focuses on the ecstatic experience in contrast to the rational; on God-awareness and self-understanding in contrast to ethical action; on transformation of the self into a spiritual rather than a rational or materialistic person. Such spirituality manifests itself in personal expressions of piety, submission to God, unquestioning belief in the Bible, expressions of joy in the face of disappointment, and trust in the face of difficulty. It is an end in itself.

From Secularity to Secularism

Chafer and his theologically like-minded friends were not operating in a vacuum. The modern secularist paradigm they found so problematic was, and remains, a big part of the problem, for it offered only truncated and rationally constructed categories within which to define theological concepts. Beginning with the rational elimination of a transcendent reality, which its scientific methodology cannot investigate and verify, secularism limited truth to quantifiable scientific data. It equated reality with empirical (sense) experience, classified experience into distinct either-or categories, and progressed only by means of rational and mathematical speculation based on inductive research. Of course, all of this has been very productive for the advance of empirical knowledge, but it has proved quite inadequate for religious and moral evaluation.

Unfortunately, the liberal-fundamentalist debates of the twentieth century's first half proceeded largely along these lines, with fundamentalism readily adopting the rational and dualistic categories of natural/supernatural, knowledge/belief, individual/communal, Spirit-led/humanistic, and spiritual/social in the course of defining and defending its positions. Fundamentalist theologians thus failed to recognize the subtle but crucial difference between what Christopher Kaiser calls "biblical secularity" and modern secularism, an oversight that led them to make unnecessary ontological distinctions between the spiritual and the social.[17] Today's postfundamentalist evangelicals continue to be plagued by this semantic confusion, even though Kaiser's distinction provides them and others with a meaningful way out.

In "biblical secularity," Kaiser explains, God and spirit are integrally, even ontologically, related to the secular process of historical development.[18] Heaven is part of what we today call the universe; God is king, directing the political life of the nation; and charismatic servants, judges, and prophets carry out God's purposes in the political life of the nation. Even angels serve as agents in the historical process, for while they may be invisible, they are nonetheless real, thus belonging to the realm of the secular, that is, the reality of this age.

According to this biblically informed understanding of reality, God's spiritual laws regulate the political society, and social ethics are matters of spirituality. Economic and juridical justice, agricultural practice, and military strategy (along with temple ritual and individual worship) are matters of one's personal relationship with and responsibility before God. Since the theocratic rule of Yahweh marks out the parameters of spirituality, it would be strange, if not unthinkable, to separate spirituality and social justice. As Paul observed in Rom 14:17, the kingdom of God (a spiritual reality) is a matter of "righteousness [justice as a personal-social ethic] and peace and joy in the Holy Spirit." Notice how naturally these fit together!

In contrast, the contemporary Western division of the sacred and the secular effectively separates these realms. In the historical process we know as secularization, the natural was first separated from the supernatural, then public social life from individual private life. Instead of nature and supernature being dimensions within a holistic environment, they became two separate spheres. The supernatural (nonempirical or spiritual) was relegated to the individual (the private, subjective sphere), and the social or public sphere was secularized.

All of this had significant consequences for the nature and mission of the Church, for the Church quickly became associated in many Christians' minds with the supernatural realm, and its primary work was deemed to be spiritual in nature. Especially in the United States, where constitutional law separates Church and state, the Church became identified with the individual private sphere. This, of course, was not true of John Calvin's reform, nor was it true of Wesleyan holiness with its emphasis on sanctification, even though John Wesley himself operated within a dualistic paradigm. But since the early twentieth century, American Christianity in general and evangelicals in particular have been beset by this radical disparity of the two realms.

Early twentieth-century fundamentalists exemplified this problem most clearly, for they subjectivized the spiritual and separated themselves from the public order, thus functionalizing the rift between social and spiritual. Moreover, fundamentalists individualized the meaning of person, reducing it to an individual-in-private capacity. With respect to the work of the Church, they defined the gospel as a purely spiritual message and evangelism as the verbal proclamation of that message. Not surprisingly, they designated church professions "spiritual," and branded professions such as law, medicine, teaching, and social work "secular," even if practiced by Christians.

The fundamentalists' divide between the spiritual and the secular even had consequences for their apologetic work. In their well-intentioned attempt to contextualize biblical terminology, many fundamentalist theologians embraced empirical definitions of modern secularism to explain biblical narratives and teachings. For instance, they defined biblical miracle as an empirical category—that is, the spiritual phenomena reported in the Bible as publicly attested acts of God (miracles) were understood to be empirical, historical events caused by supernatural powers that interrupted natural causation.[19] Many of these theologians argued that with the end of the apostolic writings, such miracles ceased. They henceforth made a theological distinction between the natural and the supernatural, the temporal and the spiritual, whether or not any empirical distinction could actually be observed.

The acceptance of this rationalistic paradigm further reinforced the schism between the spiritual and the historical-social. Those who embraced this paradigm limited the miraculous to the experience of personal salvation—understood as a private, individual, subjective event that, strictly speaking, could only be believed and confessed.[20] Correspondingly, they classified social acts of compassion and justice as humanitarian good works and disregarded them as necessary aspects of authentic spirituality. In other words, they considered social action, however good and desirable, to be secular or humanistic apart from the miracle of spiritual new birth. For them, professed intellectual belief and verbal confession of receiving Christ, more than a distinguishable lifestyle or a compassionate mode of living, constituted the evidence of spiritual renewal. Consequently, they deemed laboring for the miraculous salvation of the world to be the Church's primary work, a mission accomplished by preaching and prayer. The social gospel was, in their rendering, an ersatz humanitarian gospel because it did not manifest the definable spiritual characteristics.

The Paradigm Shift

At least since the publication of Carl F. H. Henry's *The Uneasy Conscience of Modern Fundamentalism* (1947), evangelical leaders have been cognizant of the problem evangelicals have had in integrating spiritual ministry and social service. Fundamentalist churches, of course, had long encouraged philanthropic activity (e.g., charitable relief) to accompany their evangelistic work, but they nonetheless considered denominational social service programs suspect. Henry decried fundamentalism's "embarrassing divorce from a world social program," and he called for a renewed fundamentalism to compete on the world scene as "a vital world ideology . . . project[ing] a solution for the world's most pressing problems."[21] Still, Henry saw "no need for Fundamentalism to embrace liberalism's defunct social gospel,"[22] and instead based his strategy, which he labeled "supernatural redemptionism," on the uncompromising assumptions of dualistic supernaturalism.[23] In fact, Henry built his call for social involvement on a definition of the evangelical task that was entirely within fundamentalism's traditional understanding of spiritual priorities. "The evangelical task primarily," wrote Henry, "is the preaching of the Gospel, in the interest of individual regeneration by the supernatural grace of God, in such a way that divine redemption can be recognized as the best solution of our problems, individual and social."[24]

This priority continues to be the identifying characteristic of the evangelical movement.[25] In the 1960s and 1970s, evangelical parachurch organizations such as World Vision were rationalized as "pre-evangelism," and more holistic programs such as the Sojourners Community remained on the margins of the movement. In the 1970s and 1980s, John R. W. Stott enunciated what Nancey Murphy has since called "holistic dualism"[26] and was instrumental in persuading most evangelicals that an integrated social service and spiritual witness were essential to the expression of genuine Christian *agape*. Nevertheless, Stott continued to use the both-and (evangelism and social service) terminology of traditional dualistic theology. Similarly, contemporary evangelical social programs such as Ronald J. Sider's Evangelicals for Social Action and Franklin Graham's Samaritan's Purse are embraced as legitimate *evangelistic strategies* under the traditional slogan "evangelism and social service."

This both-and rationale reveals an inherent ambivalence and implies a need to strike a proper balance between two aspects of holistic Christian ministry, namely, verbal presentation and active demonstration of the gospel. By implication it forces an ideological judgment about the relative importance of social ministry and evangelism. Granted, sociologist James Davison Hunter reports a growing conviction among evangelical college and seminary students that social ministry has an "intrinsic worth . . . *apart* from ultimate spiritual concern."[27] But while Hunter's finding may be welcomed as recognition of social ministry as a distinctly Christian responsibility, the rhetorical separation of these two values—"intrinsic worth" and "spiritual concern"—signals the problem inherent in a dualistic theological rationale. To the contrary, the intrinsic worth of social ministry stems from the spiritual reality and value of human life as affirmed in Christ. It is precisely participation in the ministry of Christ through the dynamic of his Spirit/spirit that gives secular ministry intrinsic worth. To be sure, institutional priorities need to be defined and ministries distinguished for practical purposes, but the theological rationale undergirding and guiding Christian ministry should always be unitive.

It is therefore my contention that locating an adequate theological rationale for holistic spiritual service requires a paradigm shift that begins with our very conception of spirit and spirituality. The modified dualism of evangelical theologians still leaves us with an ideological contrast that requires a choice of priorities and a need to "balance" Christian ministries. As long as spirit (*pneuma*) is identified solely with eternal being—immortality, infinity, perfection—in contrast to body (*sarks*), which is physical, temporal, finite, and corruptible, the recognition of humans as holistic, personal creatures in God's image will remain elusive. So too will a holistic Christian ministry to the body (*soma*, which includes the dimension of spirit).

This paradigm shift will require, at the very least, a redefinition of divine immanence and transcendence and a more nuanced distinction between biblical secularity and modern secularism. The older dualism between the spiritual and the temporal inherited from the Greeks will need to give way to a more holistic (*pneumo-somatic*) view of human reality. Beginning already in the mid-twentieth century, some philosophers and theologians (who are sometimes referred to as "neoclassical") began to probe the possibilities of a more careful statement of God's relation to the universe of matter. In the interest of defending theism against the criticism of secular rationalism, they began to use terms such as "dipolar" and "panentheistic" to describe God's relation to the created universe.[28]

More recently, Roman Catholic theologian David Tracy has advocated the use of "panentheism." In an interview with the *Christian Century*, Tracy argues that "panentheism, the doctrine that all is in God but God's inclusion of the world does not exhaust the reality of God, is the best way to render in modern concepts God's relationship to us as described in the Bible."[29] Whatever philosophical term we use, it seems obvious that we need to reimage God's relationship to the world and humankind. The use of Neoplatonic categories of transcendence as they have played out in modern rational empiricism does not adequately represent "biblical secularity."

By the same token, and as part of the shift, Christians will need to revise their conception of humans having been made in the image of God. Theologian Nancey Murphy, who has used terms such as "holistic dualism" to describe "the most common position in church history, at least from Augustine to the present century," proposes the more precise term "nonreductive physicalism" to describe and contextualize the biblical understanding of humanity.[30] Murphy argues, both for theological and scientific reasons, that "there is only one entity, the *person*, who is clearly a physical, biological organism," and that "such an organism is indeed capable of all of those higher human capacities that have been attributed to the soul."[31] It is precisely this creature "in the image of God" that can recognize the voice of God and respond to God's will for the world.[32]

I therefore propose a theological conception of spirituality that begins with spirit as a *dimension* of the total human being created in God's image, not as a *distinct part* in conflict or even in tension with the rational soul and the physical body.[33] Too often Christians have substituted the Stoic concept of the image as a "divine spark" *in* human beings for the biblical image of "human beings *in* the image of God," thus equating the *imago Dei* with some faculty or part of the human being (e.g., Stoic reason or gnostic spirit) to the exclusion of the physical body. The implication of the Genesis conception of human beings in all their physicality, including sexual identity, seems to have eluded us.

In order to more adequately integrate the christocentric spiritual experience and its social expression, contemporary Christians will need to think outside the old dualistic parameters of faith and works, spiritual and ethical, salvation of souls and reconciliation of persons, private virtue and public action, and *agape* and justice. Social concepts such as biblical righteousness, justice, and holiness must be reconnected to our concepts both of spirituality and salvation. In sum, we will need to reframe the eschatological social vision of salvation as the restoration of the rule of God expressed in Eph 1:10. Indeed, the very concept of the "kingdom of God" as Jesus announced it already conflates the historical-social (secular-temporal) and the spiritual (transcendent-eternal). As Paul writes so eloquently, when the kingdom finally becomes universal reality, then God "will be all and in all" (1 Cor 15:28). Maranatha!

Summary

The dualistic traditions strongly influenced by Neoplatonism and gnostic Christianity make personal piety the requisite expression of spirituality and, correspondingly, devalue the spiritual character of social ministry. According to this conception of the Christian life, the fruit of the Spirit in a person's life may provide motivation for social action, but spirituality is not immediately identified with compassionate social action. Instead, spirituality is associated with ascetical, monastic community (in contrast to secular-temporal society), mystical contemplation, devotional piety, evangelistic witness, and charismatic worship. This theological bifurcation of the spiritual and social-psychological, I have contended, develops almost inevitably from an inadequate conception of the ontological relationship between the historical-temporal (empirical) and the transcendent-eternal (unseen). It is a consequence of the sharp dualism of the spirit and the material-physical, that is, a consequence of conceiving of spirit as a distinct aspect of human beings combined with an animal body.

A more adequate conception of Christian spirituality begins with an understanding of the spiritual person as one who experiences life in its totality under the influence of God's enabling presence. In this rendering, one's spiritual character expresses itself in a spirit of compassion and a profound sense of grace. It emphasizes *praxis* in following the nonviolent way of Jesus, and it strives for God's justice and the coming of God's kingdom (Matt 5:6). In short, it incarnates Micah's call to do justice, love compassion, and walk humbly with God (Mic 6:8). While Christians must never negate the vertical dimension of the Christian life (i.e., the work of the Spirit of God in influencing and enabling the

Christian life), lived expression must be considered the essential identifying mark of Christian spirituality. Indeed, true spirituality is the fulfillment of the image of God in its full individual and societal gestalt—personal, social, political. That this attainment is the gift of the Creator-Savior God, who is the sustaining spiritual dynamic of life, we freely and thankfully recognize.

Notes

1. In his article entitled "Christian Supernaturalism," first published in 1897, Warfield wrote, "The supernatural is the very breath of Christianity's nostrils." This article was reprinted in Samuel Craig, ed., *Biblical and Theological Studies* (Philadelphia: Presbyterian & Reformed Publishing Co., 1952), 1–21.

2. This distinction between the natural and the supernatural, between spiritual and psychosomatic realities, between the "personal" and the "social," may have been present in traditional Protestant orthodoxy, but it was exacerbated by the modernist-fundamentalist debate in the early twentieth century. In these years, the "social gospel" became an oxymoron for Christian fundamentalists. For them, the Church was a spiritual, "heavenly" reality not to be confused with the ecclesiastical institution, and "saving souls" was its business.

3. See, for example, David Van Biema, "Missionaries under Cover," *Time*, June 30, 2003, 36–44.

4. Robert Grant, "Gnostic Spirituality," in *Christian Spirituality: Origins to the Twelfth Century* (ed. Bernard McGinn and John Meyendorff; New York: Crossroad, 1987), 56.

5. Peter Brown, "The Notion of Virginity in the Early Church," in McGinn and Meyendorff, eds., *Christian Spirituality*, 428, 429.

6. Quoted in Brown, "Notion of Virginity," 432.

7. Lewis Sperry Chafer, *Systematic Theology* (vols. 1–8; Dallas: Dallas Seminary Press, 1947–1948).

8. See C. Norman Kraus, *Dispensationalism in America: Its Rise and Development* (Richmond, Va.: John Knox, 1958).

9. James W. Jones, *The Spirit and the World* (New York: Hawthorn Books, 1975), 148–49.

10. At Explo '72, organized by Youth for Christ at the Dallas Cowboys' stadium, these two perspectives came to an explosive climax when Pentecostals, who had refused a display booth, entered the grounds with signs reading, "Expose '72." Chafer's perspective was enshrined in the "Four Spiritual Laws," which were promoted at this convention as a superior evangelistic tool.

11. Lewis Sperry Chafer, *He That Is Spiritual* (Our Hope Publisher, 1918), 56.

12. Ibid., 44.

13. Ibid., 45–46, 48.

14. Ibid., 49.

15. Andrew Murray (1828–1917) was a Dutch missionary pastor whose writings became popular in conservative pietistic circles. His *Absolute Surrender*, published in London in 1895, was widely used in the United States and continued in print well into the twentieth century.

16. Chafer, *He That Is Spiritual*, 55–56.

17. See Christopher Kaiser, "From Biblical Secularity to Modern Secularism: Historical Aspects and Stages," in *The Church between Gospel and Culture: The Emerging Mission in North America* (ed. George R. Hunsberger and Craig Van Gelder; Grand Rapids: Eerdmans, 1996), 79–112. Kaiser's seminal article explains the significant difference between "biblical secularity" and modern secularism. I have used his insights to develop my own description of the subtle but significant ontological difference between biblical concepts of miracles (and the relation of the spiritual realm to history) and modern fundamentalism's empiricist translation of these concepts.

18. Kaiser explains, "By 'biblical secularity' I mean the positive value placed on time, temporal events, and temporal goals in Holy Scripture. God created the world of space and time as a medium of divine self-expression and self-revelation to humanity. God also gives some space and time to each creature as an opportunity for self-fulfillment and service to others. Therefore, the seasonal times of

individual life and the historical times of communal history are viewed in Scripture as being filled with theological significance." Noting the difficulty of defining modern secularism, he writes, "Personally, I am persuaded by scholars like Thomas Luckmann and Peter Berger, who define secularism not as the decline of religion but as a redefinition of its role in such a way that religious beliefs are dissociated from the secular processes of world-structuring, and secular values are alienated from the sphere of religion." Kaiser, "From Biblical Secularity to Modern Secularism," 79, 82.

19. For example, they interpreted creation as a historical event that could be chronologically located in time, the virgin birth as an empirical exception to genetic processes, and revelation as an empirical communication between God and humans.

20. The Pentecostal movement largely accepted the dispensational hermeneutic of biblical literalism, the separation of the spiritual and social, and the emphasis on individual supernatural salvation. It modified the position, however, by allowing individual ecstatic experience of the Spirit's work to count as evidence of supernatural new birth. This reintroduced the possibility of miracles (speaking in tongues, prophecy, and healing) as experiential signs of spiritual rebirth and Spirit endowment. In the United States, these signs were rarely social in character. Pentecostals in impoverished cultures have been much more open to the spiritual validity of "gifts" of social services.

21. Carl F. H. Henry, *The Uneasy Conscience of Modern Fundamentalism* (Grand Rapids: Eerdmans, 1947), 68, 76.

22. Ibid., 85.

23. The sociopolitical programs of the contemporary Religious Right seem designed to fulfill Henry's challenge, although Henry himself did not champion their causes.

24. Henry, *The Uneasy Conscience*, 88.

25. Sociologist James Davison Hunter observes that "when asked to choose the most important priority for Christians today, nine out of ten Evangelical seminarians chose priorities of a spiritual nature." Hunter, *Evangelicalism: The Coming Generation* (Chicago: University of Chicago Press, 1987), 41.

26. Nancey C. Murphy, *Reconciling Theology and Science: A Radical Reformation Perspective* (Kitchener, Ont.: Pandora, 1997), 36–37, 58–59.

27. Hunter, *Evangelicalism*, 45 (emphasis added).

28. Philosophers such as Charles Hartshorne and theologians such as Schubert Ogden, Norman Pittenger, and John Cobb are associated with this position. In his last volume of theology, Paul Tillich, who was sometimes criticized for being too *pantheistic*, introduced the term "eschatological panentheism" in order to preserve the personal dynamic in the relation of God to the universe. See Tillich, *Systematic Theology* (vol. 3; Chicago: University of Chicago Press, 1963), 421. Van A. Harvey, in his *Handbook of Theological Terms* (New York: Macmillan, 1964), explains the intended meaning of the term panentheism: "Just as a person is both the sum of all his experiences and parts and yet more than they, so God has all the finite being as part of his being and experience but transcends it" (172).

29. David Tracy, "The Impossible God," *Christian Century*, February 13–20, 2002, 24. See also David Tracy, *Blessed Rage for Order: The New Pluralism in Theology* (San Francisco: Harper & Row, 1988).

30. Murphy, *Reconciling Theology and Science*, 58–59.

31. Ibid., 59.

32. Ibid. Murphy continues: "I believe nonreductive physicalism is close to the ancient Hebrew conception of the person. It maintains the *holistic* view of the person found in both the Old and New Testaments. It has theological advantages over dualism. Most important, it forces us to attend to New Testament teaching about bodily resurrection as the source of Christian hope for eternal life" (ibid.).

33. See C. Norman Kraus, *An Intrusive Gospel? Christian Mission in the Postmodern World* (Downers Grove, Ill.: InterVarsity Press, 1998), 69ff., 84–86.

3

THE LOVE OF GOD AS THE SOURCE OF SPIRITUALITY AND SOCIAL JUSTICE

— David Rensberger —

The connection between spirituality and social justice is often mystifying. Indeed, for many people there hardly seems to be any connection at all. Rather than asking how we may put spirituality and social justice together, however, I want to ask what it is that *already* connects them, what it is that already holds them together.

It is easy to cite a host of examples—from the twentieth century back to the beginnings of Christianity—of people in whose lives spirituality and social justice have been two aspects of an indissoluble whole, a unity, the Christian life. Some names from recent Christian history recall for us entire movements: Desmond Tutu, Martin Luther King Jr., Dorothy Day, Oscar Romero. In earlier centuries, we can point to abolitionists and women's rights campaigners, the Anabaptist reformation, John Wycliffe and the Lollards, Francis of Assisi and his followers, the Waldensians, Martin of Tours, and numerous others. Many of the New Testament writers can be called on as witnesses to this unity, which one of them sums up in two commandments: Believe in Jesus Christ and love one another (1 John 3:23). And of course it is Jesus himself who stands at the head of this series, with his appeal to the two commandments of love for God and for one's neighbor (Mark 12:28–31); but in so doing, even he points further back, to the prophets and lawgivers of Israel.

I take it for granted, then, that within the Christian tradition, and reaching back beyond the beginnings of Christianity, social justice and spirituality have been viewed and lived as two aspects of one thing, two streams flowing from a single source, two stems growing from a single root, two rays radiating from a single central point. Moreover, in many practical respects, they are not two separate things at all; there is only one thing, the Christian life, and when you look at it, you cannot say whether it is about spirituality or about social justice.

I start, then, with a highly unoriginal perception: Everything that God wants from us and everything that God offers us is at bottom all one thing. From a conceptual standpoint, we may designate parts of it as contemplation and action, evangelism and discipleship, faith and works, spirituality and social justice, but fundamentally it is all and only one single thing. If we can see that one thing whole, if only for a moment, we will understand better what we are doing as we work at any of the particular parts. That unified vision is my subject here. I want to consider what that one thing is, the one thing that comprises both spirituality and social justice. What is that source, that root, that center point from which both radiate? I suggest that that one thing is the love of God.

Defining Our Terms

As we begin this exploration, three questions of terminology come quickly to mind regarding "spirituality," "social justice," and "the love of God." The term "spirituality" has by now acquired so many connotations that any serious consideration of the term requires that it first be defined. What follows is certainly not intended to be the only or even the best possible definition of spirituality, but simply the one being employed for present purposes. In this essay, I use "spirituality" to mean *the experiences of a life lived in relationship with God, and the practices that constitute and sustain that relationship*. With reference to a specifically *Christian* spirituality, I add that this relationship with God exists and has its particular character because of Jesus Christ, and is lived out within a community of other people who share a similar relationship.[1]

In this understanding, spirituality is more a practical thing than a theoretical one. It is not theology, but rather theology lived out both in practice and in experience. Philip Sheldrake offers the following formulation: "Spirituality is understood to include . . . a conscious relationship with God, in Jesus Christ, through the indwelling of the Spirit and in the context of the community of believers. Spirituality is, therefore, concerned with the conjunction of theology, prayer and practical Christianity."[2] For Bradley P. Holt, spirituality "refers in the first place to lived experience. . . . The starting point is the spirit of Christ living in the person, but the person is always considered in the context of a community, the body of Christ. Spirituality describes a particular *style* of Christian discipleship."[3]

Spirituality in this sense is an explicitly relational thing. People who hold a Trinitarian theology will have a spirituality in which they are in relationship with the three persons of God: Creator, Christ, and Holy Spirit. They will also be in community with others who have a similar relationship. They will experience this relationship in various ways, including prayer, congregational worship, and encounter with nature, and they will carry out various practices in the course of living out the relationship, for example, meditation, Bible reading, and singing. Thus, I speak of spirituality not as something purely individual and interior, but rather as something that connects a person's deepest individuality with a great Other, the triune God, and with many others, the person's fellow Christians and fellow creatures.

As for "social justice," definitions of it are not easy to find or devise. Let me, however, suggest a few parameters for how I understand it here. It must be concerned to create and maintain social arrangements in a way that is just, that is, impartial (not arbitrarily favoring some over others) and equitable (so that goods are available to all, the weak as well as the strong). Correspondingly, one scholar has suggested that justice in the Hebrew Bible "refers to basic human rights."[4] I believe that social justice should be construed in a broad sense, to include not only human society but the natural world as well, so that human strength is not allowed to destroy other creatures. I would also link social justice to peace among human beings, both individuals and societies. Warfare and violence generally have their roots in injustice, in persons and nations seeking or holding on to what is not properly theirs, and violent means of seeking justice seem invariably to result in further injustices.

A preliminary word is also needed on the expression "the love of God," for there is a problem connected with it that is familiar to biblical scholars but may be less obvious to other readers of the Bible. Phrased in exactly that way, "the love of God," it is an ambiguous expression. Does it refer to God's love for us, or our love for God? Is it love that comes from God, or love that is directed toward God?

In the Bible, of course, there are many cases in which there is little or no ambiguity. When Paul writes in Rom 8:39 that nothing in creation "will be able to separate us from the love of God in Christ Jesus our Lord," he clearly has God's love for us in mind. On the other hand, Luke 11:42—"you . . . neglect justice and the love of God"—clearly envisions human love for God.

Other biblical texts, however, are more ambiguous. In Rom 5:5, for example—"The love of God has been poured out in our hearts through the Holy Spirit that has been given to us" (my translation)—is the subject love for God, or love that comes from God? Or what about John 5:42: "You do not have the love of God in you"? Similarly, 1 John 3:17: "Whoever has worldly riches and sees their brother or sister in need and closes their heart against them, how does the love of God abide in that person?" (my translation). The letters of John are filled with little conundrums like this.

Of course, both of these meanings, love *for* God and love *from* God, are vitally significant for human relationship with God. However, I will be primarily emphasizing our love for God and how it works to create and hold together Christian spirituality and Christian work for social justice. This is because both spirituality and action for justice are human activities, and it is the connection between these activities that is of interest to us here.

Two Mistakes

Before examining this connection, I want to address what I consider to be two erroneous ways of conceiving it, one probably more dangerous to earlier generations, the other a pressing problem today.

In medieval European Christianity, it was common for wealthy persons to give assistance to the poor. This was understood to be an act of social justice, in that the poor deserved to have their lives sustained by the surplus of the rich. This view was confirmed in canon law by Gratian's *Decretum* in the twelfth century, but it goes all the way back to St. Ambrose in the fourth century.[5] Such giving was not understood as an act of social transformation or even reformation; there was no question of a reordering of the social hierarchy. Primarily, this assistance was understood as a spiritual act, with the rich gaining merit for their souls by acts of charity. The concern was not so much for improving the lot of the poor as it was for saving the souls of the rich. Indeed, the view that "the most important issue is the spiritual welfare of the giver rather than of the recipient" was expressed already by St. Ambrose.[6]

In this understanding, spirituality and social justice were connected, and each was practiced in relation to the other, but the concerns of justice were intrinsically subordinated to those of spirituality. The connection thus established between the two was a false one, precisely because of this subordination. Rather than seeing the claims of social justice as standing on their own, as part of God's will for human life, only the so-called "spiritual" realm was valued.

In the process, spirituality itself risked being debased by being cut off from its genuine character as a relationship with God lived out in freedom and obedience, worship and commitment, love and faith. The aim was to accrue merit with God, which is certainly a relationship, but not a relationship of love and freedom, and therefore not a relationship of true obedience either. There was also a chance that the other person, the recipient of the benefaction, would be seen only as an instrument of attaining salvation for the benefactor and not in his or her own wholeness and reality as a child of God, thus diminishing the possibility of relating to God through and in that person. The relational character of spirituality was distorted, both with respect to God and with respect to other people. In sum, the subordination of the concerns of social justice to those of spirituality failed to truly serve the ends of either one.

In some ways this false connection between social justice and spirituality is still with us. Whether we are rich or middle class, we can easily see our acts of charity as transactions more between ourselves and God than between ourselves and the poor. These acts *are* transactions between ourselves and God, of course, but if we perform them primarily as a means of "becoming better Christians," or of allaying our own guilt, we are still subordinating justice to a somewhat dubious spirituality and thus falsifying the connection between the two.

The opposite mistake, however, is probably far more tempting today, especially for Christians of a liberal social-ethical persuasion, namely, subordinating the concerns of spirituality to those of social justice. I am referring to the commonly heard promotion of prayer, Bible study, retreat, and other spiritual disciplines as means of "recharging the batteries" or "refreshing the souls" of those who labor in the vineyard of social justice. Here too we have an instrumental understanding: Spirituality is good because it helps us be more faithful activists or because it prevents burnout.

I understand the reasons for this instrumental approach; it sometimes seems the only way to get activists seriously interested in prayer at all. But prayer is not good because it refreshes us or recharges us. That would reduce it to something like a New Age meditation technique for stress management to help busy people stay productive and successful. Prayer is good because it is prayer. Relationship with God—spirituality—is important because it is what we are created for. Prayer does indeed refresh and restore us, because it puts us in contact with the source and the purpose of our existence, and we do need that contact in order to work for justice. But we need it primarily in order to live fully human lives at all.

The purpose of spirituality is not to enable us to work for justice, any more than the purpose of social action is to improve our spiritual condition. Spirituality and social action do have these good effects on each other. But spirituality should not be made an adjunct to social justice work, nor should social justice be subordinated to spirituality. The two are related, but the relationship is not one of subordination. Rather, both are simply the outworking of the love of God.

God's Love as the Starting Point for Spirituality and Social Justice

Although my emphasis is primarily on the love of God as *our love directed toward God*, the other meaning of the phrase—*the love of God for us*—remains the fundamental starting point for the Christian message, Christian theology, and Christian life. We say that it was God's love that sent Jesus into the world; we say, indeed, that God is love; and we say that we live in the confidence that God loves us. It is God's love that calls forth our love in response, so that God's love for us is the ultimate basis for both Christian spirituality and Christian social justice activities.

Where did this characteristic feature of Christian teaching, experience, and life originate? The message of Jesus focused largely on the kingdom of God, that is to say, on the sovereignty or the reign of God. Interestingly, though, we rarely read of Jesus speaking to God or about God as "King." Instead, he typically spoke of God as "Father." Moreover, he emphasized the compassionate nature of God: "Be merciful, just as your Father is merciful" (Luke 6:36). The parables of the Lost Sheep, the Lost Coin, and the Prodigal Son picture God as eagerly seeking after those who have gone astray, and welcoming them home with joy (Luke 15).

Why did Jesus teach about God in this way? There are, after all, other ways of picturing God than as loving, merciful, and benevolent. How did Jesus know that God's kingdom or reign is one of compassion? He might have gained this knowledge from the Hebrew Scriptures, for example, from Ps 103, which speaks of a God who has "compassion" on Zion, or perhaps from Ps 145:8–11:

> The LORD is gracious and merciful,
> slow to anger and abounding in steadfast love.
> The LORD is good to all,
> and his compassion is over all that he has made.
> All your works shall give thanks to you, O LORD,
> and all your faithful shall bless you.
> They shall speak of the glory of your kingdom,
> and tell of your power.

However, Jesus is never reported as quoting these or any other biblical texts as justification for his understanding of God, nor as citing tradition or any other source. The closest he comes to giving any basis for his teaching about God is his observation that God "is kind to the ungrateful and the wicked" (Luke 6:35), or in Matthew's version, that God "makes his sun rise on the evil and on the good, and sends rain on the righteous and on the unrighteous" (Matt 5:45).

In other words, it was apparently Jesus' *experience* and *observation* of God and God's ways that led him to focus on the compassionate nature of God's sovereignty.[7] God's love was a matter of experience for Jesus, and his experience issued in practice. God's kindness to the wicked was the basis for Jesus' precept that his followers should likewise love their enemies (Matt 5:43–48 = Luke 6:27–36). Jesus' social-ethical practice of love was derived from an experience of God's sovereignty as loving and compassionate; in other words, God's love was part of his spirituality. It is quite in keeping with this that Luke portrays Jesus as healing the slave whose ear was cut off by one of his disciples when he was being arrested, and as forgiving those who crucified him (Luke 22:50–51; 23:34). Thus, the emphasis on God's love that is the starting point for both Christian spirituality and Christian work for social justice has its roots in the spirituality, the teaching, and the life and death of Jesus himself.

God's love for us creates the possibility of Christian spirituality when the God of love—Creator, Redeemer, and Sustainer—initiates a relationship of love with us. Our spirituality is practiced within the framework of this love, amounting basically to our living in the loving relationship with God that we enjoy and seek to maintain. Christianity is essentially just this: to know that we are beloved children of God because of Jesus Christ, and to live accordingly. Because we know God as love toward us, we seek a spiritual life that is characterized by love and the joy and peace that flow from a relationship of love. Both the existence and the nature of Christian spirituality are created and conditioned by the fact of God's love.

We understand this divine love to be a just love, in the sense I suggested earlier. God's love is impartial, not favoring some over others because of their achievements, and seeks a just order in the world, in which the goods of creation are freely available to the weak as well as the strong. Clearly, such an understanding of the justice of divine love also implies that God's justice is itself loving and compassionate. God's love is just, and God's justice is loving, and so the love of God for us and for all creation is as much the basis of Christian actions for social justice as it is of Christian spirituality.

Love for God as the Source of Spirituality and Social Justice

I will now turn to our love for God as the fundamental unifying factor between spirituality and social justice, the source or center point from which they both emerge. I was tempted here to proceed under two headings, first spirituality and then social justice. But since my point is precisely that our love for God is a single thing that incorporates both of these, I will continue without making a division between the two.

If the definition of spirituality that I have given—"the experiences of a life lived in relationship with God, and the practices that constitute and sustain that relationship"—is taken at its broadest, it implies that every loving response to God's love for us is a part of our spirituality. The practice of actions for social justice proceeding from a heart that loves God would then surely come under that definition. Social justice would thus be incorporated under spirituality, though not subordinated to it as in the medieval way of thinking I described earlier. In this understanding, social justice work is seen as having its own value as a loving response to God's love, as a spiritual discipline important in itself, and not as an auxiliary field of activity subordinated to other, more truly "spiritual" categories. In this sense, then, spirituality, at its most inclusive, would encompass action for social justice.

I want to be careful, however, not to short-circuit the discussion and miss the point of what this volume is trying to achieve. Let me therefore focus on the particular terms of my definition of spirituality: "the *experiences* of a life lived in relationship with God, and the *practices* that constitute and sustain that relationship." Thus, we may speak of spirituality in a narrower sense, as encompassing the incidents of the spiritual life on the one hand, and on the other hand the practices commonly referred to as spiritual disciplines, practices such as contemplative prayer, spiritual reading or *lectio divina*, silence, fasting, self-examination, and corporate worship.[8] This may in fact be closer to what many people mean by the spirituality that is being considered in relation to social justice in this volume.

"You shall love the Lord your God with all your heart, and with all your soul, and with all your mind, and with all your strength. . . . You shall love your neighbor as yourself" (Mark 12:30–31). By selecting these two commandments from the Torah as the most central ones for a life of faithful relationship with God, Jesus laid the groundwork for understanding the Christian life as a life of both spirituality, in the narrower sense just described, and justice. For Jesus, the necessary human response to God's sovereign love is our joyous and delighted love for God in return, and likewise our compassionate love for our neighbors and even our enemies. Love for God is thus the proper starting point in the Christian quest for justice and for peace. It is also the starting point of the quest for communion with God that we call spirituality.

Christian spirituality begins and ends in relationship, and by focusing on a love for God that takes up the whole of the human person, Jesus indicated that the defining quality of this relationship is total and self-abandoning love. Christian spirituality is an outpouring of love that begins in the depths of the human heart and extends to the divine heart that brought forth the cosmos. Every relationship begins with an encounter between two persons, and every relationship requires some means of continued encounter to sustain it, some kind of contact, communication, communion. Particularly in a relationship of love, this communion, this ongoing encounter of two hearts, is an essential part of what holds the lovers together. Encounter with God, then, both initially and on a persistent basis, is fundamental to Christian spirituality.

Lest this language of two hearts be misunderstood, let me emphasize that encounter with God has never, in any healthy expression of Christianity, been understood as one that requires or even allows an individual to isolate himself or herself from the body of Christ. My definition of Christian spirituality specifies that relationship with God is lived out within a *community* of other people who share a similar relationship. Even hermits, in all but the most extreme cases, have maintained contact with others and sought to be of benefit to them. The spiritual life of the individual Christian takes place within the spiritual life of the Church as a whole, although no individual can claim that the life of the Church makes it unnecessary to nurture her or his own relationship with God.

Christian tradition has given quite a number of answers to the question of how the ongoing encounter that sustains our relationship with God takes place. This encounter may be said to occur in our engagement with the Word of God, whether written or preached; or in the gathered community of believers; or in the liturgy and the sacraments, especially the Eucharist; or in the actions of a life of discipleship; or in mystical prayer; or in the created world; or in meeting the needs of other persons. It is one of the tragedies of the post-Reformation Church that we have so often felt obliged to defend one or another of these as the superior, or the fundamental, or the ultimate means of divine encounter, rather than simply rejoicing to encounter God in any and every opportunity that we have been given.

Often enough we encounter God at times and in manners that we do not anticipate, like Moses at the burning bush (Exod 3:1–6) or Mary Magdalene at the empty tomb (John 20:11–18). Because it is fundamentally a relationship, Christian spirituality is not tied to rituals, contemplative practices, or asceticism. Yet it can encompass all these and other ways of soliciting encounters with God, of "seeking the presence of the Lord," as the psalmists say (Pss 24:6; 27:8; 105:4). As noted above, it is such spiritual disciplines that we often mean concretely when we speak of spirituality. The disciplines do not by any means *guarantee* that we will find communion with God, as frustrating as this may be to the achievement-oriented spirit of the modern world. They simply provide a framework within which we may seek God's presence and learn to look for God's coming in all places and all circumstances.

Actions aimed at furthering social justice can also provide this framework. If we understand the life of discipleship and the needs of others, in particular the cry of the oppressed for justice, as "places" where God can be encountered, then the activities of discipleship, of meeting needs and seeking justice, are quite evidently means of seeking God's presence. Under the broadest definition of spirituality, they are themselves spiritual disciplines, ways of entering into and sustaining relationship with God. Under a narrower definition, they stand alongside such supposedly more classical spiritual activities as fasting, *lectio divina*, and prayer. Work for social justice is a means of communion with God.

But it does not have to be; it is not automatically a path to divine encounter, any more than skipping meals, reading a book, or even contemplative stillness automatically lead to such an encounter. I may fast until I keel over, I may spend days and nights among the homeless, but I will encounter God only if I am *open* to that encounter, only if I believe that there can be such an encounter and if it is love for God rather than my own heroic virtue that motivates me. It is ultimately, then, love for God that makes either spiritual practice or social justice work a means of divine encounter and divine communion. It is because we love God and desire God that we seek God's presence, and it is when we seek God that we enter into this communion with our Beloved, whether through prayer, in Scripture, at the Lord's Supper, or through social action.

Christian spirituality is rooted in a love that seeks out the love at the heart of the cosmos, but it does not pass by the other creatures that make up this cosmos on its way there. It encompasses them as well, embraces them on its lifelong journey toward its divine source. It is this embrace of love, initiated by God and destined to end in God, that generates, empowers, and guides particular Christian actions for social justice. These actions are not grounded in or limited by social, political, or economic principles, and thus they are not constrained by ideology or group interests. Nor do they have one particular set of strategies or tactics that are valid in all times and places. They cross lines of nationality, ethnicity, institution, even religion—indeed, even species. They are driven by the love of God and shaped and bounded only by what is consistent with this self-giving, compassionate, and tenderhearted love.

The connection between spirituality and social justice in Christian life is not an artificial one. Both kinds of activity emerge organically from the love that comes from God and is reflected back to God, and form the core and the engine of all that is Christian. When love has its proper place at the Christian center, it would require a painstaking effort to distinguish, let alone choose, between spirituality and social justice—and none at all to see and inhabit their unity. The Christian life is one life, one simple and complex, plain and mysterious, active and contemplative life. Each of us has a particular calling and particular gifts within this one life, and few if any of us do all things equally well or equally gladly. But each of us is also a piece of the wholeness of the Christian reality, and each of us has that wholeness available to be a guiding vision of what the integrated human life lived in relationship with God should be. Worship, peacemaking, evangelism, care for the earth, discipleship, prayer, and the quest for justice are all one thing, one single and beautifully multifaceted acting out of our love for God.

Notes

1. On the definition of spirituality, see Kenneth J. Collins, introduction to *Exploring Christian Spirituality* (ed. Kenneth J. Collins; Grand Rapids: Baker, 2000), 11–14. In the same volume, see also Philip Sheldrake, "What Is Spirituality?" 21–42; and Walter Principe, "Toward Defining Spirituality," 43–59.

2. Sheldrake, "What Is Spirituality?" 40.

3. Bradley P. Holt, *Thirsty for God: A Brief History of Christian Spirituality* (Minneapolis: Augsburg, 1993), 6.

4. Temba L. J. Mafico, "Just, Justice," in *The Anchor Bible Dictionary* (ed. David Noel Freedman; New York: Doubleday, 1992), 1:1128.

5. Miri Rubin, *Charity and Community in Medieval Cambridge* (Cambridge: Cambridge University Press, 1987), 59, 62.

6. Abigail Firey, "'For I Was Hungry and You Fed Me': Social Justice and Economic Thought in the Latin Patristic and Medieval Christian Traditions," in *Ancient and Medieval Economic Ideas and*

Concepts of Social Justice (ed. S. Todd Lowry and Barry Gordon; Leiden: Brill, 1998), 340. See also Rubin, *Charity and Community*, 64, 89-90; Leo L. Dubois, S.M., *Saint Francis of Assisi: Social Reformer* (New York: Benziger, 1913), 20–21; and Leonardo Boff, *Saint Francis: A Model for Human Liberation* (New York: Crossroad, 1982), 54–55.

7. On Jesus' spiritual experience, see Marcus Borg, *Jesus: A New Vision* (San Francisco: HarperSanFrancisco, 1987), 39–56 (though Borg may somewhat overstate what can be said about such experience); and Stephen C. Barton, *The Spirituality of the Gospels* (London: SPCK, 1992), 144–45.

8. Two excellent popular treatments of the classical spiritual disciplines are Richard J. Foster, *Celebration of Discipline: The Path to Spiritual Growth* (New York: Harper & Row, 1978); and Marjorie J. Thompson, *Soul Feast: An Invitation to the Christian Spiritual Life* (Louisville, Ky.: Westminster John Knox, 1995). In addition, in *Thirsty for God*, Bradley P. Holt combines exercises in such disciplines with a study of the history of Christian spirituality. Two interesting collections of studies relate spiritual disciplines to particular denominations and other traditions within Christianity: Robin Maas and Gabriel O'Donnell, O.P., eds., *Spiritual Traditions for the Contemporary Church* (Nashville: Abingdon, 1990); and E. Glenn Hinson, ed., *Spirituality in Ecumenical Perspective* (Louisville, Ky.: Westminster John Knox, 1993). The latter includes a chapter by Tilden Edwards entitled "Spiritual Perspectives on Peacemaking."

PART II

THEOLOGICAL RESOURCES FOR CONNECTING SPIRITUALITY AND SOCIAL JUSTICE

4

JUSTICE, SPIRITUALITY, AND THE CHURCH: THE ATONEMENT CONNECTION

— J. Denny Weaver —

At first glance, the relationship between spirituality and justice or ethics would seem obvious: the more spirituality, the more ethics, and hence the greater justice. In fact, the connection is frequently lacking. Consider, for example, the findings of Ohio pastor John Dey. In preparation for teaching a college course called "Discipling and Mentoring," Dey examined more than one hundred discipleship paradigms designed to promote the Christian life. He observed that they focused almost exclusively on individual spiritual growth or a personal relationship with Jesus, but they struggled to make sense of a call to discipleship based on the life and teaching of Jesus. Dey linked the problem to atonement theology, observing that "by far the majority" of the paradigms or ways of understanding discipleship assumed substitutionary atonement, but that following Jesus (i.e., discipleship) made little sense when salvation was understood as a personal, spiritual relationship based on the cross understood as a "punctiliar" event.[1]

The absence of ethical discernment in discipleship paradigms is a multidimensional problem. This essay deals with two of those dimensions. The first concerns the relationship of spirituality to ethics and the fact that spirituality and a "personal relationship with Jesus Christ" do not necessarily result in ethical discernment based on Jesus' life. (For a historical example, remember Bernard of Clairvaux, known among other things for his writings on spirituality, but who also preached the second crusade against Muslims). More specifically, this essay argues that an inadequate atonement theology, as pointed to by John Dey, is an important contributor to the separation of justice and spirituality.[2] Discussion of the atonement will lead us to a second question about discipleship and spirituality. This second question concerns the appropriate venue and mode for the practice of spirituality: Is it primarily an individual enterprise, or a communal enterprise?

Two assumptions underlie many discussions about keeping spirituality and ethics together. One is that spirituality does have something to do with being Christian, and the more "spirituality" one exhibits, the more "Christian" that person is. The second, more problematic assumption is that spirituality is an independent entity, capable of being detached from justice or whatever other entity is under discussion. When the problem is detachment or separation, the answer is connection or reconnection. Finding the answer then becomes the search for a super glue that will ensure that the two will stay connected. But I believe that searching for a super glue is the wrong conceptualization of the problem (and not just because "super glue" is not a theological term!). Why it is the wrong conceptualization will become clear in the course of this chapter.[3]

Being Christian

Stated succinctly, to be Christian means to be a disciple of Jesus. A disciple is one who learns from and patterns his or her life after Jesus.

In Jesus, the reign of God was (and still is) present in the world. Therefore, to know about God one looks to Jesus. Jesus was in the world as the embodiment of God, to make God's rule visible to the world that does not yet acknowledge that rule. Thus, the reign of God made visible in Jesus poses a contrast to the world (including the natural order, which is fallen or sinful) and is the beginning of its restoration.[4] Jesus' teaching depicts life under the rule of God, a rule that began in its fullness in Jesus' life, teaching, death, and resurrection. In sum, to be a disciple of Jesus is to live in and to be shaped by the story of Jesus, whose life, teaching, death, and resurrection made (and make) visible the renewal and restoration of all creation.

Being a disciple of Jesus thus means living in relationships—a relationship with Jesus as well as relationships with others who are also disciples of Jesus. Jesus' teaching—which dealt with the treatment of poor people, sick people, Samaritans, and women—involved both social issues and personal relationships. Moreover, it supplied resistance strategies by means of which people without power could turn the tables nonviolently on military occupiers and oppressors. In Jesus' life and teaching, we see the beginning of a social movement that received specific visibility when Jesus called his disciples to follow him. Later,

Jesus sent these same disciples into the world to invite others into a community whose primary function was to make visible the rule of God on earth.

Old Testament Precedents

The community inaugurated by Jesus was not altogether new, but rather represented a new stage in a community's life that began with God's call of Abraham. The corporate, peoplehood character of salvation appears clearly in the exodus, the paradigmatic event in God's calling of a people that came to be named Israel. The Old Testament recounts the story of Israel and the Israelites' efforts to understand who they were and how they were to live as God's people. The failures, doubts, and disobedience of the patriarchs, the office of kingship as a failure to trust God's rule, the disobedience and obedience of kings, the accounts of violence alongside triumphs without resort to violence—these narratives and themes comprise the story of Israel's efforts to understand and live as God's people, the human entity through which God works in the world.

The Babylonian exile that followed the capture of Jerusalem in 587 B.C.E. introduced a new element to this story. The new challenge was for the people of God to "seek the welfare of the city where I have sent you into exile, . . . for in its welfare you will find your welfare" (Jer 29:7). As John Howard Yoder has explained, the exiles from Israel were "to settle in, to buy land and plant gardens and vineyards, to marry off their children and enjoy their grandchildren"—the point being that they could "renew the life of faith anywhere" without needing to be masters of society's direction.[5] As they lived that life of faith, God assured them, they would bless the host society even as they witnessed to the rule of God. Stories about Daniel, Esther, and Daniel's three friends recount acts of faithfulness in the course of being civilly disobedient to empire.[6] In all these cases, they honored God's call *not* to assimilate, maintaining their identity as God's people while living and working within the Babylonian culture.

Jesus inherited this community and gave it additional substance with his teaching about the rule of God, a rule that rejected the use of violence to control the outcome of history. It is this community of God's people, extending from the Babylonian exile into the early centuries of the Christian era, that was undone when the Church embraced empire, symbolized most clearly by the fourth-century emperor Constantine.[7]

Discipleship Ecclesiology

Until the fundamental change that occurred with Constantine—that is, the linking of Church and civil authorities—being related to the God of Israel and Jesus meant living in the community of God's people.[8] That was the calling of

Abraham, a conception of God's people that entered a new stage with the life and teaching of Jesus. In this new stage, God's people were now identified by faith in and acceptance of Jesus as the Messiah, a theological revision that opened the way for receiving into the community people who were not Jews. Even so, the people of God was the continuation of the people Israel, and the identifying mark of this people was a life lived by the rule of Yahweh. Now, however, the acknowledgment of Jesus as Messiah meant that his life and teaching became the norm for the life of that community.

In Luke 4, we not only see Jesus' appeal to his continuity with Israel—after reading from Isa 61, which speaks of the coming of God's salvation, Jesus tells his listeners, "Today this scripture has been fulfilled in your hearing"—we also encounter the content of his newly inaugurated ministry: "good news to the poor," "release to the captives," "recovery of sight to the blind," and freedom for the "oppressed" (Luke 4:18). This proclamation of justice was more than an empty claim. Surveying Jesus' work as recorded in the gospels reveals that his ministry for and with his disciples was a ministry of justice that challenged the oppressive character of the purity system of his time (through such things as Sabbath-day healings and consorting with people the code deemed unclean), elevating the status of women and Samaritans, and caring for the poor and the outcast. Indeed, Jesus' acts and the relationships he developed were intrinsically characterized by justice. Justice cannot be separated from this ministry; if justice is lacking then the ministry no longer witnesses to the reign of God.

To relate to Jesus, then, is to be a disciple of Jesus in this justice-seeking community. The mission of this people is to continue the mission of Jesus to make present the reign of God in the world. This community is formed around and through Jesus Christ, and is shaped by the life and teaching of Jesus. It is therefore not possible to relate to Jesus or to accept Jesus as Messiah without being part of this community and doing the justice that characterizes it. To assume that one could relate to Jesus without becoming a disciple of Jesus would be like proclaiming oneself a basketball player but never attending practices and games. Being Christian, being identified with Jesus, means to live as a disciple of Jesus in the community that Jesus' teaching depicted and that his life exemplified. Following Jesus is not something *added to* an experience of Christ, or something that one does *along with* an experience with Christ. Following Jesus is what it means to be Christian.

Moreover, if justice made visible is a characteristic of the community of the people of God, then the idea of Christian faith without justice is not possible. If one has to ask how to add justice to Christian faith, then one already has a distorted version of Christian faith. Correspondingly, if one has to ask how to bring justice into the experience of the Church, one has a faulty understanding of the nature of the Church. When the Church is faithful, the relationships that it displays witness to and make visible peace and justice. This witness involves both its own visible structures and its challenge to unjust structures in the larger world. If the people of God do not display justice in these regards, then this community is failing its mission. Moreover, since justice deals with relationships between people and among people and structures, justice is not the work of lone individuals. Rather, justice is a work of the people as community.

If we use the term "ecclesiology" to describe this community, then it is a *discipleship ecclesiology.* One's relationship to Jesus and thus to the God of Israel and of Jesus is not defined exclusively (or even primarily) by an inner, spiritual relationship to Jesus and to the God of Jesus. Although one can certainly meditate about the life of discipleship, the practice of this life—living what Jesus taught and exemplified rather than meditating about it—defines the relationship to Jesus.

Narrative Christus Victor

When considering the place of justice in the Church—discipleship ecclesiology, as I have called it—we must also consider what theologians call "the work of Christ," that is, the atonement. In his person and in his work, Jesus was the embodiment of the reign of God on earth, a reign that inevitably confronted the rule of Satan in the world. What is more, the teaching and the life of Jesus revealed how the reign of God confronts the rule of Satan. It is, the gospel writers tell us, a confrontation that happened without Jesus' resort to coercion or violence. That the confrontation was without violence is evident in Jesus' rebuke of Peter for drawing a sword when the mob came to arrest Jesus (Luke 22:49–51; John 18:10–11) and is further evident in Jesus' ironic comment to the arresting mob, "Have you come out with swords and clubs as if I were a bandit?"(Luke 22:52), a comment that implies that, had they truly understood him, they would have known that weapons were unnecessary.

In this confrontation, the powers of evil were eventually provoked to the point of murder. They killed Jesus. On the third day thereafter, God raised Jesus from the dead. This resurrection was nothing less than God's triumph over the powers of evil, establishing forever that the reign of God controls the fate of the universe.

In the earthly dimension of this confrontation, the community of Jesus—the Church, with Jesus as its head—is the structure that represents the reign of God. The Roman Empire, the earthly structure ultimately responsible for killing Jesus, represents the reign of evil, that is, all the structures of the earth that have yet to acknowledge the rule of God. Jesus' life, lived in confrontation with Jewish religious codes and the Roman Empire, is thus an earthly confrontation with cosmic dimensions. In the gospels we read of this confrontation from an earthly perspective, that is, from the standpoint of the people who walked the dusty roads of Palestine with Jesus. In the book of Revelation, we read of the same confrontation from a cosmic perspective—as the confrontation between the reign of God and the reign of Satan.

This confrontation between the reign of God and the reign of evil, with Jesus' resurrection as the triumph of the reign of God, constitutes an atonement motif that I have elsewhere called "narrative Christus Victor."[9] In this motif, to experience salvation is to participate with Christ in the confrontation between the reign of God and the rule of evil. To experience salvation means to live in the way of Jesus in confrontation with (and in witness to) the structures of evil that do not acknowledge the rule of God. Building on a *discipleship ecclesiology*, narrative Christus Victor presents a *discipleship atonement* motif: One cannot experience salvation in the reign of God without living in the reign of God. And since the reign of God in narrative Christus Victor concerns justice, one does not live according to the reign of God without doing justice.

The Atonement Connection

At the beginning of this chapter, I pointed to the problem of the separation of spirituality and ethics. It is important to see how narrative Christus Victor avoids this separation. For narrative Christus Victor, sin consists of living on the side of the rule of evil in opposition to the reign of God. That is the beginning position of every human being. It means that all of us, as sinful human beings, participate in the rule of evil that crucified Jesus. We thus share responsibility for the death of Jesus.

To experience salvation in the reign of God requires changing sides in the struggle between the reign of God and the rule of Satan. Changing sides functions as a metaphor for accepting Jesus or experiencing salvation in the reign of God. Changing sides is more than a mere change in status. It is an actual transfer of loyalty and allegiance that embraces the task of learning a new way to live. As Paul wrote, "He has rescued us from the power of darkness and transferred us into the kingdom of his beloved Son, in whom we have redemption, the forgiveness of sins" (Col 1:13–14). Taking this new way means becoming a disciple of Jesus, whose life and teaching made present the reign of God in human history. One cannot experience this salvation without actually taking up a new way of life any more than one can switch from football to basketball without actually going to basketball practice and learning the game. Within the paradigm of narrative Christus Victor, a spirituality focused on a "personal relationship with Jesus" that does not issue in an ethical life transformed by the reign of God made visible in Jesus does not constitute an authentically Christ-related spirituality. In other words, it is not conceptually viable in narrative Christus Victor to envision a Christian spirituality that accommodates conduct in opposition to Jesus' teaching and example, such as killing in capital punishment and killing in war.

The idea of changing sides implies some level of human responsibility in the process of salvation. What does personal responsibility look like for changing sides? On the one hand, God created all human beings with a free will, which makes us responsible for our actions. We need to make a conscious choice to leave a sinful way of life and to join and live by the reign of God made present in Jesus' life. Moreover, we are responsible for the choices that align our actions with the structures and powers of the rule of Satan. In other words, while this change of sides may begin with a decision at a certain point in time, it involves ongoing, daily choices to continue to live within and by the narrative of Jesus. In this conceptualization, human beings are continually responsible, and an understanding of salvation and Christian faith distinct from living as a disciple of Jesus is inconceivable.

At the same time, we must recognize that sinful human beings cannot save themselves; they cannot, under their own power and authority, overcome the rule of Satan. To the contrary, changing to the side of God can occur only under the call and the power of God. Similarly, sinful human beings cannot undo their participation in Jesus' death; they can only beg forgiveness. God incorporates them onto the side of God in spite of what they have done, without those sinful human beings having any capacity to return anything to God in compensation for their participation in the cross. Participating in the salvation of the reign of God is therefore an experience of grace. It is an unearned, unmerited gift of God's call, accomplishing in sinners that which they cannot accomplish through their own power. In this conceptualization, human beings live by grace as disciples of Jesus, and an understanding of salvation and Christian faith distinct from living as a disciple of Jesus is inconceivable.

If certain elements of the previous two paragraphs seem to contradict each other, that perception is correct. These paragraphs present a genuine paradox—two contradictory statements that are both true. Narrative Christus Victor makes visible the paradox of grace that is expressed in Paul's statement: "I worked harder than any of them—though it was not I, but the grace of God that is with me" (1 Cor 15:10).

Contrast these observations about narrative Christus Victor, discipleship, and salvation to that of satisfaction atonement. The satisfaction atonement motif has dominated atonement theology for much of the past millennium, since its first articulation in Anselm's *Why the God Man?* in 1098. Satisfaction atonement focuses on the death of Jesus understood as a punctiliar event. Nothing of Jesus' life and teaching, or resurrection, figures in atonement. The death of Jesus is aimed toward God. In Anselm's version of atonement, Jesus' death was necessary in order to satisfy the offended honor of God and restore order in the universe. In a later Protestant version of this atonement model, Jesus bore the punishment that sinful humankind deserved. His death had the divine law as its target, rather than God's honor, and it satisfied the law's requirement that sin be punished.

In both of these satisfaction motifs, salvation consists of a change in status before God. For Anselm, sin distorted the order of creation and offended God's honor, thus estranging sinful humankind from God. In this early rendition of satisfaction atonement, Jesus' death, by satisfying God's honor and restoring the order of creation, changes the sinner's status before God, that is, the sinner is restored to God's favor and no longer needs to die. In the later Protestant version, the sinner deserves the punishment of death. When Jesus dies in the sinner's place, the sinner has escaped his or her rightful punishment and is consequently restored to fellowship with God as one who no longer needs to die.

For our purposes in this essay, satisfaction atonement's rendering of salvation poses a marked contrast to participation in the reign of God as represented in the narrative Christus Victor model. In any variant of the Anselmian motif, salvation concerns a status change that happens apart from any discussion of discipleship or of Jesus' life and teaching. The saving work of Jesus involves *only* the event of his death, and consideration of the life of discipleship comes later, if at all. It is at this juncture that the problematic separations occur—separation of salvation from justice and ethics, or separation of spirituality from justice and ethics. In Anselmian atonement, salvation is a matter of *being*, of standing in a new status before God. Indeed, a satisfaction atonement motif is intrinsically one in which ethics, living as a disciple, is conceptually distinct from a saving relationship with Jesus. That is how justice is separated from spirituality.

Stated very directly, if justice and spirituality (or justice and Christianity) should be inseparable, it will be necessary to change our atonement motifs. The predominant atonement motifs of satisfaction or substitutionary atonement have already separated justice and spirituality. Since satisfaction atonement is an inadequate paradigm for discipleship, churches in the discipleship tradition and persons concerned about salvation *and* ethics should abandon satisfaction atonement. I offer narrative Christus Victor as a helpful biblical alternative.[10]

Spirituality and Justice

I am now in a position to address the question of spirituality. The two atonement paradigms, satisfaction and narrative Christus Victor, understand the individual sinner's relationship to God quite differently. Satisfaction atonement focuses on the individual and his or her status before God. In this rendering of the Christian faith, the serious Christian devotes much effort to cultivating this individual relationship and a consciousness of God. The higher this God-consciousness, the better (i.e., the "more Christian"). This, I take it, is what much of North American "Christian spirituality" is about. This status with and before God is not intrinsically a statement of ethics and discipleship. Ethics and discipleship are something else to engage in, after and/or alongside one's altered status before God. In light of this understanding of salvation, it is quite obvious how persons can conceive of ethics, justice, becoming separated from spirituality. The answer to this separation is not a matter of finding a better glue to hold spirituality and justice together. The separation is intrinsic to the underlying atonement motif, and no glue will ultimately stick together two separate and conceptually different entities.

What we need is an atonement motif that does not separate justice and relationship to God. Salvation, as conceptualized within the motif of narrative Christus Victor, successfully integrates a relationship to God with being a disciple of Jesus. In this motif, doing justice is an intrinsic dimension of a relationship to God, so that if justice is lacking, it is clear that one is no longer living in a way formed by the reign of God.

This approach to justice and spirituality has important implications for many dimensions of the Christian life, for it shifts the focus of salvation, ethics, and spirituality from the individual to the reign of God. Since satisfaction atonement focuses on an individual's relationship to God and to Jesus Christ, it inevitably encourages those who embrace it to examine and cultivate their feelings and their consciousness of God. What is God doing in my life today? What is God's will for my life? These are the questions that predominate in such a scheme. Unfortunately, such questions reveal an egocentric orientation that assumes that God exists for the individual and that the individual's response to God is the focus of God's acts in history.

In contrast, narrative Christus Victor focuses on the reign of God and then asks about the individual's relationship to that reign. The individual sinner still experiences salvation—that is not in doubt—but the focus is now on the reign of God. Instead of examining one's *inner* life for signs of a relationship to God, one examines one's *entire* life to see if it is being lived in and oriented by the rule of God made present in Jesus. Instead of asking, "What is God's will for my life?" the disciple asks, "Is my life in line with God's will for the world?" This formulation is not spirituality reconnected to justice. It is neither ethics without a savior nor salvation by human effort. It is salvation that is justice lived in the paradox of grace that is narrative Christus Victor.

Communal Spirituality

Finally, I come to the point of discussing the spirituality, the God-consciousness, of the people of God. If, as I have argued, the people of God constitute the primary means by which individuals experience God, then corporate worship, rather than individual experience, emerges as the primary spirituality of those in the community. In other words, the primary means and place for individuals to experience God should be in the Church and through the Church's corporate worship. Correspondingly, the inner experience of individuals should never be considered the *primary* spirituality of Christian faith. If one has to lose oneself in a prayer closet or embark on a private retreat to find God, then one has lost track of the fact that the primary experience of God and of Jesus Christ is in the corporate belonging to the people of God, as imperfect as they might be.

To be sure, many Christians find prayer closets and private retreats spiritually helpful. I do not mean to discount those experiences or to render them
intrinsically unhelpful. My point, however, is that such retreats and practices
are not complete in and of themselves, nor are they the essence of Christian
experience. Such practices can and should serve as preparation for the full
experience of Christian identity in the community of God's people and in that
community's practice of justice, for it is in community that people experience
and express the God-consciousness of participating in the reign of God.
People find God and people experience salvation by participating in this community that is formed around Jesus Christ. This worship of God includes the
doing of justice and living as disciples of Jesus. If that dimension of the experience of God is lacking, then it is not really Christian experience. Indeed, it is
not Christian faith.

Notes

1. My sources for John Dey's work include personal conversations, e-mail correspondence, and
the draft of a new discipleship paradigm.

2. My approach to this separation builds on the analysis of atonement in my book *The Nonviolent
Atonement* (Grand Rapids: Eerdmans, 2001).

3. I have described the function of spirituality without defining it. Why a precise definition is
unnecessary will become clear in the remainder of the essay.

4. Since the natural order shares in the fallenness that God is restoring, I part company with the
belief in the Reformed tradition that "orders of creation" establish the state and certain vocations and
estates in life. As symbols of creation's fallenness, consider birth defects and natural disasters (torna-
does, hurricanes, and earthquakes) that cause harm haphazardly and indiscriminately.

5. John Howard Yoder, "See How They Go with Their Face to the Sun," in *For the Nations: Essays
Public and Evangelical* (Grand Rapids: Eerdmans, 1997), 53.

6. Ibid., 57.

7. Ibid., 69–70.

8. The seminal article on the changes in the fourth century is John Howard Yoder, "The
Constantinian Sources of Western Social Ethics," in *The Priestly Kingdom: Social Ethics as Gospel* (Notre
Dame, Ind.: University of Notre Dame Press, 1984), 135–47. See also Yoder, "The Otherness of the
Church," in *The Royal Priesthood: Essays Ecclesiological and Ecumenical* (ed. Michael G. Cartwright;
Grand Rapids: Eerdmans, 1994), 53–64. Recent historical work has challenged Yoder on certain details
of the Constantinian shift but has not fundamentally altered his theological analysis of the changes that
occurred.

9. See Weaver, *Nonviolent Atonement*, 19–69. Developing the earthly facet of this confrontation on
the basis of the gospels distinguishes *narrative* Christus Victor from the classic version of Christus
Victor, which envisioned only the cosmic dimension and, over the centuries, disregarded the earthly
dimension. The book that stimulated the twentieth-century discussion of what I have here called the
classic version of Christus Victor is Gustaf Aulén, *Christus Victor: An Historical Study of the Three Main
Types of the Idea of Atonement* (trans. A. G. Herbert; New York: Macmillan, 1969).

10. Satisfaction atonement has other problematic dimensions relative to violence that I consider
even more significant than the issues raised in this essay. For a discussion of these problems, see
Nonviolent Atonement. A shorter version is J. Denny Weaver, "Violence in Christian Theology,"
CrossCurrents 51 (2001): 150–76.

5

ECCLESIAL DISCIPLESHIP AND THE UNITY OF SPIRITUALITY AND SOCIAL JUSTICE

— Richard D. Crane —

The endeavor to connect spirituality, discipleship, and social justice through an account of the nature and mission of the Church faces formidable obstacles. If popular religious discourse is any indication, the most striking similarity between spirituality and discipleship is their *lack of connection* to the Christian community. Consider, for instance, the renewed North American interest in spirituality, a renewal punctuated by claims of personal relationships with God and searches for God within the self.[1] This brand of spirituality is frequently defined in opposition to organized religion and participation in a faith community. While numerous critics have complained that such versions of spirituality reflect the worst features of a narcissistic consumer culture, the word "spirituality" nonetheless remains widely associated with the individual quest for personal fulfillment.[2]

Similarly, the word "discipleship" is frequently assumed to be a matter of the individual's attempt to determine "What would Jesus do?" In his analysis of Charles Sheldon's classic novel *In His Steps* (1896), Michael Cartwright identifies assumptions about discipleship that remain prevalent in North American Christianity a century after the book's publication. In the novel, Sheldon's protagonist pastor invites his congregation's members to *voluntarily* ask themselves, "What would Jesus do?" Sheldon thus presents discipleship as an optional practice of heroic achievement above and beyond ordinary Christian life. In addition, the novel places the locus of decision making in each individual's private conscience rather than in the gathered community of disciples.[3]

Although the corporate Christian life seems to many North Americans to be peripheral, even antithetical, to discipleship, spirituality, and the struggle for justice, I contend just the opposite, namely, that connecting Christian spirituality and an authentically Christian social witness depends upon the recovery of the ecclesial character of both discipleship and salvation. Our goal, then, is to provide a theological framework for linking spirituality and social justice, a goal I will pursue by weaving together themes from the Synoptic Gospels and the Pauline corpus. This, I believe, is the crucial task of constructive theology. Since the Christian canon is a diverse collection of texts, constructive theological reflection necessarily entails "piecing together" various New Testament strands in order to articulate a coherent Christian vision. Theologically speaking, the task of reconnecting spirituality and the social witness of the Church demands a creative, synthetic imagination, an ability to discern connections rarely made in our context.[4]

Discipleship and Social Justice

In *The Politics of Jesus,* John Howard Yoder argues that Chalcedon's affirmation of Christ's full divinity and humanity means this: that Jesus is both normatively human and the ultimate revelation of the character of God. Against certain trends in Christian social ethics, Yoder thus maintains that the primary authoritative norm for Christian ethics should be the call to imitate God's character as revealed in the gospel accounts of Jesus' life, death, and resurrection.[5] In the following pages, I assume the validity of Yoder's argument (recognizing, of course, that following Christ can never mean a simple repetition of his actions, but rather requires judgments about how to be faithful in a given context). And if Christ's life, message, and self-sacrificial death provide the normative pattern for Christian living, it is imperative for us to risk an interpretation of the meaning of Jesus Christ for the identity and mission of the Church.

Matthew 12:22–29 might seem a strange starting point for this interpretive work, but its narrative content provides clues about the relationship between Christ's words and deeds and social justice. In this short passage, Jesus expels an evil spirit from a man, restores the man's vision and speech, and thereby provokes the accusation that he is in league with Beelzebul, the prince of demons. Jesus rejects the accusation, of course, and offers a climactic declaration: "But if it is by the Spirit of God that I cast out demons, then the kingdom of God has come to you."

This healing/exorcism, like others in the gospels, is best interpreted in light of first-century Jewish eschatology and demonology, which interpreted history in terms of two ages. According to this scheme, the present evil age constituted a period of conflict between God and the evil spirits, who had formed a unified kingdom under Satan's leadership. Illness, misfortune, suffering, and oppressive social and political structures were construed as manifestations of Satan's stranglehold on human life. Israel's messianic hope lay, then, in the glorious age to come, when Satan's power would be broken and God's intentions for human wholeness would be fully realized.[6]

The connection between the Holy Spirit, Jesus, the kingdom of God, and the expulsion of evil spirits is significant. The Synoptic Gospels interpret Jesus' ministry as an act of aggression against the Evil One's stronghold, a challenge to the powers that enslave, torment, and damage human beings.[7] By the power of the Spirit, who makes all things new, the eschatological kingdom of God dawns *in the present evil age* as Jesus delivers people from multiple forms of bondage. That this is Jesus' mission is evident in his self-identification as the one anointed by the Spirit to open blind eyes, release captives, proclaim good news to the poor, and announce the Jubilee Year of economic justice (Luke 4:19). When asked by the Baptist's disciples, "Are you the one who is to come, or are we to wait for another?" Jesus points to his deeds that signal the messianic age anticipated in Isaiah: the blind receive sight, the lame walk, the deaf hear, the dead are raised up, and the poor have the gospel preached to them (Matt 11:2–5).

Because Jesus construed the Mosaic law's purpose to be mediating God's concern for human wholeness, he opposed interpretations of the law that functioned to exclude from the covenant community persons and groups considered unclean. Contrary to the separatist spirit of the Essenes and segments of the Pharisees, Jesus enacted a gracious inclusion of tax collectors and sinners, the ritually impure, the blind, lame, and deaf, and others written off as beyond the pale of God's covenant love. Indeed, his table fellowship with such marginalized persons represented an anticipatory participation in the festal banquet of the age to come.[8]

In Jesus' ministry, then, we find no bifurcation between spiritual, physical, and social matters. He forgave sin, healed diseased, taught people how to pray, fed the hungry, and called his listeners to practice the economic provisions of the Jubilee Year. His well-documented confrontations with the religious establishment emerged as he opposed social practices and arrangements that excluded, dehumanized, and oppressed human beings. He criticized certain scribes and Pharisees for their status-driven behavior, their lack of compassion for human suffering, and their exploitation of economically vulnerable widows (Mark 12:38–40). The cleansing of the temple constituted an act of prophetic protest against the corrupt Sadducean establishment. In the parable of the Rich Man and Lazarus, Jesus expressed in the strongest possible terms God's opposition to those who lived luxurious lives indifferent to the misery of their fellow human beings.[9]

The canonical gospels not only bear witness to Jesus' words and actions, but they also constitute discipleship manuals for the communities for which they were written.[10] Jesus commissions his disciples to participate in a ministry in continuity with his own, and so he sends them to raise the dead, heal diseases, expel demons, and cleanse lepers. The "praxis of the Kingdom of God," Edward Schillebeeckx argues, consists in deeds of deliverance, the setting free of one's fellow human beings.[11] In the parable of the Good Samaritan, which concludes with the command to "go and do likewise," discipleship demands compassion for, and deeds designed to deliver, human beings in danger, suffering, and distress.

This much, then, is clear: Jesus' proclamation of God's reign was inseparable from his inauguration of a *new kind of community*. This community, which was to be characterized by mutual service rather than domineering authority (Mark 10:42–45), was charged by Jesus to follow, in different historical and social contexts, his words and deeds. The mission of the Church, therefore, includes sharing Jesus' concern for the poor, the marginalized, and the vulnerable. If Jesus opposed the exploitation of widows in first-century Palestine, then contemporary Christians should stand in opposition to global economic arrangements that allow some to accumulate massive wealth while millions lack the resources for a humane existence. If Jesus came to deliver persons from bondage, twenty-first century Christians must exhibit a commitment to delivering persons from malnutrition, torture, racist and sexist social arrangements, the violence of war, and domestic violence. The Church is appointed, as Jesus was, to defend human dignity by opposing whatever dehumanizes and destroys. In sum, Christian concern for social justice is not based upon a general philosophical concept of justice; rather, it is based upon Jesus' concrete demonstration of compassion for human beings in distress.

We should not overlook, of course, the soteriological implications of Jesus' proclamation and embodiment of God's kingdom. The salvation Jesus brings is not merely a matter of the individual's relationship with God. As the redemption, healing, and transformation of all creation, this salvation is eschatological and cosmic in scope. Ultimately, salvation is the new creation anticipated in the book of Isaiah and other prophetic writings as an age of justice, peace, reconciliation, human wholeness, and deliverance from every form of oppression (e.g., Isa 2:2–4; 9:3–7; 11:1–9; 61:1–2).

Discipleship, Salvation, Church: Pauline Themes

The theme of discipleship is not limited to the Synoptic Gospels. Within the Pauline corpus, it is difficult to draw a line of demarcation between Paul's theology and his ethical teachings.[12] Paul's writings manifest an intimate connection between the indicative (what God has done in Christ) and the imperative (how

Christians should live). Christ's death on the cross, as an act of loving, self-sacrificial obedience, is consistently upheld by Paul as paradigmatic for the obedience of all Christians.[13]

In contrast to Paul's theological ethics, however, many North American
Christians tend to reduce discipleship to a peripheral matter, logically subsequent to and only tenuously connected to the message of salvation in Christ.
One contributing factor to this tendency has been the dominance within
North American Protestant soteriological thought of the Lutheran tradition's
concept of justification as a quasi-juridical declaration of the sinner's righteousness before God. According to the Formula of Concord, justification is
imputed righteousness, absolution that changes the legal status of the sinner
(*coram Deo* = before the face of God) but does not include the transformation
of the sinner.[14] Luther himself was reticent to affirm an ethic of *imitatio Christi*
because he feared a reintroduction of works righteousness into the salvation
experience.[15] The unfortunate consequence has been the compartmentaliza-
tion of justification, on the one hand, and sanctification and discipleship, on
the other. Correspondingly, the ethical imperatives of the Christian life have
been reduced to secondary status, unrelated to the reality of salvation.

Luther's warnings against works righteousness should be taken seriously.
Salvation is a gift of grace, and to view discipleship as heroic moral achievement would be an error as serious as dismissing the New Testament's discipleship motif. The challenge, then, is to set forth a more comprehensive vision of
the meaning of salvation that avoids these errors yet incorporates discipleship
as integral to the salvation process.[16]

Salvation Is Incorporation into Christ/Christ's Body

Paul viewed the Christian's relationship with God in terms of solidarity
with, participation in, or belonging to Christ.[17] From a Pauline perspective,
then, salvation is the Christian's living union with the crucified and risen Christ,
and to be baptized into Christ is to be incorporated into Christ, to participate
in Christ's death and resurrection. Accordingly, Paul tells the Corinthians that
their bodies "are members of Christ" (1 Cor 6:15–16), reacting with horror at
the thought of sexual immorality because it is unthinkable to join bodies, which
are members of Christ himself, to a prostitute. He even goes so far as to identify the intimate sexual union in which husband and wife become one flesh as
an analogy of the union between Christ and Church (Eph 5:31–32).[18]

Incorporation into Christ does not merely entail a relationship between
Christ and the individual. To be joined to Christ is simultaneously to be
incorporated into Christ's body, the Church (Rom 12:4–5; 1 Cor 12:4–31). In
the Church, Christians are one body in Christ and members of one another.
The unity of this community should be such that "if one member suffers, all
suffer together with it; if one member is honored, all rejoice together with it"

(1 Cor 12:26). John Milbank's assertion that "the unity and inter-communion of Christians is not just a desirable appendage of Christian practice, but is itself at the heart of the actuality of redemption" is compatible with the irreducibly ecclesial character of Pauline soteriology.[19]

Union with Christ includes both reconciliation with God and reconciliation between previously hostile persons and groups. The reconciliation of Jews and Gentiles within Christ's own broken and risen body is not a positive by-product of salvation, but is itself the salvific goal of Christ's redemptive death (Eph 2).[20] The socioeconomic, gender, ethnic, or racial categories that divide persons through alienated relationships of domination, social stratification, and mechanisms of exclusion are overcome through the formation of this new and reconciled humanity "in Christ" (Gal 3:28; Col 3:11).

In Christ: The Transformation of the Self

For Paul there is no union with Christ without the transformation of the self. To be "in Christ" is to have one's life conformed to the self-giving love enacted on the cross. Paul speaks of being crucified with Christ and transformed such that "it is no longer I who live, but it is Christ who lives in me" (Gal 2:20). Baptism into Christ's death is the event in which the old self, enslaved to sin, is crucified with Christ in order that Christians might be liberated from the tyranny of sin. The imperatives of Rom 6:12–23, in which Christians are exhorted not to let sin reign in their bodies and to offer themselves to God as instruments of righteousness, are not optional. To be alive to God in Christ is to be dead to sin. Throughout the Pauline corpus (e.g., Rom 8:5–14; Gal 5:16–26), the sharpest antithesis is drawn between the Christian's former way of life, the practices of the old self, and life according to "the flesh," on the one hand, and transformed existence in Christ, on the other. This transformed existence is the conformation of the self to Christ (e.g., Rom 8:29), which involves living lives patterned after Christ's generosity, his sacrificial self-offering to God and "for us," and his radical concern for others at great cost to himself (e.g., Rom 15:1–3, 7; 2 Cor 8:7–12; Eph 5:1–2).

This transformation is not a private matter, but takes place in and through incorporation into Christ's body. The very point of God's saving and reconciling work in Christ is that the Church might become the righteousness of God, embodying in its communal life the reconciling love of Jesus (2 Cor 5:21).[21] Paul explicitly connects this transformation to Christians' status as members of one another. The "new self" has put away the destructive vices— lying, theft, bitterness, slander, malice—that destroy community. Instead, he or she speaks words designed to edify and is kind, tenderhearted, forgiving, and truthful *because* "we are members of one another" (Eph 4:25). The self is transformed for the very purpose of participation in this communal life of reconciliation, mutual edification, mutual responsibility, and bearing one another's burdens (Eph 4:1–4; Rom 14:19; 1 Cor 10:23–24; Gal 6:1–2). The basis for this communal way of life is discipleship: the imitation of the pattern of Christ's self-sacrificial love, obedience, and willingness to adopt the posture of a servant (Phil 2:1–11).

The Gift of the Holy Spirit

In the Pauline corpus, salvation is the reception of the gift of new life in the Holy Spirit. Indeed, it is having the Spirit that defines and determines that someone is "in Christ" (Rom 8:9–10).[22] Therefore, we should expect to discover a link between the Spirit and the two soteriological motifs of incorporation into Christ and Christ's body, on the one hand, and the conformation of the self to Christ, on the other. In 1 Cor 12:13–27, Paul affirms that Christians are baptized by one Spirit into the body of Christ. The Holy Spirit is the bond of unity and the basis for Christian fellowship (Eph 4:3–4; Phil 2:1), as well as the agent of rebirth and renewal (Titus 3:5–7). Christians are saved through the sanctifying work of the Holy Spirit (2 Thess 2:13), and transformed existence is "living according to the Spirit" (Rom 8:5–13).

In the Synoptic Gospels, the Holy Spirit is the eschatological power of God at work in Jesus' deeds of deliverance. First-century Jewish expectations for the glorious age to come included the hope for the resurrection of the dead. Jesus' resurrection, as an act of the Spirit (Rom 1:3–4; 8:11), constitutes for Paul the inauguration of the eschatological new creation. Through incorporation into Christ and by virtue of participating in the Spirit, Christians are drawn into this new creation in the here and now (e.g., 2 Cor 5:17). New Testament scholar James Dunn characterizes the work of the Spirit as analogous to a bridge between the present and future, the "already" and the "not yet." The gift of the Spirit, who attests to our adoption as children of God (e.g., Rom 8:23; 2 Cor 1:22), is the beginning of the process that will reach its ultimate end with the resurrection of the body. In other words, this process of eschatological transformation, in which we already participate, is ultimately fulfilled only when the Spirit fully duplicates in us what the Spirit has already done in the resurrected Christ as the New Creation.[23]

Pulling the Strands Together

As future reality, salvation is God's ultimate eschatological victory over the principalities and powers that enslave and oppress human persons, a victory attained through Christ's death and resurrection (e.g., Rom 8:18–23; Col 2:14–15). In the present age, salvation involves incorporation into Christ, who has been raised from the dead by the power of the Spirit. Salvation, as incorporation into Christ, is an eschatological process of healing and transformation into which we have been drawn and, by God's grace, invited and empowered to participate. Our participation in this process of divine deliverance takes place within the Church, the new humanity that has been rescued from the dominion of darkness and inserted into the kingdom of the Son (Col 1:13–14). Within this community, salvation is the lifelong process of the conformation of the ecclesial self to Christ by virtue of the transforming power of the Holy Spirit.

The recovery of these communal and eschatological dimensions of salvation has important implications for our thinking about discipleship. Much of the anxiety about works righteousness finds it roots in individualistic conceptions of salvation. However, by recovering the communal and eschatological dimensions of salvation we quickly discover that the point of sanctification/discipleship is not meritorious human achievement. Rather, we recognize that salvation (understood as inclusion in the new social reality that God has brought into being "in Christ" *and* the correlative transformation required for such participation) is a gift of grace, a gift that allows human beings to participate in God's transformation of the entire creation.

I have argued that salvation and discipleship are inseparable, that the Spirit's transforming work has as its focus and end the conformation of the Christian's life to the pattern of Christ. But how do we connect this Pauline motif of salvation with the theme of discipleship in the Synoptic Gospels and its possible political implications? The connection is to be found in the fact that Paul, though he did not have the canonical gospels, refers back to the Jesus traditions that were available to him. For example, in Rom 12, Paul encourages Christians to obey Christ's teachings by blessing those who curse them, returning good for evil, and relinquishing revenge. The later inclusion of the gospels in the canon represents the Church's theological judgment that these particular narratives were indispensable for the Church's identification with Jesus Christ, a judgment that requires us to integrate Pauline language of conformity to Christ with the gospels' portrayals of Jesus' words and deeds. If Christ provides the pattern for the transformed communal existence that is the life of the Church, then the conformation of the self to Christ should include the alignment of the self with the priorities and commitments of Jesus, such as an active concern for the poor, the marginalized, the excluded, and the oppressed. If Jesus' mission was to engage in conflict with the powers that enslave, torment, afflict, and otherwise damage human persons, then being conformed to Christ means feeding the hungry, working for more equitable global economic arrangements, and putting an end to the torture of racism and political oppression. If the process of salvation is one of being transformed into his likeness (2 Cor 3:18), then Christians should share Jesus' commitment to the deliverance of "the least of these my brethren," that is, those who are hungry, thirsty, sick, imprisoned, and otherwise lacking in basic human necessities (Matt 25:40 KJV).

Spirituality

After linking discipleship and social justice, and both concepts to salvation, the final piece of the puzzle is to link discipleship and spirituality. One would presume that one of the primary goals of Christian spirituality is sanctification, "the Christian's progressive attainment of likeness to God's character and intentions for humanity."[24] The process of sanctification is nothing other than the salvific process of the conformation of the self to Christ discussed in the previous section. Therefore, the point of spirituality is not individual self-improvement. Rather, it is the alignment of oneself with God's purposes for the Church as witness to, embodiment of, and instrument in God's eschatological design.

Rodney Clapp observes that it is contrary to our habits as North Americans, shaped and molded by modernity and capitalism's consumeristic ethos, to view ourselves as overlapping members of one another.[25] However, the recovery of this insight is crucial if North American Christians are to be faithful to the ecclesiological reality of salvation. While an authentic Christian spirituality is concerned with the individual's spiritual growth, the primary concern, if the letter to the Ephesians is any indication, is spiritual maturation as a *communal* reality. According to Ephesians, the eschatological sovereignty of Christ over every rule and authority, power and dominion is manifest in the Church (1:19–23). This community is a work in progress, to be sure, but spiritual growth means nothing less than growing together in love (Eph 2:19–22; 3:14–17). It is the mutual love and compassion for one another, and the interethnic reconciliation embodied by this community, that make manifest God's wisdom to the "rulers and authorities in the heavenly realms," that is, the powers that enslave humanity in opposition to God's good purposes.[26]

In sum, spirituality is concerned with the entire Christian community's maturation such that this community embodies the quality of life characteristic of God's ultimate eschatological purposes. This would suggest that *corporate* spiritual practices—worship, the sacraments, fellowship, group prayer, Christian formation, group Bible study, and participation in mission and service activities—are of primary importance for Christian spirituality. These corporate practices are designed to bind Christians more closely to Christ and to one another and to form a people whose life together comprises a faithful witness to the ultimate purposes of God: to deliver the entire creation from forces that enslave, wound, and destroy.

Concluding Reflections:
Communal Spirituality and Social Justice

While the primary goal of this essay has been to outline a *theological* framework for linking spirituality and social justice, this last section seeks to delineate (in a very abbreviated form) some implications of this framework for Christian social and political engagement. The recovery of the *ecclesial* character of spirituality, salvation, and discipleship is urgently needed in our consumer-oriented North American culture. In his recent work, *The (Magic) Kingdom of God*, Michael Budde describes the dominance of the global culture industries, pointing out that the entertainment and advertising industries have a large stake in promoting a consumerist ethos in general and profligate levels of consumption in particular. Long before Budde's book appeared, historian Christopher Lasch and philosopher Alasdair MacIntyre had similarly observed that the market economy contributes to an ethos characterized by individualism, acquisitiveness, competitiveness, and narcissism. Americans are simply not trained to subordinate their interests to those of others; in fact, they are trained to do just the opposite. In this context, Budde laments that Catholic and mainline Protestant churches have tended to neglect Christian formation, leaving their members to cobble together their own eclectic spiritualities from commercial culture, nationalist ideologies, and fragments of the Christian tradition. The result, Budde notes, are spiritualities that privilege the acquisitive, feel-good messages of the culture industries, spiritualities incapable of practices aimed at peace, care for the poor, or any other goal transcending self-interest.[27] The problem does not lie with Catholics and mainline Protestants alone, however. Evangelical tendencies toward the individualization of salvation tend to promote a similar cultural ethos of personal fulfillment and self-absorption.

The recognition that salvation is nothing less than an eschatological process of healing and transformation of the entire creation provides an important corrective to the pervasive individualism of North American Christianity. In a culture that tends to market Christianity as a commodity for self-fulfillment, there exists an urgent need to recover this more comprehensive soteriological vision, one that insists the gift of salvation is joyous participation in a reality greater than one's own life. The gift of salvation is life together in a community that bears witness to an existence that God has made possible in Christ. Therefore, an authentically Christian spirituality is not a program of individual self-improvement, but rather is concerned with the formation of a community of disciples whose life together witnesses to God's purpose of delivering the whole creation from forces that enslave, wound, and destroy.

From a political standpoint, then, the ecclesiology set forth in this essay calls the Church to be an alternative community, bearing witness through its communal life to a radically different way of being human. As a political entity in its own right, the Church is called by God to provide a sample of the kind of humanity within which the destructive effects of the powers (e.g., poverty and racism) are overcome, a place where Christ's triumph over the powers becomes visible in a concrete way of life. That being the case, the Church's characteristic practices, such as worship, baptism, and the Lord's Supper, are themselves crucial to spiritual formation and ecclesial discipleship, since these practices serve to conform the Christian community to Christ. For example, eucharistic table fellowship, which celebrates and remembers Christ's generosity in laying down his life, should contribute to the formation of a generous people. In this regard, the first Christians actually celebrated the Eucharist in the context of a shared meal, meaning that the Lord's Supper was itself the practice of generosity—the sharing of food at a common meal.[28] In this way and others, the Church is called by God to model a new way of being human, which includes economic sharing, egalitarian relationships, racial reconciliation, and peaceful modes of conflict resolution.

Some critics, of course, have charged that the formation of an alternative community is not sufficient. For the African-American woman ordered to the back of a bus, Sunday's sermon about one's freedom in Christ will not suffice. For the laborer who works a ten-hour shift in an unsafe factory, the sharing of resources within the church community is not enough. The achievement of racial and economic justice demands changes in social, political, and economic policies and structures—something that the endeavor to create an "alternative community" cannot directly achieve.[29]

While these critics' challenges must be taken seriously, we must nonetheless respond that it is quite unnecessary to frame the issue as an either-or choice: *either* the Church as an alternative social formation *or* activism on behalf of the poor and oppressed. As John Howard Yoder has so aptly noted, "The church is called to be today what the world is called to be ultimately," and what the world is called to be ultimately is prefigured in Jesus' actions on behalf of human wholeness, his inclusion of the outcast, and his deliverance of human persons from every form of bondage.[30] So the critics are right: A church that is content merely to form an alternative community has not embraced the responsibilities of discipleship in a world of massive suffering. Even so, it is precisely those Christian communities that take seriously the task of embodying justice, equality, and generosity *in their communal lives* that are in the best position to produce disciples who pursue the commitments of Jesus and, as a result, affect society in ways that reflect God's purposes in the here and now.[31]

Notes

1. For an example of this, see Benjamin Shield and Richard Carlson, eds., *For the Love of God: Handbook for the Spirit* (New York: MJF Books, 1999).

2. See Robert Wuthnow, *After Heaven: Spirituality in America since the 1950s* (Berkeley: University of California Press, 1998). See also L. Gregory Jones, "A Thirst for God or Consumer Spirituality? Cultivating Disciplined Practices of Being Engaged by God," *Modern Theology* 13 (1997): 3–28. In this article, Jones notes that Thomas Moore's *Care of the Soul* displays little need for the practices and friendships of the Christian community (or any other community).

3. Michael G. Cartwright, "The Once and Future Church Revisited," in *Embodied Holiness: Toward a Corporate Theology of Spiritual Growth* (ed. Samuel M. Powell and Michael E. Lodahl; Downers Grove, Ill.: InterVarsity Press, 1999), 115–44.

4. William C. Placher, *The Domestication of Transcendence: How Modern Thinking about God Went Wrong* (Louisville, Ky.: Westminster John Knox, 1996), 197–99.

5. John Howard Yoder, *The Politics of Jesus: Vicit Agnus Noster* (Grand Rapids: Eerdmans, 1972), 100–106, 239; Nancey C. Murphy, "John Howard Yoder's Systematic Defense of Christian Pacifism," in *The Wisdom of the Cross: Essays in Honor of John Howard Yoder* (ed. Stanley Hauerwas et al.; Grand Rapids: Eerdmans, 1999), 52–53, 63–65.

6. For an exploration of first-century Jewish eschatology, see Edward Schillebeeckx, *Jesus: An Experiment in Christology* (New York: Crossroad, 1979), 183–84. Ched Myers argues that this apocalyptic vision is closely connected to political realities, the kingdom of Satan being a symbolic accentuation of the negative experiences of earthly rule. Ched Myers, *Binding the Strong Man: A Political Reading of Mark's Story of Jesus* (Maryknoll, N.Y.: Orbis, 1988), 165.

7. Schillebeeckx, *Jesus*, 184.

8. James D. G. Dunn, *Jesus' Call to Discipleship* (Cambridge: Cambridge University Press, 1992), 12–15.

9. Although this essay cannot explore the passion narratives and the saving significance of Christ's death on the cross, Christ's crucifixion should also be understood in terms of his struggle against oppressive religious and political power structures in the name of God's reign.

10. In this regard, see the essays in Richard Longenecker, ed. *Patterns of Discipleship in the New Testament* (Grand Rapids: Eerdmans, 1996).

11. Schillebeeckx, *Jesus*, 227.

12. I will include in this section insights from Ephesians and Colossians, even though many New Testament scholars question their Pauline authorship.

13. See Richard Hays, *The Moral Vision of the New Testament: Community, Cross, New Creation: A Contemporary Introduction to New Testament Ethics* (San Francisco: HarperSanFrancisco, 1996), 27–28. One example is Paul's use of the primitive Christian hymn in Phil 2:5–11. The hymn observes that, instead of seizing God-likeness, Jesus emptied himself of personal prerogatives and embraced suffering, servanthood, and death on the cross. These actions then serve as Paul's rationale for admonishing the church in Philippi to relinquish competitive self-promotion in favor of humility. Similar Pauline examples include Gal 6:1–2; Eph 4:32; 5:1; Rom 15:1–3, 7; and 2 Cor 8:7–12.

14. It is important to distinguish between subsequent Lutheran theology and Martin Luther's own more complex understanding of justification. Finnish scholars, led by Tuomo Mannermaa, have questioned the notion that Luther embraced a notion of justification unrelated to the actual transformation of sinners. See Carl E. Braaten and Robert W. Jenson, "Preface: The Finnish Breakthrough in Luther Research," and Simo Peura, "Christ as Favor and Gift (*donum*): The Challenge of Luther's Understanding of Justification," in *Union with Christ: The New Finnish Interpretation of Luther* (ed. Carl E. Braaten and Robert W. Jenson; Grand Rapids: Eerdmans, 1998), viii, 45.

15. Willard M. Swartley, "Discipleship and Imitation of Jesus/Suffering Servant: The Mimesis of New Creation," in *Violence Renounced: René Girard, Biblical Studies, and Peacemaking* (ed. Willard M. Swartley; Telford, Pa: Pandora Press U.S.; Scottdale, Pa.: Herald Press, 2000), 219.

16. Douglas Harink points out that Krister Stendahl opened new vistas in Pauline scholarship, shifting attention away from typically Lutheran (Protestant) themes of justification, guilt, grace, and

faith to the more concrete, historical issues of the relationship between Jews and Gentiles. See Douglas Harink, *Paul among the Postliberals: Pauline Theology beyond Christendom and Modernity* (Grand Rapids: Brazos, 2003), 13–16.

17. J. Paul Sampley, *Walking between the Times: Paul's Method of Moral Reasoning* (Minneapolis: Fortress, 1991), 12.

18. The recovery of the Pauline soteriological theme of union with and participation in Christ invites reflection on the relationship between the Eastern Orthodox doctrine of *theosis* (deification) and Protestant soteriologies. For a recent consideration of this, see Veli-Matti Kärkkäinen, "The Ecumenical Potential of the Eastern Doctrine of *Theosis*: Emerging Convergences in Lutheran and Free Church Soteriologies," *Sobornost/Eastern Churches Review* 23, no. 2 (2002): 45–77.

19. John Milbank, *Theology and Social Theory: Beyond Secular Reason* (Oxford: Basil Blackwell, 1990), 403. Milbank asserts elsewhere that "the church is not primarily a means of salvation, but rather is a goal of salvation. Our way back to God is through our incorporation into the historical body of the redeemed." John Milbank, "An Essay against Secular Order," *Journal of Religious Ethics* 15 (1987): 204.

20. See John Howard Yoder, "The New Humanity as Pulpit and Paradigm," in *For the Nations: Essays Public and Evangelical* (Grand Rapids: Eerdmans, 1997), 44.

21. Hays, *Moral Vision of the New Testament*, 24.

22. James D. G. Dunn, *The Theology of Paul the Apostle* (Grand Rapids: Eerdmans, 1996), 414, 423.

23. Frank D. Macchia, "Justification as New Creation: The Holy Spirit and the Doctrine by Which the Church Stands or Falls," *Theology Today* 58 (2001): 211–12; Dunn, *Theology of Paul the Apostle*, 403, 469; Sampley, *Walking between the Times*, 21.

24. E. C. Blackman, "Sanctification," in *The Interpreter's Dictionary of the Bible* (ed. George Buttrick et al.; Nashville: Abingdon, 1962), 4:210.

25. Rodney Clapp, "Tacit Holiness: The Importance of Bodies and Habits in Doing Church," in Powell and Lodahl, eds., *Embodied Holiness*, 70, 72.

26. Although it is impossible in this essay to do justice to the Pauline language of principalities and powers, these powers entail (among other things) sociopolitical realities, the pagan religious structures undergirding Roman and other societies, and the intellectual, moral, political, and economic structures that hold sway over people's lives. The powers, though created good, are fallen, and therefore enslave and damage humanity.

27. Michael Budde, *The (Magic) Kingdom of God: Christianity and the Global Culture Industries* (Boulder, Colo.: Westview, 1997), 25–26, 32–37. See also Alasdair MacIntyre, *After Virtue: A Study in Moral Theory* (Notre Dame, Ind.: University of Notre Dame Press, 1980); and Christopher Lasch, *The Culture of Narcissism: American Life in an Age of Diminishing Expectations* (New York: W. W. Norton & Co., 1978).

28. Various scholars have noted that one of the purposes of the early Church's eucharistic meal was to ensure that no community member lacked the basic materials to sustain life. See Harink, *Paul among the Postliberals*, 116–17, 125–28, as well as chapter 15 of this volume.

29. For a critique, see Robin Lovin, "Religion and American Public Life: Three Relationships," in *Religion and American Public Life: Interpretations and Explorations* (ed. Robin Lovin; New York: Paulist Press, 1986), 18–19.

30. John Howard Yoder, *Body Politics: Five Practices of the Christian Community before the Watching World* (Nashville: Discipleship Resources, 1992), viii–ix.

31. Michael Budde argues that the common denominator in Christian movements against slavery, apartheid, the arms race, the exploitation of women, and economic injustice is the faith-based passion of persons deeply invested in the role of disciple. See Budde, *(Magic) Kingdom of God*, 1–2.

6

HOLISTIC SPIRITUALITY
AS WITNESS

— *Brad J. Kallenberg* —

Central to Christian belief is the assertion that the physical realm is not all there is. For many, this assertion entails a commonsensical corollary: Human beings have two components, a physical body and an immaterial soul. This view is called body-soul dualism. Naturally, persons with this view hold that the soul is more important than the body; regardless of the state of the body, the state of one's soul is what really counts. Using this line of reasoning, Augustine (d. 430) concluded that that the rape of women by invading barbarians did not cost them their chastity. He reasoned that chastity is primarily a property of the soul that becomes the body's by association: "Not only the souls of Christian women who have been forcibly violated during their captivity, but also their bodies, remain holy."[1]

Christian thinkers quickly got into the habit of making interiority the locus of spirituality.[2] Although Meister Eckhart (d. 1327) stood on the margins of orthodoxy, he aptly expressed what theology had come to believe: Properties of the soul (such as chastity) and powers of the soul (such as memory) lie near the soul's surface. Deeper than knowledge, deeper than memory, deeper even than volition is the essence of the soul, that quiet place where God the Son is eternally being born. "But if it doesn't happen *in me*, what does it profit me? What matters is that it shall happen in me."[3] If authentic spirituality takes place here, in the "little castle" of the soul, what is the external world but a source of distraction, danger, and idolatry?[4]

Many have claimed that this emphasis on interior spirituality erected a conceptual barrier that prevented later generations of Christians from thinking of "spiritual" activities as belonging to the same class as those activities that serve the interests of social justice. It is just this barrier that many hope to pierce by discovering ways of reconnecting spirituality and social justice. However, as heirs of Augustine, we too easily assume that the two can be reconnected by simply adding one to the other. Very often the plea is made for us to beef up private spirituality on the assumption that the efficacy of social justice activity depends simply and crucially upon the spiritual preparation first undertaken in private. Thomas Merton once advised, "It is in deep solitude that I find the gentleness with which I can truly love my brothers and sisters. The more solitary I am, the more affection I have for them."[5] Merton is suggesting that the contemplative journey of interior spirituality arms the Christian for service. Similarly, nineteenth-century Baptist theologian Hezekiah Harvey emphasizes the effectiveness of attending to the interior life: "Spiritual force comes from within, from the hidden life of God in the soul. . . . The soul's secret power with God thus gives public power with men."[6] We can see in Harvey's words how easily a priority on interiority gets commuted into a type of individualism. In other words, the social sphere cannot be transformed until first the individual is changed. "Acquire inner peace," wrote St. Seraphin, "and a multitude around you will find salvation."[7]

A recent intellectual development challenges the hegemonies of both *dualism*, the view that human beings are souls housed in bodies, and *individualism*, the idea that social transformation reduces neatly to the transformation of each and every individual agent that comprises the community. These notions are hegemonic precisely because they seem to compel the conclusion that justice on the social level depends vitally on spirituality at the private level. Let us call the development that challenges these notions "anthropological holism."[8] However, I want to argue here for one particular application of anthropological holism, namely, for the plausibility of seeing private and corporate spirituality as *internally related* (rather than causally so).[9] By assembling some reminders of the way the word "spirit" enters our conversations, I hope to shed fresh light on the way we see the work of God's spirit at the level of social transformation.[10] As we shall see, social justice is not causally dependent on private spirituality because authentic spirituality is not private at all.

The Grammar of "Spirit"

Concepts get a grip on our lives in practical ways. A concrete noun, such as "shoe," takes on conceptual significance through our interaction with shoes. We learn that shoes are for buying, lacing, pairing, losing, finding, kicking off, and outgrowing. It makes sense, therefore, to speak of shoes in these contexts but not others. In fact, we learn what shoes are by speaking of them in these contexts in ways that befit shoes. Someone who uses the word "shoe" in the wrong context or manner will be speaking gibberish. After all, we would not know what to make of someone who asked whether a given shoe was "malicious" or whether another one was "timely."

Surprisingly, we learn the meaning of abstract words, such as "pain," in concrete ways as well, because what matters for learning words is not the concreteness of the concept but the *concreteness of our behavior*, namely, our speaking the word in specific contexts. When a child skins her knee, her crying is a form of communication with the parent. The parent who comforts the child with the words, "There, there. I know it hurts," is teaching the child a different way to communicate with others. Eventually, phrases such as "Ouch!" "It hurts!" and "I have a pain right here," go proxy for crying. "Pain" is not simply a verbal label that we attach to a sensation; words such as "pain" and "ouch" are tools we learn how to use through our interaction with others.[11] (In fact, one can only point to an instance of pain if he or she already knows how to use the word "pain.")

The fact that meanings of words grow out of our varied use of words both limits and enables divine revelation. The bad news seems to be that God has limited himself to using coarse, crude, creaturely language as the means to communicate with humans. The good news is that human language is adaptable and can be enriched over time. This flexibility gives revelation a toehold; as our form of life together alters, new concepts can emerge and grow. When a concept's evolution becomes noticeable, we can begin to get an inkling of where the concept is headed even when we cannot fully grasp its entirety.[12] For example, the notion of "resurrection" did not simply pop into existence three days after Calvary. Rather, it first entered Jewish culture as a retrospective way to understand the healing of the Shunammite woman's son by the prophet Elisha (2 Kgs 4:32–36). Later, resurrection became a metaphor for the restoration of the people of God (e.g., Ezek 37:1–14). The concept further expanded and gained greater circulation during the intertestamental period, during which era it foretold the return to life of martyred faithful Jews (e.g., 2 Macc 7).[13] This conceptual evolution was the backdrop against which the disciples, dull witted as they were, recognized the raising of Jesus as more than a temporary healing or the resuscitation of a corpse, but rather as the first fruit of a universal resurrection.

Like "resurrection," the concept of "spirit" has also undergone a conceptual evolution. While Christians today offhandedly describe the Holy Spirit as the Third Person of the Trinity, we must remember that earlier believers struggled mightily to say this correctly. As late as the fourth century, Augustine used "grace" and "the bond of love" (*vinculum caritas*) as synonyms for the Spirit.[14] As important as it might be to trace the conceptual history of "spirit," I want to focus my comments on its contemporary uses, for the grammar of ordinary language can help us see that the concept of "spirit" transgresses the arbitrary boundaries thought to disconnect spirituality and social justice.[15]

"Spirit" in the English Language

Let us first consider various uses of the English word "spirit." Most English speakers are quite familiar with uses of the concept that emphasize individuality. When we say someone "expired" (*ex spirare*) or "gave up the ghost," we mean that something about a particular individual changed, namely, he died. Alternatively, when we refer to a horse as "spirited," we mean that this particular horse acts in an unusually lively manner. What is under consideration is *this* horse, not *that* horse, or horses in general. A third way that we employ "spirit" individualistically is when we speak of an artist as "inspired." Here we mean that *this* artist, here and now, exhibits creative genius. Our comment says something about her as an individual. Finally, when a mild-mannered gentleman lashes out in a fit of jealous rage, we describe him as having been overcome by "a spirit of jealousy." Once again, this common idiom says something about the individual and his behavior.

Just as common, however, are those uses of "spirit" that have corporate connotations, a reality that, as we shall see, offers helpful resources for conceiving spirituality correctly as something exterior rather than merely interior to individuals. Consider first the phrase "holiday spirit." When we exhort someone to "get into the holiday spirit," we do not mean only that she should go about her daily business with a countenance of smarmy sentimentality. In fact, the spirit of the holidays constitutes the entire pattern of human activities that surrounds our celebration of Christmas—activities such as gift giving, forgiving grudges, sending chatty letters to forgotten relatives, singing carols, volunteering for charity work, and attending parties. This spirit is not a hidden interior state; rather, it is worn on our sleeves, embodied in human actions. That the holiday spirit tends to be contagious provides further evidence of its public nature.

Second, we sometimes describe a course of action as done "in the spirit of so-and-so." This means more than simply acting in someone's memory. As an example of the latter, we might erect a monument in tribute to St. Francis. But if we were to act *in the spirit* of St. Francis, we would need to imitate the manner in which he lived, perhaps by opening an animal shelter or giving our shoes to a homeless person. This use of the word "spirit" indicates the publicly recognizable and imitable pattern of St. Francis's mode of living. Similarly, if we were to live in the spirit of Mother Teresa, who became Christ to the poor of Calcutta, we would need to live in such a way that we bore a resemblance to her and the Christ she worshiped. It follows that a good place to begin when thinking about the spirit of Christ, then, is the characteristic pattern of Christ's actions that has been in some sense reproduced in lives such as Mother Teresa,

St. Francis, or the Apostle Paul. The similarities between these believers and Jesus are not as much something internal as they are something externally visible, something found in the weave of their interpersonal relationships. To say the same thing differently, the spirit of Christ is recognizable *between* believers as much as it is *in* them individually. This is not to say that the Holy Spirit is to be identified with interpersonal relationships. It is to say that we cannot understand "spirit" apart from concrete instantiations. God remained *Deus absconditus*, the hidden God, until God was manifest in Christ's incarnation. This incarnation is in an important sense extended by the embodiment of Christ's spirit in the *ekklesia*, the believing community that Paul tells us is the temple in whom the Spirit dwells corporately (see Eph 2:21–22). Thus, our knowledge of Christ's spirit is corporately assisted.

In addition to speaking of "holiday spirit" and acting "in the spirit of so-and-so," we commonly recognize the corporate dimension of "spirit" in phrases such as "school spirit" and "team spirit." The group that possesses these may or may not achieve success or victory. But they will be marked by loyalty. Perhaps the notion I have in mind is best captured by the term *esprit de corps*. Combat units possessing *esprit de corps* not only display uncommon loyalty to group members, they also embody faithfulness to the code of honor in a manner that distinguishes their group's persona from others. The strong sense of spirit that emerges within combat units explains why Paul so naturally describes Christian life in military terms (see, e.g., 2 Tim 2:3–4; 1 Cor 9:7; Phil 2:25). Paul does not use this metaphor to suggest that each Christian wages war as a lone soldier against dark spiritual forces. Rather, he is commanding Christians to "hold rank" (*stoicheō*) with each other and thus with the spirit of the team, which in this case is identified with the Holy Spirit (Gal 5:25; 6:14–18). The formation we hold is neither a line nor a phalanx but a cross. Listen to Paul's words in Gal 6:14–18:

> But may it never be that I should boast, except in the cross of our Lord Jesus Christ, through which the world has been crucified to me, and I to the world. For neither is circumcision anything, nor uncircumcision, but a new creation. And those who will walk (*stoichēsousin*) by this rule (*kanōn*), peace and mercy be upon them, and upon the Israel of God. From now on let no one cause trouble for me, for I bear on my body the brand-marks of Jesus. The grace of our Lord Jesus Christ be with your spirit (*tou pneumatos humōn*), brethren. (NASB)

Paul is here expressing his wish that his sufferings as a Christ follower comprise the very pattern or canon (*kanōn*) of relationships within the community that is itself the new creation of God.[16] Just as Paul elsewhere identifies the believing community as the "body of Christ," so too here; it is the whole community—

the distinctive manner of living the members have with each other—that manifests the cruciform pattern ("spirit") of the Savior. Paul ends by underscoring *esprit de corps*, for by wishing the grace of the Lord Jesus to be with their spirit, which is to say their *corporate* spirit (the pronoun *humōn* ["you"] is plural), he is affirming that the achievement of Christlikeness at the corporate level is an achievable, though not easy, task.

"Spirit" in the New Testament

With this last example I have moved from English into Greek. I cannot pretend that my simple grammatical remarks constitute proof of some sort. My initial claim was much less robust; I simply wanted to demonstrate that the English notion of "spirit" retains both individual and corporate senses. So what? I suspect that once we concede this is the case in English, we might be less surprised to discover the same possibilities are exemplified by biblical texts. I will discuss two.

First, we must carefully rethink the uses of the plural phrase "in you all" (*en humin*). In Rom 8:8–11 we read:

> . . . and those who are in the flesh cannot please God. However, you (*humeis*) are not in the flesh but in the Spirit, if indeed the Spirit of God dwells in you (*en humin*). But if anyone does not have the Spirit of Christ, he does not belong to Him. And if Christ is in you (*en humin*), though the body is dead because of sin, yet the spirit is alive because of righteousness. But if the Spirit of Him who raised Jesus from the dead dwells in you (*en humin*), he who raised Christ Jesus from the dead will also give life to your mortal bodies through His Spirit who indwells you (*en humin*). (NASB)

One common, albeit unsuitable, stance for reading this text is body-soul dualism. In such a view, our bodies are merely containers. In a pre-Christian state, the container is empty and thus incapable of leading one into moral righteousness. But when the individual comes to faith in Christ, a miracle is said to occur: The formerly empty container becomes occupied by the spirit of Christ. Thereafter, living with an exterior eye, with one's finger on the pulse of bodily passions, leads to death. Living with an interior eye, a mind set on the internal Spirit, yields righteousness, a life capable of pleasing God.

While this dualistic interpretive strategy has the advantage of treating the spirit realm as ontologically real, it runs into exegetical problems once we recognize that all the "yous" of the text are plural.[17] This plurality makes a difference in verse 9: "*The whole lot of you people* is not fleshly, but *corporately* spiritual if the Spirit of God dwells *among you all*—and indeed he does!" And verse 11: "But if the Spirit of him who raised Jesus from the dead dwells *among you all,* he . . . will give life to your mortal bodies through his Spirit who dwells *in the midst of you all.*" This more precise translation teases out the possibility that the location of the Spirit's dwelling is *between* persons rather than internal to each disconnected individual.[18]

Some will insist that I am making too much of the use of plural pronouns by biblical writers. After all, the Epistles were generally addressed to groups. What should we expect but plural objects? Nevertheless, a writer intending to single out individual action or responsibility customarily employed the qualifier "each" (*ekastos*). Since this term occurs throughout Scripture with roughly the same frequency as the plural pronoun phrase "in you,"[19] we cannot conclude that the term "each" was particularly uncommon among biblical authors. In other words, it is significant that the term *ekastos* is used infrequently—actually only twice—to designate an *individual* as a recipient of the Spirit's ministry.[20] Consequently, we must pay close attention to its absence in the passages under consideration and conclude that the use of the plural pronouns in the absence of *ekastos* signifies the community as the recipient of the Spirit's ministry.

Others will say, "Surely you must be joking. If there is a distinctive mark of the Spirit's mode of ministry under the new covenant, it is that the Spirit fills individuals as the rule rather than the exception. Peter was, after all, full of the Holy Spirit on the day of Pentecost." I do not dispute this. However, one searches in vain for a passage that unambiguously describes Spirit-filling *apart* from a social context. Even the *locus classicus* of the concept of Spirit-filling, Eph 5:18, must be considered in light of the greater context. The command to be filled (also plural!) with the Spirit is the last in a string of twenty-seven imperatives that are issued rapid-fire in the space of twenty-nine verses (the hortatory pericope of 4:25–5:21). Each of these commands is plural both in lexical form and semantic content. As such, the command to be filled is the capstone command that summarizes the previous twenty-six imperatives dealing with intracommunal living (do not lie, do not let anger fester, be kind, etc.). Moreover, the imperative itself (*plērousthe*) is qualified by five participles, two of which in particular—namely, "speaking with others" (*lalountes eautois*) and "being subject to one another" (*hupotassomenoi allēlois*)—unambiguously emphasize the *social* nature of being filled with the Spirit.[21]

In light of this biblical evidence, Christians would be well served to invert the priority that modernity has mistakenly bestowed upon the individual. In modernity's view, individuals are thought to constitute the Church, and the Church exists purely for the sake of the individual. The real action takes place at the level of the individual, while the Church is, at best, a means for helping the individual cultivate individual righteousness or spirituality in advance of putting it into practice.[22] I am suggesting this is backwards. If we adopt a holistic view of spirituality, then *individual* spirituality becomes a misnomer;

spirituality is a team sport. This means at least two things. First, it means that individuals are constituted by the Church and not the other way around.[23] Individuals are redeemed precisely to the extent they are caught up into a narrative weave much more substantive than individualism can supply. Except for authentic participation in the life of the believing community, there is no salvation. This, of course, threatens to become a form of works-righteousness so long as "participation" is understood as "voluntary engagement," something that depends on the will of the agent. But I am using the term "participation" in a more passive sense whereby God, by means of the Spirit, baptizes the believer into the community of believers (1 Cor 12:13), thereby making believers participants (*metochoi*; Heb 6:4) or copartakers (*summetocha*; Eph 3:6) with other believers in the life of the Spirit. Second, holistic spirituality means that the Church, the believing community, is itself the end (*telos*) or final purpose of the individual. As we shall see shortly, both of these aspects come together in the "practices" that constitute the Church.

Stated as a theological reversal, the two claims I have just made—that individuals are constituted by the Church and that the Church is the final purpose of individuals—run the risk of being just as reductionistic as those they are meant to replace. However, this reversal need not be reductive, because there is more to the second claim than meets the eye.

Practices as the Form of Spirituality and Social Justice

Scholars concede that individualism made its main entrance into theology through the pen of Augustine.[24] When Augustine writes that he desires "absolutely nothing" more than "to know God and the soul,"[25] he is prejudicing his entire theological project by the assumption that we have souls, or more properly, that we are souls who happen to be temporarily trapped in bodies (a fact that for Augustine makes physical death the "greatest boon"[26]). Augustine's anthropological dualism can be traced to vestiges of Neoplatonic philosophy still clinging to his mind from his pre-Christian days. Surprisingly, the earliest of Plato's own writings show resources for overcoming the bifurcation of soul and body.

In the first place, Plato reports that Socrates conceived human persons, both body and soul, as isomorphic (i.e., similarly shaped) with the human community. In describing the polis first as isomorphic with the human *body*, he chided those philosophical pretenders, the Sophists, for engaging in pseudopractices that more closely resembled pastry baking than community formation (*politikē*). Socrates asserted that true practices contribute to the health of both the individual and the human community.[27] For instance, the practice of medicine (*iatrikē*) builds health by driving disease out of the body. Consequently, there is a corporate analogue to medicine called retributive justice (*dikaiosunē*), which drives evil out of the polis by driving wickedness out of the wrongdoer.[28] In a similar fashion, the practice of exercise (*gumnastikē*) adds health by increasing muscle tone and coordination. The corporate analogue to exercise is legislation (*nomothetikē*), which, by ordering civic life, increases its strength and vitality. In Socrates' mind, the human body is isomorphic with the body politic.

In addition to making these connections between the human body and the body politic, Socrates also found the polis isomorphic with the human *soul*. The political excellencies of organization and order brought about by the proper practice of governing makes the city a *just* city. Similarly, persons achieve excellence when order and organization of the soul is procured. The person whose soul is well-ordered and self-controlled is a *just* person. Thus, the community is isomorphic with the human individual. This isomorphism demonstrates that there is at least a *formal* connection between individual persons and the communities they constitute: Just persons and just cities both participate in the form of justice. This formal connection is one reason to resist a hasty bifurcation of soul and body.

A second Socratic resource for overcoming body-soul bifurcation can be seen in Socrates' disinclination to bifurcate the *city's* soul and body. We see this most clearly by his use of the notion of "practice" in a way that overlaps both domains. Recall that for Socrates, the practice of retributive justice contributes to the physical health of the body politic by driving out disease. While this sort of disease could be driven out of the city literally through the execution or banishment of criminals, it could also be driven out by corporal punishment (e.g., public flogging), a course of action that in Socrates' mind actually redeemed the criminal while simultaneously ridding the city of disease. Socrates therefore advocated that the wrongdoer "not keep his wrongdoing hidden but bring it out into the open, so that he may *pay his due and get well*."[29] We see here, then, that for Plato and his teacher, the practice of retributive justice overlaps both domains; it can cure the soul as well as the body. My point is that the connection between just persons and just cities is not merely formal but *praxic* or practical. In other words, some of the practices that constitute community life have simultaneously to do with both soul-care and body-care, with both internal righteousness and external ethics, with both spirituality and social justice.

While Socrates' followers may or may not be to blame for an overly strong distinction between the inner and outer life, the practices that constitute the Church show promise for holding these two together, a promise made more urgent by the grammatical remarks I made earlier.[30] There I demonstrated that the concept of "spirit," employed both by contemporary believers and by New Testament writers, is at least as much at home in references to the community as it is in references to the individual. Perhaps more so. This fact need not spawn speculative claims about the conditions, location, or intensity of the Holy Spirit's presence in community, lest in defending such claims we press language in directions it cannot go. Rather, the close connection between the language of "spirit" and "community" means, first, that talk about "spirit" (whether Holy, corporate, or both) requires as the condition for its intelligibility particular descriptions of the community's form of life. We would not know what to make of claims regarding the Holy Spirit's presence if, for example, accounts of forgiveness between persons are entirely absent. Of course, conversely, no description of authentic reconciliation in the name of Jesus could possibly be complete without acknowledgment of the Holy Spirit's role. In that very regard, second-century apologist Aristides asserts the Holy Spirit's presence, but not until he has spent several pages describing the marvelous ways that Christians treat each other.[31] Likewise, a vocal despiser of sixteenth-century Anabaptists reluctantly concluded:

> Among the existing heretical sects there is none which in appearance leads a more modest or pious life than the Anabaptist. As concerns their outward public life they are irreproachable. No lying, deception, swearing, strife, harsh language, no intemperate eating and drinking, no outward personal display, is found among them, but humility, patience, uprightness, neatness, honesty, temperance, straightforwardness, in such measure that one would suppose that *they have the Holy Spirit of God*.[32]

In both cases, the manner in which Christians treated each other serves as the backdrop against which claims about the Holy Spirit become understandable and without which backdrop such claims are simply unintelligible.

As a grammatical remark, the connection between the language of "spirit" and that of "community" means, second, that any distinctive sense to *our*, that is *Christian*, use of these terms can only be found in those aspects of our community life that are distinctively Christian. In other words, if we are willing to grant that language emerges in tandem with the form of life that a community shares,[33] then first-order religious claims, as well as theological reflection on these claims, can never be reduced to mere sociological descriptions. This is so because the form of life constitutive of the Christian community differs significantly from that form of life upon which the language of social-scientific description depends. So while believers may find common ground with nonbelievers over the use of "holiday spirit" and "team spirit," we must guard against assuming that notions such as "spirit" and "spirituality," so commonplace today, have identical connotations for nonbelievers and Christians alike. As Wittgenstein reminds us, "*Practice* gives the words their sense."[34] In other words, as Christians use the words "spirit" and "spirituality" in distinctive ways, this distinctiveness can only be learned by looking to the practices that constitute the particular form of life that we call Christian. In Christian practices, writes Reinhard Hütter, "we not only unquestioningly encounter 'church' but also the Spirit's concrete works." Indeed, says Hütter, "these practices *are* the Spirit's works through which the Holy Spirit enacts his sanctifying mission in the triune economy of salvation."[35]

But what exactly is meant by the semitechnical term "practices"? Ever since Plato, thinkers have debated ways in which certain human activities, such as medicine, differ significantly from others, such as taking long showers. For his part, philosopher Alasdair MacIntyre identifies at least four important characteristics that distinguish practices from other human activities. First, practices develop skills or virtues for practitioners who patiently pursue excellence in these activities. Second, it is not a rulebook but actions of expert practitioners that embody the standards of excellence.[36] Third, practices are marked by goods that are internal rather than external to the practice.[37] Fourth, genuine practices improve over time.[38]

While Christian thinkers have long insisted that Christians must attend to the constitutive practices of the believing community, they have not always agreed on which practices are most crucial. Martin Luther's list of community-constitutive practices included proclamation of God's word, baptism, the Lord's Supper, ordination, prayer, and discipleship.[39] To this list other Christian theologians have added contemplation,[40] interpretation,[41] forgiveness,[42] and pacifism.[43] My purpose here is not to settle whose list of practices is correct or to assemble a comprehensive list. Rather, it is to make the related points that *social practices are the form that spirituality takes*, and *social practices are the form that social justice takes*. These two claims come together in the work of John Howard Yoder.

In his book *The Christian Witness to the State*, Yoder argues that social justice has to do with corporate practices.[44] In the questions he raises against political theologian Reinhold Niebuhr, who maintained that religious *individuals* are the agents of change in society,[45] Yoder asserted that the Church itself is properly the agent of social change. The type of action taken by the Church is "witness." Witness has two elements. On the one hand, witness is the prophetic message by which the Church forth-tells the truth to the world.[46] On the other hand, such truth telling requires the living out of Christian convictions in community. These lived-out convictions are the material conditions for understanding Christian speech on its own terms. Thus, the secular statesman or policymaker, having no innate knowledge of objective moral norms by which to govern, can observe in the concrete life of the Church what justice amounts to. To be sure, misunderstandings are bound to occur; Christian *agapē*, for instance, will be mistaken for mere fraternity, and so on. Nevertheless, secular justice, when modeled after the Church, may begin to approximate Christian love. The upshot of Yoder's view is that the best way for the Church to "seek the welfare of the city" (Jer 29:7) is for the Church to be a distinguishable alternative to that city.

According to Yoder, Christian distinctiveness hinges on five social practices: reconciliation, breaking bread, baptism, the fullness of Christ, and community discernment.[47] In addition to constituting the Church's witness, these practices are simultaneously the form of Christian spirituality, for in them we meet not only the Church but the Spirit at work among us. The practice of reconciliation, for instance, is the means that Jesus specified for conflict resolution in the Church (Matt 18:15–20). While this particular practice demands keen moral discernment from humans because its purpose is reconciliation rather than retribution, the gospel text affirms that the community's actions are at the same time the activity of God; whatever is bound or loosed on earth also is so in heaven.[48] Similarly, the communal breaking of bread commemorates not only Jesus' Passover meal with his disciples, it also calls to mind the feeding of the multitude in the desert, the common meals shared daily by first-century believers, and the resolution of the dispute involving the Hellenistic widows (Acts 2:42–46; 6:1–7). The same Spirit that came upon Jesus for reinstating the Jubilee (Luke 4:18–19) is met in this practice precisely because, in the breaking of bread, Christians reenact the economic leveling that characterizes Jubilee.[49]

In a strikingly parallel fashion, the other three practices that Yoder lists—baptism, community formation, and discernment—also contribute to the content of Christian witness even as they entail the work of the Spirit. For its part, baptism is a political act that "initiates persons into a new people," achieving a unity that transcends all prior identity markers.[50] This sounds innocuous enough, but the radical implications of the practice of baptism were not always so easy to overlook. For example, slaveholders in the American South feared that if baptism were practiced among converted slaves, the slaveholders might be obligated to set them free. (Apparently, reports of such behavior in the Portuguese colonies in Africa had reached American shores.) As a result, some slaves were prompted to take an oath *during the rite of baptism*:

> Do you declare in the presence of God and before this Congregation that you do not ask for the holy baptism out of any design to free yourself from the Duty and Obedience that you owe your Master while you live, but merely for the good of Your Soul and to partake of the Graces and Blessings promised to the members of the Church of Jesus Christ?[51]

Clearly the social justice edge is taken off the practice once baptism is turned into a private affair.

In the practice of community formation (what Yoder calls "the fullness of Christ"; Eph 4:11–13), the Spirit is met when Christ-followers welcome one another as divine gifts vital for the achievement of the common good. This "new mode of group relations"[52] runs counter to our natural inclination to index a person's honor to his or her utility. Rather, the good of the Church is to be found precisely in this new pattern of relationality, especially in the reliance of more honorable members upon the less honorable, believing that we are all "members of one another" (Rom 12:5; Eph 4:25). Finally, the practice of discernment, that is, the means by which the believing community makes decisions, is rightly deemed a spiritual practice. Genuine consensus, especially when the stakes are high (as they were in Acts 15), is so rare that achieving it can only be attributed to the action of God's spirit—which the New Testament Church did when it claimed in the same breath, "It has seemed good to the Holy Spirit *and* to us" (Acts 15:28).

While the practices detailed by Yoder sound narrowly parochial, this is not borne out in everyday life. To take one example, the Mennonites are widely known for disaster relief that benefits non-Christians as often as Christians. But these practices are humble. They are about forgiveness, eating, inclusion, teamwork, and decision making. In Yoder's mind, these five practices are the material conditions for speaking intelligibly of spirit and spirituality, because we meet God's spirit wherever these are practiced. In that respect, social justice is not simply one practice of the five or ten or twenty that constitute the Church. Nor is the Church's social justice work causally dependent upon the exercise of private spirituality. Rather, the web of all the practices that constitute the Christian community is simultaneously the practice of spirituality *and* the practice of social justice, for in these practices both practitioners and recipients meet the spirit of God *and* the Church, which is our own true end and God's radical alternative to the world.[53]

Notes

1. Augustine, *City of God* 1.16–19 (trans. Gerald G. Walsh et al., ed. Vernon J. Bourke; Garden City, N.Y.: Doubleday, 1960), 53.

2. For an outstanding recent study, see Philip Cary, *Augustine's Invention of the Inner Self* (Oxford: Oxford University Press, 2000).

3. Meister Eckhart, *Meister Eckhart, from Whom God Hid Nothing: Sermons, Writings, and Sayings* (ed. David O'Neal; Boston: Shambhala, 1996), 45 (emphasis added).

4. Eckhart used the term "little castle" in his treatise "God Enters a Free Soul," in *Meister Eckhart: A Modern Translation* (ed. and trans. Raymond Bernard Blakney; New York: Harper & Row, 1941), 207–11.

5. Quoted in John Dear, *Living Peace: A Spirituality of Contemplation and Action* (New York: Doubleday, 2001), 21.

6. Hezekiah Harvey, *The Pastor* (Rochester, N.Y.: Backus, 1982), 164.

7. Quoted in Dear, *Living Peace*, 7.

8. For a recent theological application of anthropological holism, see Warren S. Brown, Nancey Murphy, and H. Newton Malony, eds., *Whatever Happened to the Soul? Scientific and Theological Portraits of Human Nature* (Philadelphia: Fortress, 1998).

9. See Brad J. Kallenberg, "All Suffer the Affliction of the One: Metaphysical Holism and the Presence of the Spirit," *Christian Scholar's Review* 31 (2002): 217–34.

10. The sort of linguistic philosophical analysis I undertake here is an extension of the work of Ludwig Wittgenstein and J. L. Austin. Wittgenstein helps us to see that language constrains the possibilities of thought. Austin taught that the language we speak, insofar as it has a sufficient history, has evolved into a reliable map for navigating human experience. Together these thinkers are pillars of what has become known as "ordinary language philosophy."

11. See Ludwig Wittgenstein, *Philosophical Investigations* (ed. G. E. M. Anscombe and Rush Rhees; New York: Macmillan, 1953), para. 244.

12. This is called disclosure. For example, I cannot draw a perfect circle, but I don't need to draw one in order to communicate features about a circle. From the series of figures—triangle, square, pentagon, hexagon, etc.—an observer can grasp in a flash where the series is headed, namely, toward a regular polygon with an infinite number of equal sides. As the number of sides increases, the length of each side gets smaller until—voilà!—a circle. For more on disclosure, see Ian Ramsey, "Talking of God: Models Ancient and Modern," in *Christian Empiricism* (ed. Jeffrey H. Gill; London: Sheldon Press, 1974).

13. See Robert Martin-Achard, "Resurrection (OT)," in *The Anchor Bible Dictionary* (ed. David Noel Freedman; trans. Terrence Prendergast; New York: Doubleday, 1992), 5:680–84; and George W. E. Nickelsburg, "Resurrection (Early Judaism and Christianity)," in *Anchor Bible Dictionary*, 5:684–91.

14. The fact that picturing the Holy Spirit is mind-numbingly impossible is a clue that *relational* metaphors may be the best way for us to understand who the Spirit is.

15. For an account of the conceptual development of "soul," see John W. Cooper, *Body, Soul, and Life Everlasting: Biblical Anthropology and the Monism-Dualism Debate* (Grand Rapids: Eerdmans, 1989).

16. On the community as the new creation, see the corporate use of "new man" in Eph 2:14–15: ". . . that in Himself He might make the two into one new man (*hena kainon anthropon*) thus establishing peace" (my translation).

17. There are eighty-nine instances in the Nestle-Aland text of "in you" (*en humin*) in which the "you" is plural, compared with only twenty instances in which the "you" (*en soi*) is singular. Only two of these twenty are in the context of passages mentioning the Spirit: the coming of the Spirit on Jesus (Luke 3:22) and the gift (*charismatos*) indwelling Timothy (1 Tim 4:14). Kurt Aland et al., eds. *The Greek New Testament* (4th rev. ed.; Stuttgart: Deutsche Bibelgesellschaft, 1994). Grammatical analysis by the GRAMCORD Institute for Accordance Bible Software (version 4.5, 2000).

18. A similar revelation emerges four chapters later, in Rom 12, where Paul exhorts the Romans to present their bodies (plural) as a living sacrifice (singular).

19. *ekastos* is used eighty-two times in the New Testament.

20. 1 Cor 12:7, 11. The reading strategy I am proposing is not new. For an Eastern Orthodox version, see J. Zizioulas, *Being as Communion: Studies in Personhood and the Church* (Crestwood, N.Y.: St. Vladimir's Seminary Press, 1985). See also Martin Buber, *I and Thou* (trans. Walter Kaufmann; New York: Charles Scribner's Sons, 1970).

21. The other participles—singing (*adontes*), psalming (*psallontes*), and thanking (*eucharistountes*)—may be carried out in isolation, but as speech-acts they cannot properly be considered privatized behavior, for the acquisition of fluency in a conceptual language depends upon participation in a form of life.

22. For a critique of this view, see Reinhard Hütter, "The Church," in *Knowing the Triune God: The Work of the Spirit in the Practices of the Church* (ed. James J. Buckley and David S. Yeago; Grand Rapids: Eerdmans, 2001), 25.

23. See Stanley Hauerwas, "What Could It Mean for the Church to Be Christ's Body? A Question without a Clear Answer," in *In Good Company: The Church as Polis* (Notre Dame, Ind.: University of Notre Dame Press, 1995), 19–32.

24. See Cary, *Augustine's Invention of the Inner Self.*

25. *Soliloquies* 1.2.7, quoted in William Placher, *History of Christian Theology* (Philadelphia: Westminster John Knox, 1983), 108.

26. Augustine, "The Greatness of the Soul," in *Ancient Christian Writers* (ed. Johannes Quasten and Joseph C. Plumpe; trans. Joseph M. Colleran; Westminster, Md.: Newman Press, 1950), 33.76.

27. Plato, *Gorgias* (Indianapolis: Hackett, 1987), 23–26 (lines 463a–466a).

28. Ibid., 49–50 (lines 479e–480e).

29. Ibid., 49–50 (line 480c); emphasis added.

30. Although it is common to blame dualism on the Platonists, the sort of dualism that afflicts us today is probably attributed better to Descartes. I have taken the more popular account for ease of argument and because the connection between Augustine and Neoplatonism is so clear. Compare Charles Taylor, *Sources of the Self: The Making of the Modern Identity* (Cambridge, Mass.: Harvard University Press, 1989), with Fergus Kerr, *Theology after Wittgenstein* (Oxford: Basil Blackwell, 1986).

31. "But the Christians . . . show kindness to those near them; and whenever they are judges, they judge uprightly. . . . They do good to their enemies. . . . If one or other of them have bondmen and bondwomen or children, through love towards them they persuade them to become Christians, and when they have done so, they call them brethren without distinction. They do not worship strange gods, and they go their way in all modesty and cheerfulness. Falsehood is not found among them; and they love one another. . . . And he, who has, gives to him who has not, without boasting. And when they see a stranger, they take him in to their homes and rejoice over him as a very brother. . . . And if they hear that one of their number is imprisoned or afflicted on account of the name of their Messiah, all of them anxiously minister to his necessity. . . . And if there is among them any that is poor and needy, and if they have no spare food, they fast two or three days in order to supply to the needy their lack of food. . . . Such, O King . . . is their manner of life. . . . And verily, *this is a new people, and there is something divine in the midst of them.*" Aristides, "The Apology of Aristides the Philosopher," in *Ante-Nicene Fathers*, 1st ser. (ed. Allan Menzies; Grand Rapids: Eerdmans, 1965), 10:276–78 (emphasis added).

32. Franz Agricola, quoted in Harold S. Bender, "The Anabaptist Vision," *Church History* 13 (1944): 16 (emphasis added).

33. This point is misunderstood as often as it is contested. See Brad J. Kallenberg, *Ethics as Grammar: Changing the Postmodern Subject* (Notre Dame, Ind.: University of Notre Dame Press, 2001), esp. 161–214.

34. Ludwig Wittgenstein, *Culture and Value* (ed. G. H. von Wright and Heikki Nyman; trans. Peter Winch; Oxford: Basil Blackwell, 1980), 85e.

35. Hütter, "Church," 34, 35 (emphasis added). Hütter uses Hannah Arendt to claim that a political community, whether the Greek polis or the Christian community, is marked by normative convictions that are embodied in constitutive practices directed toward a distinctive telos (40). In other words, what makes the Christian community distinctive is not merely that we have unique primitive reactions or even different reflexes to external stimuli but also that Christians give these reflexes and behaviors certain descriptions in the context of a community of practitioners who share a form of life.

36. Thus, there are rules of play for tennis, but no rules of excellence. For example, there is no rule for how high to throw the ball when serving. Principles for serving must be "read off" the play of experts.

37. For example, in the practice of music, the point of playing music with excellence is not money or fame but excellent music.

38. MacIntyre's treatment of these characteristics is in *After Virtue: A Study in Moral Theory* (Notre Dame, Ind.: University of Notre Dame Press, 1984). In his later works, MacIntyre is careful to attribute this fourth mark to whole traditions rather than simply to practices. Traditions "improve" over time in the sense that later moments in a historical tradition are able to out-narrate earlier versions yet in a way that maintains continuity with earlier versions (see, e.g., MacIntyre, *Whose Justice? Which Rationality?* [Notre Dame, Ind.: University of Notre Dame Press, 1988]). Since criteria are internal to traditions, it is more fitting for the Christian tradition to require its practices be faithful than effective. Hence, Martin Luther is correct to preserve baptism and Eucharist as tradition-constituting practices without requiring that these somehow show improvement over time in the same way medicine has improved.

39. Martin Luther, "On the Councils and the Church (Part III)," in *Martin Luther's Basic Theological Writing* (ed. Timothy F. Lull; Minneapolis: Fortress, 1989), 539–76.

40. See A. N. Williams, "Contemplation," in Buckley and Yeago, eds., *Knowing the Triune God*, 121–46.

41. See David. S. Cunningham, "Interpretation," in Buckley and Yeago, eds., *Knowing the Triune God*, 179–204. See also Stephen E. Fowl and L. Gregory Jones, *Reading in Communion* (Grand Rapids: Eerdmans, 1991).

42. See L. Gregory Jones, *Embodying Forgiveness: A Theological Analysis* (Grand Rapids: Eerdmans, 1995).

43. For an account of Christian practices, see Nancey Murphy, Brad J. Kallenberg, and Mark Thiessen Nation, eds., *Virtues and Practices in the Christian Tradition: Christian Ethics after MacIntyre* (Valley Forge, Pa.: Trinity Press International, 1997).

44. John Howard Yoder, *The Christian Witness to the State* (Newton, Kan.: Faith and Life Press, 1964).

45. See Reinhold Niebuhr, "Christian Faith and Social Action," in *Faith and Politics* (ed. Ronald H. Stone; New York: George Braziller, 1968), 119–37.

46. In addition to the proclamation of the gospel, truth telling may take the form of negative criticism rather than constructive advice, because constructive advice could only be offered on the basis of a theological definition of an *ideal* state. But since the state is a postfall institution, it has no ideal form. See John Howard Yoder, *The Original Revolution* (Scottdale, Pa.: Herald Press, 1971), 79.

47. See John Howard Yoder, *Body Politics: Five Practices of the Christian Community before the Watching World* (Nashville: Discipleship Resources, 1992).

48. Yoder, *Body Politics*, 1.

49. Ibid., 16–25.

50. Ibid., 28.

51. Quoted in Danielle Harley, "Bishop Daniel Payne: Educating Black Saints in Ohio" (master's thesis, University of Dayton, 2002), 13–14.

52. Yoder, *Body Politics*, 47.

53. I would like to thank Terrence Tilley and Therese Lysaught for their helpful comments on this essay.

PART III

HISTORICAL RESOURCES FOR CONNECTING SPIRITUALITY AND SOCIAL JUSTICE

7

LIVING OUT THE PEACE OF GOD: THE APOSTLE PAUL'S THEOLOGY AND PRACTICE OF PEACE

— Raymond H. Reimer —

Consider a common understanding of Jesus, thoroughly meek and mild. He pats little children on the head and blesses the pigeons and doves. He says nice things about how people ought to get along, never raising his voice in the process of saying them (well, there was that one time in the temple yard, but they were *asking* for it!). He's always gentle, always calm—and he's savior of the universe!

Then there's Paul, a big, brazen bully. He's arrogant, thinks he has all the answers, and won't let anyone else get a word in edgewise. Almost every congregation he visits degenerates into an uproar by the time he leaves. When people question his authority or his fundamental claim that Gentiles don't have to become Jews to join the movement he's building, he's in their faces right away. "Are you differing with *me*? I'm an apostle from God, and what I say goes!"

This simple dichotomy I have concocted is thoroughly fraudulent, of course. Jesus wasn't that nice. He was run out of one town after another, his ministry led to congregations and families being torn apart, and the authorities were constantly accusing him of disturbing the peace. By some accounts, that is what led to his crucifixion.

And Paul wasn't that bad. He was quite interested in building enduring relationships with people, and he was pretty good at it, too. You don't get to be called the apostle to the bulk of the world if you don't have any people skills. He didn't just tear communities apart. A goodly portion of his writing focuses upon healing hurts, fixing brokenness, and calling people to unity—in other words, making peace. Paul the peacemaker. It's not the usual image, is it?

After Jesus, Paul was perhaps "the most energetic, articulate, and dynamic leader in the early church. He was a church organizer, an untiring worker, . . . a conceptualizer." To be sure, he became involved in controversies, but fundamentally he was a person "who took personal relationships seriously enough so that when peace between human beings was disrupted he sought to res' it."[1] Although this essay focuses upon Paul's vision of peace and practic peacemaking, I intentionally chose that concentration as a lens through wl to consider his approach to the wider topic of social justice. Paul does not r ily fit into traditional definitions and interpretations of social justice f either the first century or today. Some see his approaches to topics suc women, slavery, and relations with the state as excessively cautious, even r tionary. Others consider him to be an innovator, pressing for liberating tr within a movement still defining its direction. Whatever the final determ tion, it is clear that Paul was willing to stir the pot in redefining the issue consider just relationships and social change from a new perspective, nan the vantage point of apocalyptic hope, sustained by his abiding spiritu: Paul recasts the debate about what social justice is and means in new te: and such transformation has always discomforted people. Some, regrett: have chosen to dismiss or ignore him. My thesis is that Paul developed wi the emerging Christian movement a fresh and creative understanding of p that is largely overlooked by twenty-first-century Christians. The insight garner from both his theological understanding of this dynamic and the he demonstrated its power within his own life can enrich our own faith and practice of spirituality and social justice.

Paul's Theology of Peace

Paul's understanding of peace is understandably shaped by the context in which he lived, a context markedly different from our own. Both the social setting and the lexical background of first-century Mediterranean understandings of peace have been explored extensively and need not be replicated here, but they serve as the backdrop for all that follows. At the very least, the effect of a volatile interchange of a Hebraic notion of *shalom* and a Roman notion of *pax* must not be underestimated.[2] I focus first upon the particular way in which Paul shaped this complex of thought into something new as he explored in his writings themes of peace—*eirēnē*—as found between God and creation and specifically between people, then I proceed to consider the prospect of Paul as a peacemaking person in his own life and relationships.

Paul's understanding of peace does not start with human beings. It starts with God. Let me begin with a lexical observation: The English terms "justification" and "righteousness" both attempt to translate the same Greek word, *dikaiosunē*, and that word itself seeks to translate the Hebrew terms *mishpat* and *tsedaqah*—"justice" and "righteousness." All of these words are roughly synonymous, having to do with restoration, wholeness, setting things right, healing that which was broken, making peace—peace between humans and God.[3]

It was Paul who first described the way in which God risks making things right with people via the death of Jesus Christ on the cross. If we can trust that, if we can accept that God accepts us even though we are sinners, then we who were formerly broken off from God can be restored to wholesome relationship with God, that is, we can have peace with God. Romans 5:1 declares, "Therefore, since we are justified by faith, we have peace with God through our Lord Jesus Christ."[4] In this text, having peace with God and being reconciled to God become synonymous.[5]

Although this peace comes *from* God and is directed *toward* God, it is also initiated *by* God. This point should not be underestimated. In 2 Cor 5:18–19, God is described explicitly as the agent and instigator of reconciliation "through Christ." And this appears to be an analysis of Paul's own devising, for he is the first attested Greek author to speak of the *offended* party in a dispute initiating reconciliation, using the active voice form of the verb *katallassō*. This act or process of the one who has been offended *initiating* reconciliation is explicitly described in this passage as a ministry passed on to believers, with the expectation that they—that we—will carry it on in our lives as part of our life of faith.[6]

Arising from God's very nature, then, God's goal becomes one of peace with and among all creation. God is the right-wising, justice-bringing, brokenness-healing force that inexorably moves toward the interaction of all things in their intended relationships. Even though the cosmos itself is not at peace, God's aim, as Virginia Wiles artfully puts it, is "to put the world at peace, to 'peace' the world together."[7]

Paul's thought indicates that he sees brokenness and evil and sin as enemies of the sort of wholeness and reconciliation that reflects this peace, and yet it is the power of the resurrection that calls us to cope with evil creatively (Rom 12:9–21).[8] Paul believes the consummation of God's creation will bring peace and reconciliation to all relationships (Rom 2:9–10; 5:2–5; 15:13; 1 Thess 5:3, 23). Perhaps the clearest declaration of this is in Rom 8, where Paul observes that all nature is groaning and longing to be released from bondage and brokenness; it is yearning to be restored to God's created intent (Rom 8:12–30, esp. 18–25).[9] Elsewhere in Rom 8, he muses specifically about peace between God and humans: "To set the mind on the flesh is death, but to set the mind on the Spirit is life and peace" (v. 6). Paul understands the Holy Spirit to be that healing power of God at work in the present that makes whole the brokenness of life; it is a holy-making power. The Spirit is at odds with all enmity and contentiousness. It is what enables and empowers believers to live together cooperatively rather than competitively as true children of God (Rom 8:16–17).[10] With this understanding of the connection between the Spirit and a life of peace, it is not surprising that Paul identifies one of the foremost "fruits of the Spirit" as peace (Gal 5:22–23).[11]

Many contemporary Christians have incorrectly reduced the notion of peace to an individualistically oriented "inner peace." While Paul does address the topic of inner peace, he does so only briefly, in Phil 4:7, where he writes, "And the peace of God, which surpasses all understanding, will guard your hearts and your minds in Christ Jesus." Within the context of this passage, Paul seems to be suggesting that God's peace will be found in worship and prayer. The plural references ("your hearts and your minds") and the whole context of Philippians point to the experience of persons in community. In other words, this sort of peace is not simply individualistic. Furthermore, to believe in and seek to live out God's revelation of reconciliation, peace, and justice means that we dare to challenge our society's definition of what makes for a good human life—and this may lead believers into substantial conflict with the prevailing, unbelieving society. Nevertheless, peace *within* the lives of individual believers is valued and affirmed within the broader context of gathered human relationships.[12]

Thus far I have considered Paul's theology of peace from what might be considered to be doctrinal perspectives: a "peaceful" perspective of justification, peacemaking within the cosmos, and the Spirit's role in peacemaking. But Paul is never satisfied to leave matters in the abstract. He continually applies his theological perspective, letting it serve as the foundation of the instruction he offers about "how then to live." Paul believes peace is a gift from God, one that can be appropriated in life here and now, and so he argues it should govern relationships between believers within the congregations he has planted. As he writes to these groups, he exhorts them repeatedly to "pursue what makes for peace and for mutual upbuilding," to "be at peace among yourselves," and to walk in love with other believers (Rom 12:10, 18; 13:8–10; 14:15, 19; 1 Thess 5:13; 2 Cor 13:11).

The embrace of God's love becomes both the theological rationale for believers to relate to other believers in love, as well as the spiritual empowerment that enables them to live in such a way. Actively edifying each other, even to the renunciation of one's personal rights, ensures the wider welfare of the community of faith.[13] Treating others as one has been and is being treated by God becomes the foundation of Pauline ethics. Paul's proclamation of egalitarianism—wherein distinctions that would separate people otherwise are torn down—is well known in Gal 3:26–28, but a similar emphasis upon the equality of believers before Christ can also be found in other texts (1 Cor 12:12–13; Col 3:9–11—if the latter is to be read as a Pauline document).

This does not mean Paul is against accountability or is advocating some sort of passive quietism. In close connection with some of the passages just mentioned is the recognition that not all behavior is beneficial to the group, and the corresponding notion that believers are right to challenge each other to holy living. For Paul, then, an interest in *eirēnē* is not divorced from an interest in justice or righteousness (1 Cor 8:10–11; 10:23–33; 1 Thess 5:14–18). Nevertheless, this "principle of control" is pervasive, spread universally among the group of believers and not restricted to some elite, as in many religious systems. It is, in fact, the notion that underlies the flexibility and responsibility of democracy. Paul trusts the collective judgment of all, including those who are uneducated or from an economic underclass (1 Thess 5:19–22; Rom 12:1–2).

Specifically, this means that if individual believers come to have differences between themselves (and Paul is not so naïve as to assume that will not happen), he believes they should be able to find within the congregation the wisdom and the guidance through the Spirit to settle such disputes, rather than turning to secular courts (1 Cor 6:1–8). A substantial portion of 1 Corinthians stresses that everyone needs to have an appreciation for the contributions of each other, while at the same time keeping in mind the broader needs of the congregation and movement, being willing to forgo one's personal or party interests if it means that all will benefit.[14] Similarly, Romans can be read from the perspective of upholding the fellowship of a community that is struggling to balance the varied interests of believers from both Jewish and Gentile backgrounds.[15] Paul's encouragement in 1 Corinthians that the strong defer to the weak and his use of body metaphors in Romans together underscore his concern that believers must fundamentally value one another, culminating in harmonious worship of God.[16]

Paul's understanding of the life of faith does not restrict the exercise of *eirēnē* to relationships within the Christian fellowship. Some of the passages mentioned above already underscore this; they articulate Paul's interest in harmonious relations not only between people of faith but in living peaceably "with all."[17] Perhaps the most sustained focus of this theme is found in Rom 12:14–21, where Paul concludes that believers should "not be overcome by evil, but overcome evil with good." This ethic involves blessing even those who persecute you—that is, living with constructive concern for all, even for the enemy.[18]

Paul is also interested in the transformation of the world at large in order that healing come to all relationships. Practically, this means that he urges believers to live in such a way as to command the respect of nonbelievers, engaging in business with integrity, living quietly, and recognizing the legitimacy of the state to have and enforce laws (1 Thess 4:6; Rom 13:1–7; Phil 1:27).

This does not mean that believers should view the power or justice of states as absolute. Rather, Paul observes that the justice of God is not what the empire calls justice, and in Phil 3:20–21 he stipulates that the true allegiance of believers is to another realm.[19]

The way of nonviolence—the willingness to absorb hurt rather than retaliate and perpetuate a cycle of violence—is yet another allegiance turned on its head, for it appears as folly to the standards of the world (1 Cor 1:23–25). But God has other designs that reserve ultimate resolution of brokenness for God alone. Perhaps this is the best way to understand the somewhat enigmatic declaration in Rom 16:20, "The God of peace will shortly crush Satan under your feet." The God of *peace*, depicted as a *crusher*? But peace does not mean passivity for Paul, and certainly not in his apocalyptic perspective. God is quite willing to crush whatever stands in the way of peace and wholeness for creation and all that is in it, but will do so on a divine timetable.[20]

We moderns do not readily understand Paul's thoroughgoing apocalyptic, and thus we often misunderstand his theology and ethics. Given Paul's belief in the transitory nature of the present world, it was, in his eyes, relatively useless to invest one's energies toward significant societal changes. Even more, it was senseless to risk the destruction of the movement over such issues. That which is irrelevant does not set the agenda.[21] If Paul did not confront the Roman Empire and all the institutions of its political, social, and economic order as aggressively as we might have wished, this likely says far more about us than about Paul.

But one thing is clear: It does *not* mean that Paul was unconcerned for the present world. Though "passing away," it is still the place where the gospel is preached and where those who heed the gospel are called to be obedient. In 1 Cor 7:17–24, Paul advocates not obsessing about present life situations that are less than desirable, because one's fundamental calling is God's calling. Victor Paul Furnish offers an apt summary of this point: "For Paul, the Christian hope does not rob this present life of its meaning. Rather, precisely because the present is a time of confident hope, it is also the time and place for faith and faith's obedience in love. Believers are to be agents of love within the community of faith, in their serving of and caring for one another."[22]

Paul's Practice of Peacemaking

We move now to a consideration of Paul as a person. How much did he actually live out these sweet thoughts about peace and reconciliation? Is it in any way legitimate to call Paul a peacemaker? Is his theology embodied in his life, or does he fail to practice what he preaches?

I will begin with some observations about Paul's early life, before he had his personal experience of transformation on the road to Damascus and became connected with the new movement that followed after Jesus. It is hard to know what to make of Paul's earliest years. What vague references there are about his youth are suggestive at most.[23] Neil Elliott has attempted to connect childhood development theories advanced by Alice Miller and Susan Griffin with Paul's life as a youngster, suggesting some personal experience of violence within his own life that skewed his personality to react to opposition with virulence.[24] Such hypotheses are intriguing, but cannot be convincingly decided.

There does seem clear evidence that by the time Saul had become a young adult, he had internalized the exercise of violence and was directing it toward others. More specifically, he was "violently persecuting" (to use his own language) believers in Christ, combing through Jerusalem and later Damascus and elsewhere for Christ-confessing Jews, arresting them and dragging them to prison on the authority of the high priest. In retrospect he recognizes his zeal in such an endeavor as substantial, even extreme. He was explicitly trying to destroy this new movement, and was clearly ready to exercise violence to reach his goal. Fostering peaceable relations with the objects of his fury seems the farthest thing from his mind.[25]

Paul then had his visionary encounter with the risen Christ, and his life was turned around. While this experience entailed more than a rejection of violence, there was nonetheless a substantive change both in how Paul came to view other people (*all* other people) and how he attempted to relate to them, a shift that involved perceptions he came to have about God and God's peaceful goals for relating to humans. Various commentators prior to me have noted that Paul appears to have struggled with the question of how he previously could have been so violent in the name of God.[26] As Paul writes about law, sin, and justification, the key to his understanding of renewed relationships is a coherent complex that centers on healing, reconciliation, and peace—peace with God, with self, and with others. We find Paul, just as much as Jesus, arguing that God never wants violence, even declaring that the greatest commandment—the commandment that trumps all others—is to *love*.[27]

Clearly Paul became more accepting of others after his Damascus road encounter. Ironically, it was this very trait that got him into trouble with others in the newly emerging Jesus movement, who felt he was *too* accepting, too ready to reconcile and welcome others, letting down the barriers so far as to accept even Gentiles. Paul, however, wanted unity, connection, and reconciliation with this movement, with the very people that he had just been persecuting. He wished to make his peace with them.

Yet that movement itself was not all sweetness and light, as we sometimes try to convince ourselves. The image Luke presents of the earliest believers being of one heart and one soul and graciously sharing all their belongings in common is, at least in part, a literary fiction.[28] Readily apparent even in Acts is a story of tension, jealousy, disruption of the missionary successes of others, and theological disputes that resulted in divisions.[29] And this is all *before* we get to Paul's involvement in the movement. Clearly Paul is not the spoiler in the mix. While he may not have brought perfect harmony to the movement, it can certainly be argued that he worked to build and rebuild bridges, heal divisions, and reconcile disputes—at least as much as it can be argued that he set matches to tinder. To use some current vocabulary, Paul went beyond trying to manage conflict, and he even went beyond trying to resolve it. Rather, Paul endeavored to see relationships and lives profoundly *transformed* so that henceforth they would be founded upon peace and love and faith in God.[30]

In some ways, Paul's entire lifework can be described as trying to maintain unity, to find broader sweeps of peaceable relations between people. I am willing to acknowledge that Paul was not fully successful in accomplishing this, either in the congregations that he founded or in the movement at large. But then, neither were Peter or James or Matthew or John fully successful in this. Throughout his ministry, as is especially visible in his epistle to the Romans, Paul attempted to convince the predominantly non-Jewish component of a community of believers to treat Jewish believers as equals (ch. 14), and still consider the non-Christ-proclaiming Jews as God's chosen ones (chs. 9–11). Whether the outcome was fully successful or not, Paul was at least trying to find ways to bring people together, not to tear them apart.

Paul's engagement with and occasional accommodation to other people's perspectives also reflected his peace-oriented perspective. Such a willingness to interact on the playing field of ideas allowed for a degree of diversity within the communities to which he related. This does not, of course, mean that Paul was quick to compromise or to give in to others. Throughout his career as an apostle, he argued fiercely for positions and perspectives he believed rightly interpreted the gospel, and he worked hard to ensure their embrace by others.[31] But he was nonetheless willing to argue with people who differed with his perspectives. He sought them out again and again, not writing them off or giving up on his relationships with them, but always staying in communication. He even dreamed up novel strategies such as the "collection" as maneuvers to bind disparate peoples together—even people who were struggling to find togetherness in other ways.[32]

Did he become defensive on occasion? Yes. Did he brand others with virulent names, such as calling them "dogs"? Yes (Phil 3:2).[33] Paul was far from perfect. But in his humbler moments, which are definitely part of his life as well, he regretted those outbursts and perhaps sought to repent of them.[34] This is suggested by the fact that his epistles are filled with ready admissions of his imperfection and sin, his requests for forgiveness where he has wronged others, his confession that conflict brings him anguish, and his willingness to try new ideas, even to change his mind. In his correspondence with the Corinthians, for instance, he offers advice on a variety of topics and undergirds that instruction with the reasons that led him to take the positions he does; yet he also shows respect for the views of others and does not insist that they adhere to his perspective in every last detail. Thus, I would join with Michel Desjardins in suggesting that "to argue for equality and to respect other people's opinions, as [Paul] often does in his letters, is to tread the road to peace."[35]

Conclusion

Peace is pervasive in Paul's thought and practice, even if he used different language and methods from Jesus to share his understanding of it. Peace is fundamental to the gospel he proclaimed, the gospel he sought to live—peace with God and peace with other humans. Paul sought to follow God in faithfulness via imitation of Christ as best he could. His best was not perfect, and he was realistic enough to recognize that those he called to the way would not be perfect either, even as he challenged them toward that goal.[36] Paul envisioned humans becoming the righteousness of God, and that meant becoming active participants with God in bringing about God's dream of a peaceful reality to all existence, controlled by love and fundamentally reconciled.[37]

No more than any other New Testament author, or even Jesus himself, did Paul believe that complete peace—on earth, in heaven, or anywhere—could be achieved by humans via their own efforts. Yet Paul, as much as any other voice in the New Testament, held that believers must do all in their power to pursue peace, to make peace, and to be involved in maintaining and extending peace.[38] It is through Jesus Christ and in him that what Paul calls the "God of peace" (Rom 15:33; 16:20; 1 Cor 14:33; Phil 1:2; Col 1:20)[39] has made peace with humanity, so that even Jesus Christ himself in this function can be called "our peace."[40] For it is through Christ that people finally and fundamentally find peace—peace with themselves, with other human beings, with the world around them, and with God.[41] This is certainly Paul's apocalyptic hope, but it is also his fervently lived-out faith.

Notes

1. William Klassen, *Love of Enemies: The Way to Peace* (Philadelphia: Fortress, 1984), 110.
2. Good surveys of the lexical background of *eirēnē* in the first-century world can be found in Gerhard von Rad and Werner Foerster, "εἰρήνη . . ." in *Theological Dictionary of the New Testament* (ed. Gerhard Kittel; trans. and ed. Geoffrey W. Bromiley; Grand Rapids: Eerdmans, 1964), 2:400–420, esp. 400–411; and Erich Dinkler, "*Eirēnē*—The Early Christian Concept of Peace," in *The Meaning of Peace: Biblical Studies* (ed. Perry B. Yoder and Willard M. Swartley; trans. Walter Sawatsky; Louisville, Ky.: Westminster John Knox, 1992), 164–212, esp. 164–65.
3. Discussion of *dikaiosunē* is extensive within Pauline studies. See, for example, Gottfried Quell and Gottlob Schrenk, "δίκη . . .," in Kittel, *Theological Dictionary of the New Testament*, 2:174–225, esp. 202–10; and James D. G. Dunn, *The Theology of Paul the Apostle* (Grand Rapids: Eerdmans, 1998),

340–46, 366–71, and 385–86. Most commentators do not emphasize the connotations of peace connected with the term. One who does is Ted Grimsrud, *God's Healing Strategy: An Introduction to the Bible's Main Themes* (Telford, Pa.: Pandora Press U.S., 2000), 133.

4. An alternative translation of the key phrase is "Let us have peace with God." See Dinkler's comments about a weak textual tradition for the usual reading "we have peace" (*"Eirene*—The Early Christian Concept of Peace," 183).

5. Stanley E. Porter, "Peace, Reconciliation," in *Dictionary of Paul and His Letters* (ed. Gerald F. Hawthorne, Ralph P. Martin, and Daniel G. Reid; Downers Grove, Ill.: InterVarsity Press, 1993), 695–99, esp. 696; see also Ulrich Mauser, *The Gospel of Peace: A Scriptural Message for Today's World* (Louisville, Ky.: Westminster John Knox, 1992), 112–21.

6. Porter, "Peace, Reconciliation," 695.

7. Virginia Wiles, *Making Sense of Paul: A Basic Introduction to Pauline Theology* (Peabody, Mass: Hendrickson, 2000), 25.

8. This passage is extensively considered in Gordon Zerbe, "Paul's Ethic of Nonretaliation and Peace," in *The Love of Enemy and Nonretaliation in the New Testament* (ed. Willard M. Swartley; Louisville, Ky.: Westminster John Knox, 1992), 177–222.

9. See the discussion in Hubert Frankemölle, "Peace and the Sword in the New Testament," in Yoder and Swartley, eds., *Meaning of Peace: Biblical Studies*, 213–33. Dinkler suggests that 2 Cor 5:19 has a similar intent (*"Eirene*—The Early Christian Concept of Peace," 182).

10. See Klassen, *Love of Enemies*, 113; and John Ferguson, *The Politics of Love: The New Testament and Nonviolent Revolution* (Nyack, N.Y.: Fellowship Publications, 1979), 13, 110.

11. See Mauser, *Gospel of Peace*, 121–25.

12. Similar observations are made by Wiles, *Making Sense of Paul*, 130, who adds "the hope of Paul is the hope not for his own happiness and peace but, rather, for the 'glory of God' " (133).

13. See Bruce W. Winter, *Seek the Welfare of the City: Christians as Benefactors and Citizens* (Grand Rapids: Eerdmans, 1994), 174–75.

14. See 1 Cor 12–14 in particular. See also Craig Steven De Vos, *Church and Community Conflicts: The Relationships of the Thessalonian, Corinthian, and Philippian Churches with Their Wider Civic Communities* (Atlanta: Scholars Press, 1999), 226, 229–31; and Davorin Peterlin, *Paul's Letter to the Philippians in the Light of Disunity in the Church* (Leiden: E. J. Brill, 1995), 61–65, 71–75.

15. As with litigation at Corinth, there is much written about relationships in Romans. See, for example, James C. Walters, *Ethnic Issues in Paul's Letter to the Romans: Changing Self-Definitions in Earliest Roman Christianity* (Valley Forge, Pa.: Trinity Press International, 1993); and Reta Halteman Finger, *Paul and the Roman House Churches: A Simulation* (Scottdale, Pa.: Herald Press, 1993).

16. General assessments of Pauline ethics within congregational life are profuse; see Victor Paul Furnish, *Theology and Ethics in Paul* (Nashville: Abingdon, 1968), 203–6; Wolfgang Schrage, *The Ethics of the New Testament* (trans. David E. Green; Philadelphia: Fortress, 1988), 190–95; and Mauser, *Gospel of Peace*, 125–29.

17. See, for example, 1 Thess 5:15 and Rom 12:18. First Corinthians 10:33 also addresses such personal subordination, although the focus is slightly different.

18. See also 1 Cor 4:12–13. The Rom 12 passage has been studied extensively. See Luise Schottroff, "Nonviolence and the Love of One's Enemies," in *Essays on the Love Commandment* (ed. Luise Schottroff et al.; Philadelphia: Fortress, 1978), 9–39; and John Piper, *"Love Your Enemies," Jesus' Love Command in the Synoptic Gospels and in the Early Christian Paraenesis: A History of the Tradition and Interpretation of Its Uses* (Cambridge: Cambridge University Press, 1979), 102–19.

19. Among other passages, see Rom 6:13–14; 1 Cor 2:6–10; Phil 3:20–21. See also my dissertation, " 'Our Citizenship Is in Heaven': Philippians 1:27–30 and 3:20–21 as Part of the Apostle Paul's Political Theology" (Ph.D. diss., Princeton Theological Seminary, 1998). Paul's sarcastic reference to the popular belief that the *pax Romana* had brought "peace and security" (1 Thess 5:3) makes a similar point; see Helmut Koester, "Imperial Ideology and Paul's Eschatology in 1 Thessalonians," in *Paul and Empire: Religion and Power in Roman Imperial Society* (ed. Richard A. Horsley; Harrisburg, Pa.: Trinity Press International, 1997), 158–66, esp. 161.

20. Victor Paul Furnish, "War and Peace in the New Testament," *Interpretation* 38 (1984): 363–79, esp. 375; and Michel R. Desjardins, *Peace, Violence, and the New Testament* (Sheffield: Sheffield

Academic Press, 1997), 55, argue that Paul's cosmic eschatological purview kept him from advocating substantive action in the present. As Rom 16:20 is the sole passage of this tenor, I agree with those who suggest Paul simply reverted in this passage to the use of traditional apocalyptic language to describe the defeat of evil. In this regard, see William Klassen, "Peace: New Testament," in *The Anchor Bible Dictionary* (ed. David Noel Freedman; New York: Doubleday, 1992), 5:207–12, 210.

21. This is the central thesis of J. Christiaan Beker in *Paul the Apostle: The Triumph of God in Life and Thought* (Philadelphia: Fortress, 1980). See also Neil Elliott, *Liberating Paul: The Justice of God and the Politics of the Apostle* (Maryknoll, N.Y.: Orbis, 1994), 176; and Mauser, *Gospel of Peace*, 109–12.

22. Furnish, "War and Peace in the New Testament," 372–73. He cites particularly Rom 12:9–10, 13:8–10; 1 Cor 8, 12–14; Gal 5:13–14, 6:2.

23. See Martin Hengel and Roland Deines, *The Pre-Christian Paul* (trans. John Bowden; Philadelphia: Trinity Press International, 1991).

24. Elliott, *Liberating Paul*, 88.

25. Such persecution is described both by Luke (Acts 8:1–3; 9:1–2, 4–5; 22:4–5, 7–8; 26:9–11, 14–15), as well as by Paul himself (Gal 1:13; Phil 3:6).

26. See, for example, Grimsrud, *God's Healing Strategy*, 130–31.

27. Rom 13:8–9 is the central text. See Victor Paul Furnish, *The Love Commandment in the New Testament* (Nashville: Abingdon, 1972), 108–11; Joseph A. Fitzmyer, *Romans* (New York: Doubleday, 1993), 676–81 (and the bibliography indicated there); and Schrage, *Ethics of the New Testament*, 211–17.

28. See, for example, Acts 2:43–47; 4:32–35.

29. A few of the texts that expose this strata of the early Church's existence are Acts 6:1 and 1 Cor 1:12.

30. Such progression of terminology within the field of conflict practitioners is charted in Carolyn Schrock-Shenk, "Introducing Conflict and Conflict Transformation," in *Making Peace with Conflict: Practical Skills for Conflict Transformation* (ed. Carolyn Schrock-Shenk and Lawrence Ressler; Scottdale, Pa.: Herald Press, 1999), 35.

31. Any number of illustrations could be cited here. Paul and Barnabas parting company over Mark is one well-known example (Acts 15:36–41). Another is Paul's determination that sexual immorality defiles the church and must be judged (1 Cor 5:1–13).

32. Paul's metaphor of the church as a body needing all of its separate parts can be read in this light (see 1 Cor 12:14–22). The spirit in which he departed from the Jerusalem conference is not entirely clear, but it is certain Paul took that process seriously and was still seeking to live in accord with its spirit years later (Acts 15; Gal 2).

33. For a general discussion of Paul and his opposition, see Gerd Luedemann, *Opposition to Paul in Jewish Christianity* (trans. M. Eugene Boring; Minneapolis: Fortress, 1989), esp. 105–9.

34. The Pauline writings focus less explicitly upon forgiveness than do the gospels, at least in lexical usages of words such as *aphiēmi*, but Paul does advocate the process of forgiveness with vocabulary such as *charizomai* in 2 Cor 2:5–11. All of Philemon can be seen in a similar perspective. Perhaps the preeminent illustration along these lines is Paul's use of the Christ hymn, with its emphasis upon the voluntary willingness to be humbled (Phil 2:5–11). See Leon Morris, "Forgiveness," in Hawthorne et al., *Dictionary of Paul and His Letters*, 311–13; and Ralph P. Martin, *Reconciliation: A Study of Paul's Theology* (2nd ed.; Grand Rapids: Zondervan, 1990).

35. Desjardins, *Peace, Violence, and the New Testament*, 55.

36. Again, Paul is less explicit than the "Be perfect, therefore, as your heavenly Father is perfect" of Matt 5:48, but he does allude to perfection at several points, such as Gal 3:3; Phil 3:12, 15; 1 Cor 2:6; and 2 Cor 12:9; 13:9, 11.

37. See Wiles, *Making Sense of Paul*, 142.

38. For such voices across the New Testament, see Matt 5:9; Rom 14:19; Eph 4:3–6, 6:10–20; Col 3:8–15; and Heb 12:14.

39. Mauser explores with some precision what this very phrase implies for Paul (*Gospel of Peace*, 105–6; 134).

40. While Eph 2:14 is probably a deuteropauline text, I think it easily can be argued that it carries on Paul's interests.

41. Frankemölle, "Peace and the Sword in the New Testament," 230.

8

THE FULFILLMENT OF HUMAN NATURE IN EASTERN PATRISTIC CHRISTIANITY

— Lisa D. Maugans Driver —

The relationship between "the good life" and consumerism in contemporary America is both complex and troubling. For many twenty-first-century Americans, the good life consists of a mansion in the suburbs, an SUV in the garage, kids in the finest colleges, and advancement in a high-profile career that ends with early retirement in a sunny climate. Others, recently dubbed "Bobos" because of their Bohemian yet bourgeois tendencies, have claimed to reject this consumerist bent in favor of simple living, but they reject it only after attaining wealth sufficient to transform simplicity itself into a consumer ideal.[1] Still other Americans seek to defy American-style consumerism by creating a Christian counterculture, though careful inspection of this counterculture reveals that it, too, has developed its own versions of what it claims to reject. Massive youth gatherings have replaced Woodstock, Bible action figures have supplanted G.I. Joes and Barbies, and SUVs, instead of being scuttled, are sanctified with Jesus fish. Such is the good life at the dawn of the twenty-first century.

Similar problems, and similar visions of the good life, were present at the dawn of the fifth century. Consider the observations (paraphrased, of course) of Asterius of Amaseia, a bishop in the urban-centered, multicultural environment of late ancient Asia Minor:

> They parade around with Ralph Lauren and Tommy Hilfiger labels on
> their clothes. Some, the more pious, show off their WWJD and Promise

Keepers garb. And doing these things, they think they are behaving reverently and that they clothe themselves in cloaks pleasing to God. But if they accept my advice, after selling those garments (thereby discarding what should never have been bought), let them *honor the living image of God* in their fellow human beings.[2]

Many contemporary Christians assume that fourth- and fifth-century Christians were so preoccupied with asserting Christ's divine nature against the Arians that other faith issues mattered little to them. Against that assumption, this essay demonstrates that Nicene Christianity served as an important foundation for the establishment of a just society. More specifically, through an examination of Nicene homilies—that is, popular theological reflections aimed at the broadest possible audiences—this essay argues that the assertion of Christ's true divinity and true humanity served the Church well as an interpretive key for Christian social action.

In the eyes of many patristic preachers, few contexts were more theologically compelling than the yawning gap between the rich and the poor. In the paraphrase above, for instance, Asterius links his understanding of the image of God with righteous economic choices and proper relationships with both human beings and things. Similarly, Basil of Caesarea, who deemed wealth to be all things beyond necessities for survival, insisted that "to whatever extent you abound in wealth, to that extent you are lacking in love."[3] While bold critiques such as Basil's may not have been entirely typical, they cannot help but strip bare our own attempts at living out the Christian faith. With what ought we be clothed? How can we justify life's little extras?

My goal, then, is straightforward: to see how the Eastern patristic tradition can inform an authentic, Christian response to the pernicious effects of sin, especially as they contribute to economic inequality and exploitation.[4] In particular, this essay directs Christians today to the ways that faith stories can provide a foundation for social activism.[5] By concentrating on Christian stories about who we are (theological anthropology) and by briefly considering the practices that place us within those stories (catechism, baptism, and *ascesis*), this essay provides a historically grounded and theologically rich starting point for connecting the practices of Christian spirituality to issues of social justice.

Human Nature and Human Story

Theological Anthropology

Consider once again Asterius's diatribe against "designer fashions." In fifth-century Amaseia, local notables attired themselves in fine clothing that cost fifty times more than the clothing most people wore.[6] The favored treatment of such fabrics consisted of coloring them with expensive purple dyes or, better yet, weaving into them detailed pictures. While some notables gained attention by donning aristocratic hunting scenes—lions, leopards, bears, dogs, woods, and hunters—others chose to demonstrate their association with Christianity by commissioning patterns depicting New Testament stories.[7] The appearance of this clothing never failed to attract attention. Asterius says that children flocked about the walking art galleries, laughing and pointing at the pictures. Asterius likened such outfits to murals, or perhaps less complimentarily, to graffiti.[8] He realized that over fifty poor people could be clothed with the money spent for one luxurious outfit. What witnesses to Christianity better, he asked, pictures or deeds?

Early Christian preachers were not without resources as they addressed pressing social issues of their day, in particular, the problem of economic injustice. To the contrary, they found the Scriptures bristling with teachings and stories by which to impress upon their listeners the mystery of humanity: our origins and purpose, our fallenness and salvation. Without recourse to the Christian story, they argued, human beings would have no standards by which to distinguish inhumanity from humanity, things that nurture our humanity from things that destroy it. Moreover, they said, in the process of identifying what is broken, Christians can learn what it means to be whole. In sum, Asterius and his fellow preachers believed that a faithful Christian response to societal problems required an understanding of both the Scriptures' claims about humanity (created in the image of God, fallen, and saved) and God's intent for creation's material goods, including personal possessions.[9]

The starting point for all this was Paul's recognition that Christians lived betwixt and between, in a time between Christ's resurrection and their own resurrection. These fourth- and fifth-century preachers recognized that all of humanity was gifted with the image of God and that, though damaged in the fall, this image was renewed and enhanced through God's embrace of human nature in and through the incarnation. Thus, even as their listeners experienced the ongoing realities of sinfulness and frailty, both theirs and others', they could nonetheless look forward to the perfection of God's image in the kingdom to come.

The Story of the Image of God

Articulating what it meant to be created in the image of God was a fluid process within the patristic tradition, but key themes did emerge, most notably the gift of creative intelligence (*logos*) and free will. With respect to the former, Gregory of Nazianzus observed that God "has set us apart from beasts, and honored [us] with *logos*, alone of all [creatures] on earth."[10] Moreover, through Christ the Logos, each Christian is a "son of God, a co-heir with Christ, and even, I dare say, a god himself."[11] Humanity had received from God a remarkable gift that, for better or worse, placed the entire world in its care.[12] Gregory referred his listeners back to just such a "noble nature" as he considered human actions toward other human beings, indeed, toward all of creation.[13] These actions, he said, ensued from creatures who were created "free . . . and possessed of a free will."[14] Moreover, this original condition of humanity was communal rather than predatory in nature.[15] In the garden, human freedom was itself wealth because, prior to the fall, humanity recognized God's abundant provision for all of creation.[16] Such freedom, in retrospect, was also freedom from the ills that humanity brought upon itself through the fall.

Of course, fourth- and fifth-century Christians were much more familiar (as we are) with humanity in its predatory state. In the Scriptures, the story of creation is followed by the story of the fall, which quickly produced antisocial behavior to the point of fratricide. Gregory of Nazianzus observed that the flaws evident in fallen humanity, including its obsession with material things, actually compounded over time. Without accepting *logos* as its guide, he said, humanity asserted its own, more irrational nature, thereby producing a bestial social order. Instead of basic necessities being owned "in common and in abundance," things "beyond necessity" became the grounds for war.[17] Asterius saw greed at work here, and he laid much of human suffering at its feet, noting that greed brought "anomalous heights and depths" into human life, caused "men [to] lose their natural friendship to one another," and incited warfare in all its horror.[18] Greed, he said, turned humans into misanthropes. Take away greed and "all would return to the natural condition of love and friendliness."[19]

While this emphasis on the fall may seem commonsensical, Gregory of Nazianzus recognized how easy it was for Christians, especially wealthy ones, to forget the significance of the fall on social structures. Rarely did they stop to consider that economic and social stratification might itself be an evil human construction.[20] According to Gregory, the primary division within the human family was the strong versus the weak, a division exemplified by the social ills created when the strong exerted their military, economic, and physical power over the weak. In sum, he said, fallen humanity, prompted by greed, has taken repeated actions that have served to shatter its once noble nature and God's communal purposes.[21]

The Story of Possessions

For Nicene theologians and preachers, the Scriptures' claims about humanity were intimately related to the story of possessions. For instance, the Cappadocians repeatedly emphasized that responsible stewardship for the world's goods lay at the heart of humanity's job description as delineated in Gen 1: to care for the garden and to exhibit godlike dominion over God's beloved world. Gregory of Nazianzus maintained that most of God's gifts were intended for all people to have in common. Nowhere was this more true, he said, than in necessities such as air and water, which were not to be restricted by human laws or artificial boundaries.[22] With the fall, however, humans began to amass more than their needs required. By seeking and hoarding things beyond mere necessities, he said, humans abused their responsibility to tend God's gifts.

The Cappadocians' response to this abuse of responsibility varied, although their goal was the same: to encourage the generosity of their fellow Christians. As we have already seen, Basil of Caesarea manifested a deep frustration with the wealthy's ability to find "necessities" that competed with almsgiving, going so far as to level the accusation of murder against those who ignored others' suffering.[23] Although it may have come as a shock to Basil's listeners to learn they were guilty of murder because their wealth deprived others of God's riches, his stinging rebuke was not entirely unique; John Chrysostom observed that failing to share one's possessions constituted theft, swindle, and fraud.[24] Gregory of Nazianzus was less scathing, but his goal of nurturing generosity was the same. While allowing that wealth could itself be holy, he nonetheless argued that Christians should possess their things in a sanctified manner. "Possessing," he wrote, "may be sanctified through possessing well, namely, through sharing with those who have nothing."[25]

Asterius echoed the Cappadocians' concerns. Because of God's immortal, immutable nature, he said, God was the ultimate source of everything, including intangibles such as health, good repute (as judged by God, not humanity), and friends (those whose loyalty was not swayed by one's financial situation).[26] For this reason, Asterius told his congregation, "you are not your own master, but it is appropriate that you regulate word and deed and every activity of your life" according to God's desires, including activities pertaining to material possessions.[27]

The Story of Salvation

From the Fathers' perspective, Christians who understood and allowed themselves to be shaped by these stories of creation, stewardship, and the fall should be transformed in their relationships with God and the world. For instance, in light of the story of creation, all humans should see God somehow reflected in their neighbors, or at least see themselves in their neighbors.[28] Correspondingly, those with wealth should gladly apply their excess to the needs of others. Of course, simple familiarity with these stories changed nothing. In fact, the story of the fall served only to explain humanity's ongoing sinfulness and the impossibility of living in accord with the story of its lofty origins. Only with the additional story of Christ's incarnation, said the Nicene theologians, do humans receive the restoration of God's image. Only through participation in this story—through dying and rising with Christ in baptism, and through communion in his body and blood via the Eucharist—are Christians brought to growing in likeness to their Creator.

In emphasizing this possibility of growing in likeness to God, Nicene theologians built upon the Church's venerable tradition of "recapitulation" theology. As early as the second century, Irenaeus of Lyons had provided the outlines of this theology by emphasizing the possibility of becoming united with Christ:

> For it was for this end that the Word of God was made man, and He who was the Son of God became the Son of man, that man, having been taken into the Word, and receiving the adoption, might become the son of God. For by no other means could we have attained to incorruptibility and immortality, unless we had been united to incorruptibility and immortality.[29]

Irenaeus's recapitulation theology was taken up in earnest in the early fourth century by Athanasius of Alexandria, who shortened Irenaeus's idea into something of a slogan. The Word of God, Athanasius wrote, "assumed humanity that we might become God."[30] Athanasius used this slogan to underscore two truths. First, he used it to stress that in and through Christ's incarnation all of humanity had entered a new relationship with God (since, by assuming human nature, the Son had actually brought human nature into the Trinity). Second, he invoked it to underscore the renewal of human potential. Whereas in the fall humanity had lost its intimate knowledge of God and therefore its ability to remain in his likeness, Christ's incarnation had redrawn God's "portrait" within humanity, restoring human knowledge of God and rekindling a love for God's ways. In that sense, said Athanasius, the divine image can truly become ours again.[31]

These soteriological arguments were crucial to fourth- and fifth-century Christianity, particularly as they pertained to Christian discipleship. Nevertheless, Athanasius and his contemporaries did not think that merely hearing, or even knowing, the story of salvation would lead to transformed lives. To the contrary, living encounters with the Word-made-flesh were needed, encounters that occurred in and through the Church and the sacraments the Church provided. Only there, they averred, could believers be adequately nourished to follow their callings as Christians.

Formation and Commitment: Catechism, Baptism, *Ascesis*

How did early Christians learn who they were and what they were to be? Then as now, Christians learned largely from the examples and guidance of more mature believers, who both crafted and oversaw the Church's practice of telling the Christian story. The church year constituted one vehicle for this storytelling endeavor, recounting events from Jesus' life and recalling exemplary models of Christian living through festivals dedicated to saints. The liturgy, which had attained a fairly standard pattern by the mid-fourth century, likewise afforded opportunities to believers (and, to a lesser degree, inquirers) to rehearse the story of salvation on a regular basis. More fundamentally, however, Christian formation in the fourth- and fifth-century took place through the three-stage process of catechism, baptism, and *ascesis*.

Catechetical instruction in the Nicene church was serious business. In contrast to the cursory practices of some contemporary churches, catechetical instruction in the fourth- and fifth-centuries could take up to three years, concluding with a final, intensive period of preparation during Lent. The *Apostolic Tradition*, a church manual relating practices that dates to the mid-second century, outlined a three-year process whereby preparation for baptism required the sponsorship of mature Christians who participated in regular discussions with catechumens, modeled for them the Christian life, and monitored their moral lives.[32] Before infant baptism became a widespread practice during the fifth century, formation and entry into the faith often entailed the adoption of an ascetic lifestyle that, despite modern connotations of the term, focused not on separation from earthly endeavors but on living lives of simplicity and spiritual mindfulness. Correspondingly, the *Apostolic Tradition* included instructions for praying seven times a day, wherever one might be.[33]

Learning, of course, continued long after the conclusion of catechetical instruction. In some places, often at the encouragement of local bishops, small groups gathered to discuss lectionary texts, homilies, and other issues pertaining to the Christian faith. One church leader who encouraged this sort of activity was Basil of Caesarea. In his instructions to fellow church leaders, Basil noted that those who possessed "the gift of teaching" should be available outside liturgical settings to instruct "those who long to be built up by divine instructions."[34] Similarly, Basil encouraged Christians who felt their understanding of the faith was insufficient to present their questions to discussion groups or to Christian leaders.[35] Basil considered one of his primary roles as bishop to be inviting participation in educational forums that contributed to forming "complete and fulfilled [persons] of God."[36]

In addition to encouraging these educational forums, the Eastern Fathers placed a high value on the sacraments for deepening the commitment of believers to the Christian story. Surprising though it may be, the sacrament of baptism prompted more attention in this regard than did the Eucharist. Participation in the rite of baptism and, just as importantly, an emphasis on keeping one's baptismal vows served as the linchpins for Christian formation in the fourth- and fifth-century church. Not that the Eucharist was considered unimportant in the formation process; to the contrary, regular participation in the Eucharist was strongly encouraged. Nonetheless, the Eucharist was largely understood as an act that recalled what God had initiated in baptism, continuing the lifelong process of divinization (that is, the gift of participating in God through Jesus Christ) that began in baptism.[37]

Even though baptism was a common ritual, Nicene theologians and preachers were not about to take its meaning for granted. In his *Mystagogical Catechesis*, which dates to the mid-fourth century, Cyril of Jerusalem undertook to explain the deep meaning of the story into which the baptized entered. Each aspect of the baptismal ritual, said Cyril, should serve to recall various chapters in the Christian story and exemplify the participants' new identity as Christians. Consequently, Cyril's baptismal candidates approached the baptismal waters stripped bare in order to symbolize the removal of sin and in remembrance of Christ's nakedness on the cross.[38] Vowing to reject Satan, they vowed to reject not only sin in general but also the activities that distracted them from God, including athletic events, racing, hunting, and theater going.[39] The candidates then descended into a pool of water, where they underwent triune immersion as they received the Trinitarian pronouncement. Upon leaving the pool they were anointed with oil and clothed in white garments, symbolizing the gift of the Holy Spirit and the newness of life. Cyril summarized the meaning of this ritual, noting that the initiants' "birth went hand in hand with [their] death." Of course, he continued, "we did not really die, we were not really buried, we were not really crucified and raised again, but our imitation was but in a figure, while our salvation is in reality."[40] In other words, what Christ experienced, baptized Christians imitated, and by doing so they themselves became anointed ones ("christs").[41] The baptized entered the heart of the Christian story, uniting with Christ, taking his name, and becoming like the One who had first become human for them.

While the promise of Christian baptism was a lofty one, the reality of post-baptismal life was at once both daunting and mundane. Consequently, the need to encourage Christians to take their baptismal vows seriously was a significant concern in the fourth and fifth centuries, especially as it became safe, even trendy, to convert to Christianity. The Cappadocians responded to this challenge in their ascetical writings, in which they endeavored to answer the question, "Just what does it mean to be a 'christ'?" In Rule 80 of his ascetical guide *The Morals*, Basil declares that Christian disciples are those conformed "to the pattern of what they behold in Him or hear from Him." Having been "born anew through baptism of water and the Spirit," a Christian "becomes in the measure granted him that of which he has been born." This, in turn, enables the Christian to manifest a life characterized by observing God's commandments, loving neighbors, and seeking not "what is one's own but that which is to the advantage of the loved one both in body and soul." Basil concludes his ascetical summary by asking, "What is the mark of a Christian?" to which he responds, "To watch daily and hourly and stand prepared in that state of perfection which is pleasing to God, knowing that at what hour he thinks not, the Lord will come."[42]

This, in short, was Christian *ascesis*, literally, "training for the kingdom." Early Christians embraced this Greek word to describe the process of discipleship, echoing Paul's use of athletic imagery as well as his emphasis on disciplining the body in view of attaining spiritual growth. Basil of Caesarea took great pains to insist that *ascesis* was not limited to a special class of Christians, consistently refusing to use the word "monk" and advising his fellow Christians on how to live out their baptismal vows. Fighting his congregation's tendency toward spiritual complacency, Basil taught that the sacrament of baptism should initiate a change in participants' lives, enabling them to separate themselves from previous ways of life.[43] Toward that end he recommended extended retreats for the newly baptized so that they might have an opportunity to root out old habits and establish new ones, including prayer, awareness of God throughout the day, and service to others. Others, too, emphasized the importance of service in Christian *ascesis*. Asterius encouraged believers to demonstrate simplicity and hospitality, even at the risk of hosting one's persecutors. And Gregory of Nyssa emphasized the rather typical patristic link between Lenten fasting, almsgiving, and service to those in need.[44]

Making a Difference: Practicing What You Believe

What does it take for the Christian story to become one's own story? For a Christian to translate the story of the faith into daily living? While it might be theologically appropriate to say "the work of the Holy Spirit," that answer ignores the earthy and earthly ways the Spirit typically works. For the Eastern Fathers, spiritual disciplines were crucial to this transforming work of the Spirit. They believed that practicing spiritual disciplines helped practitioners not only to live more Christlike lives but also to desire such living more consistently.

Correspondingly, Nicene theologians and preachers encouraged their listeners to concentrate on the task of spiritual discipline by eliminating worldly distractions. In answer to questions regarding the "marks of a Christian," Basil linked the development of these marks to a "complete separation from and forgetfulness of old habits," including self-exile "from fleshly ties and worldly society."[45] This separation did not necessitate the adoption of a geographically cloistered existence. It did, however, demand a change of priorities that eventuated in behavior befitting a Christian. In calling for separation and exile from old habits, Basil hoped that newly baptized believers would, at the very least, modify their accustomed ways of doing business, their circles of friends, and their relationships to their possessions, including food, shelter, and clothing.

Knowing the Christian story of possessions did not always mean *living* in accordance to it, a disconnect that prompted frequent homiletic outbursts from the Fathers. These preachers saw that failure to practice simplicity and self-control betrayed both a lack of trust in God to provide and a lack of gratitude for what God had already provided. In this respect, Asterius compared the disciplines associated with self-control (e.g., simplicity and fasting) to be as necessary to Christian living as the tools of a craftsman to his trade.[46] Should such tools be set aside in preference to the world's tools, he warned, injustice would inevitably triumph over justice.[47]

As if to provide his listeners with an unmistakable object lesson, Basil's episcopal complex in Caesarea incarnated the theological content of the Christian story in a remarkably concrete way. In response to the dehumanizing effects of poverty and sickness in his community, Basil founded an episcopal complex that included a hospital with trained physicians and nurses, a job training program, and a distribution center for food, clothing, and money.[48] Perhaps most striking among the project's goals was the "rehumanization" of the region's leper population. Basil shocked his neighbors not merely by creating a place that welcomed lepers, but even more so by touching and treating them himself.[49] These lepers exemplified the most anguishing affliction of poverty, a predicament that began with anxieties caused by a lack of resources, progressed to the physical inability to provide for oneself, and culminated in being abandoned by others, indeed, becoming an object of their loathing.[50]

For Basil, *ascesis* demanded compassionate attention to society's outcasts, and he worked hard to involve other dedicated Christians (i.e. ascetics) in this humanizing endeavor. He benefited from the assistance of his fellow Cappadocians—his closest friend, Gregory of Nazianzus, and his younger brother, Gregory of Nyssa.[51] For instance, in a homily supporting the hospital's development, Gregory of Nazianzus underscored the very theological themes I have already identified as the marrow of Nicene social concern: the dignity innate to human beings created in the image of God, and the fact that all of humanity is bound together in its physical and spiritual fallenness.[52] Because of these things, said Gregory, there is no dichotomy in God's eyes between "us" (the clean, healthy, and fortunate) and "them" (the unclean, diseased, and wretched). Rather, we are all "brothers in God," all created from the same materials according to the same physical design, all liable to the same frailties, all honored with the same divine gifts beyond understanding.[53] At the close of his homily, which he entitled "On the Love of the Poor," Gregory exhorted his listeners to recall Jesus' parabolic admonition in Matt 25:

> O Servants of Christ, who are my brothers and my fellow heirs, let us, while there is yet time, visit Christ in His sickness, let us have a care for Christ in His sickness, let us give to Christ to eat, let us clothe Christ in his

nakedness, let us do honor to Christ, and not only at table, . . . not only with precious ointments, . . . not only at His tomb, . . . but let us honor Him because the Lord of all will have mercy and not sacrifice, and goodness of heart above thousands of fat lambs. Let us give Him this honor in His poor, in those who lie on the ground here before us this day.[54]

With what then are we clothed? Simplicity and good stewardship, or the acquisitiveness of North American consumer culture? How do we come to know God? Moreover, how do we learn to see God in others, especially those whom our society has deemed outcasts? These questions remain relevant today, and the answers offered to us by our fourth- and fifth-century predecessors are hardly outdated. As they would surely tell us, our response to these questions depends, on the one hand, upon our willingness to be formed by God in the Christian story through baptism, worship, and prayer. It depends, on the other hand, upon our willingness to act in ways as revolutionary as Basil's complex was in his own time.

Notes

1. See David Brooks, *Bobos in Paradise: The New Upper Class and How They Got There* (New York: Simon & Schuster, 2000).

2. Asterius of Amaseia, *Homily 1: On the Rich Man and Lazarus* 3–4. The emphasized words are a close translation, not a paraphrase. All unspecified translations in this chapter are my own. See Asterius of Amaseia, *Homilies I–XIV* (ed. Cornelius Datema; Leiden: E. J. Brill, 1970); and *Sermons for Modern Times* (homilies 1–5; trans. Galusha Anderson and Edgar Johnson Goodspeed; New York: Pilgrim, 1904).

3. Basil of Caesarea, *Homily 7: On Riches* 1. See *Saint Basile: Homélies sur la richesse* (trans. and ed. Yves Courtonne; Paris: Firmin Didot, 1935), 41.27–28. Basil suggested that necessities be limited to a simple tunic, a cloak, and one loaf of bread.

4. I develop these thoughts primarily from the writings of the Cappadocians (Basil of Caesarea, d. 379; Gregory of Nazianzus, d. 389; and Gregory of Nyssa, d. 393), with some references to their younger contemporary and northern neighbor Asterius (d. early fifth century) and their elder contemporary Athanasius of Alexandria (d. 373). Sacramental background will be taken from Cyril of Jerusalem's catechetical and mystagogical lectures (ca. 341).

5. Patristic ideas about formation and identity have been revived in recent years by ethicist Stanley Hauerwas in *A Community of Character* (Notre Dame, Ind.: University of Notre Dame Press, 1988); and philosopher Alasdair MacIntyre in *After Virtue: A Study in Moral Theory* (Notre Dame, Ind.: University of Notre Dame Press, 1997).

6. See *Edictum de pretiis* 29.17, 26.75–77, in *Diokletians Preisedikt* (ed. Siegfried Lauffer; Berlin: de Gruyter, 1971).

7. Asterius of Amaseia, *Homily 1: On the Rich Man and Lazarus* 3.3, describes hunting portraits; 4.1 describes Christian scenes, including the wedding at Cana, the woman with a hemorrhage touching Jesus' hem, and the resurrection of Lazarus.

8. Asterius of Amaseia, *Homily 1: On the Rich Man and Lazarus* 3.2. He uses the Greek term for painted or inscribed walls.

9. These early Fathers did not, of course, advocate salvation through knowledge acquisition. To the contrary, they assumed that Christ was the only means for providing saving knowledge, which in their view had more to do with loving God than with intellectually understanding God's ways.

10. Gregory of Nazianzus, *Oration 14: On the Love of the Poor* 23 (PG 35:888c). "PG" and "PL" refer to Patrologiae cursus completus, Series graeca (PG) (ed. J.-P. Migne; Paris: 1857–1868); and Patrologiae cursus completus, Series latina (PL) (ed. J.-P. Migne; Paris: 1844–1855).

11. Ibid. (PG 35:888a).

12. Ibid., 25 (PG 35:889c).

13. Ibid., 26 (PG 35:892b).

14. Ibid., 25 (PG 35:892a).

15. Ibid., 25–26 (PG 35:889–92).

16. "Freedom then, and wealth, lay simply in the observance of His single commandment: True slavery and poverty in its transgression." Gregory of Nazianzus, *Oration 14: On the Love of the Poor* 25, in *The Sunday Sermons of the Great Fathers* (trans. M. F. Toal; Chicago: Regnery, 1963), 4:56.

17. Gregory of Nazianzus, *Oration 14: On the Love of the Poor* 25 (PG 35:889c).

18. Asterius of Amaseia, *Homily 3: Against Covetousness* 2.5, 13.1, in *Ancient Sermons for Modern Times* (trans. Galusha Anderson and Edgar Johnson Goodspeed; New York: Pilgrim, 1904), 102, 103.

19. Asterius of Amaseia, *Homily 3: Against Covetousness* 2.1, 13.4, in Anderson and Goodspeed trans., *Ancient Sermons for Modern Times*, 104.

20. Gregory of Nazianzus, *Oration 14: On the Love of the Poor* 25 (PG 35:889c–d; 892a).

21. Ibid., 26 (PG 35:892b).

22. Ibid., 20 (PG 35:881c–884b); 25 (PG 35:889c).

23. Basil, *Homily 8: In Time of Famine and Drought* 7.

24. John Chrysostom, *Homily 2: On Lazarus* 4.

25. Gregory of Nazianzus, *Oration 14: On the Love of the Poor* 18 (PG 35:880d–881a). The only good of worldly excess, wrote Gregory, is the ability to give it to those in need (29, PG 35:896d–897b).

26. Asterius of Amaseia, *Homily 2: On the Unjust Steward* 1 and passim.

27. Ibid., 5.1.

28. Gregory of Nazianzus, *Oration 14: On the Love of the Poor* 26 (PG 35:892c–d).

29. Irenaeus, *Against Heresies* 3.19.1, in *Ante-Nicene Fathers* (Grand Rapids: Eerdmans, 1956), 1:448.

30. Athanasius, *On the Incarnation* 54, in *On the Incarnation: The Treatise De Incarnatione Verbi Dei* (rev. ed.; trans. and ed. Religious of C.S.M.V.; Crestwood, N.Y.: St. Vladimir's Seminary Press, 1996), 93.

31. Athanasius, *On the Incarnation*, 41–43.

32. See Paul Bradshaw, Maxwell Johnson, and L. Edward Phillips, *The Apostolic Tradition: A Commentary* (ed. Harold Attridge; Minneapolis: Fortress, 2002), 15–20.

33. Ibid., 36.

34. Basil of Caesarea, "Prologue 1," 2 (PL 103:487a). This is the prologue to the *Small Asceticon* preserved in Rufinus of Aquileia's Latin translation, *Interrogationes fratrum* (PL 103:483–554).

35. Basil, "Prologue 1," 12–13 (PL 103:487c).

36. Ibid., 6 (PL 103:487b).

37. This is how Cyril of Jerusalem described the Eucharist to those recently baptized: "Therefore with fullest assurance let us partake as of the Body and Blood of Christ: for in the figure of Bread is given to thee His Body, and in the figure of Wine His Blood; that thou by partaking of the Body and Blood of Christ, mightest be made of the same body and the same blood with Him. For thus we come to bear Christ in us, because His Body and Blood are diffused through our members; thus it is that, according to the blessed Peter, we became partakers of the divine nature (2 Peter 1:4)." Cyril of Jerusalem, *Mystagogical Catechesis* 4.3, in *Lectures on the Christian Sacraments* (ed. F. L. Cross; trans. R. W. Church; Crestwood, N.Y.: St. Vladimir's Seminary Press, 1951), 68.

38. Cyril, *Mystagogical Catechesis* 2.2, 59–60.

39. Ibid., 1.4–8, 54–57.

40. Ibid., 2.4–5, 61.

41. "Having been baptized into Christ, and put on Christ, ye have been made conformable to the Son of God. . . . Now ye were made Christs by receiving the emblem of the Holy Ghost; and all things were in a figure wrought in you, because ye are figures of Christ." Ibid., 3.1, 63–64.

42. All quotations in this paragraph are from *The Morals* as found in *Saint Basil: Ascetical Works* (trans. M. Monica Wagner; vol. 9 of *The Fathers of the Church*; Washington, D.C.: Catholic University of America Press, 1962), 203–5.

43. This theme recurs in Basil in works such as *The Long Rules* 3–8, and *Concerning Baptism*, both of which appear in *Saint Basil: Ascetical Works*, 223–337, 339–430. For the broad audience Basil envisioned for his ascetical teaching, see Paul Jonathan Fedwick, *The Church and Charisma of Leadership in Basil of Caesarea* (Toronto: Pontifical Institute of Mediaeval Studies, 1979), 15 n. 73.

44. Asterius of Amaseia, *Homily 9: On St. Phocas the Martyr* (PG 40:301a–313a); and Gregory of Nyssa, *On Good Works (Homily 1: On the Love of the Poor)* (PG 46:453–70).

45. Basil, *Long Rules* 5, in *Saint Basil: Ascetical Works*, 241–42. Basil's *Rules* seem to have arisen from his role as a theological "Dear Abby." While many commentators have assumed that Basil's questions and answers were directed toward cloistered monks, that does not always seem to be the case, especially in light of the shape of the earliest known collection.

46. Asterius of Amaseia, *Homily 14: On the Beginning of Lent* 8.1.

47. Ibid., 12.3. "He who loves the body will necessarily also be in love with money, and the money lover is unjust."

48. Described in Basil, *Letter 94*, "To Elias, Governor of the Province," in *Saint Basil: Letters* (trans. Agnes Clare Way; vol. 13 of *The Fathers of the Church*; Washington, D.C.: Catholic University of America Press, 1951), 209–11; and Gregory of Nazianzus, *Oration 43: Panegyric on S. Basil* 63–64, trans. Charles Gordon Brown and James Edward Swallow, in *Nicene and Post-Nicene Fathers* (2nd ser.; Peabody, Mass.: Hendrickson, 1995), 7:416.

49. Gregory of Nazianzus, *Oration 43: Panegyric on S. Basil* 63.

50. Gregory of Nazianzus, *Oration 14: On the Love of the Poor* 9 (PG 35:868b).

51. See Brian Daley, "Building a New City: The Cappadocian Fathers and the Rhetoric of Philanthropy," *Journal of Early Christianity* 7 (1999): 431–61. See also Susan Holman, *The Hungry Are Dying: Beggars and Bishops in Roman Cappadocia* (Oxford Studies in Historical Theology; New York: Oxford University Press, 2001).

52. Justo L. González, *Faith and Wealth* (New York: Harper & Row, 1990), 174, 179ff.

53. Gregory of Nazianzus, *Oration 14: On the Love of the Poor* 14 (PG 35:876a).

54. Gregory of Nazianzus, *Oration 14: On the Love of the Poor* 40, in Toal, trans., *Sunday Sermons of the Great Fathers*, 4:63–64.

9

THE HIDDENNESS OF GOD AND THE JUSTICE OF GOD: NEGATIVE THEOLOGY AS SOCIAL ETHICAL RESOURCE

— J. Alexander Sider —

In the spirit of Martin Buber I want to insist that the most important word in the title of this essay is "and."[1] How can we take that conjunction with its full unitive force? Does not God's hiddenness stretch or even fracture our judgments about God's justice? Can Christians struggle toward social justice in the shadow cast by the hiddenness of God? Or are all such efforts merely human and mundane, the massive projections of our own fantasies onto the screen of the divine?

The almost overwhelming interest in "spirituality" among American Christians today compounds the difficulty of these questions. Bookstore shelves (Christian and otherwise) teem with titles promising to produce spiritual depth in their readers. Churches present spiritual awareness training programs, organize spiritual retreats, and even offer yoga classes. I am suspicious of *this* interest in Christian spirituality. It seems both amnesiac and individualistic, because it isolates Christians from the history of Christian thought and protects them from external criticism. If one's spirituality is wholly inner and private, a matter of "my God and me," then it cannot be tested by others. This unassailability untethers spirituality from ethics; it disconnects spirituality and social justice. And given the extent to which Americans already conceive of Christianity as a lifestyle choice, it portends serious and unhappy consequences for the faith.

In this essay, I explore the disjunction of spirituality and social justice as it progresses along one avenue of inquiry, namely, contemporary appropriations of negative theology. One could object that I merely find social justice a useful frame on which to hang my more esoteric concerns. But social justice is not tangential to these concerns, unless we think social justice has nothing to do with discipleship to Jesus, and therefore nothing to do with Christology. So, after explaining what negative theology is and showing how contemporary theologians use it to suspend our capacity for making judgments about God, I turn to the fourth-century Cappadocian father Gregory of Nyssa to show why the negative moment in Christian theology can be conceived as a resource for, rather than an inhibition to, Christian ethics. This has to do, I suggest, with Nyssa's thought about the person of Jesus Christ, who is himself the conjunctive force of the "and" in my title. Indeed, for Nyssa, Jesus Christ is the hiddenness *and* the justice of God.

What Is Negative Theology?

Simply put, negative theology is an account of how human speech always fails to make adequate reference to God. In this respect it is an ancient undertaking, for Christian theology has always labored under the burden of criticisms dealing with the accountability of its own speech. In what way can creaturely statements made with a creaturely set of tools by creatures themselves point to the uncreated God who created all that is? If God is the unlimited source of all being, how can limited beings claim to speak responsibly about God? Negative theology traffics in these questions. They are undeniably abstract questions, so perhaps we should take the time to clarify them with reference to a particular thinker within the Christian tradition.

The sixth-century Syrian-speaking monk we now know as Pseudo-Dionysius (or Denys) is one of the best candidates for this job, despite the fact that we do not know exactly who he was. He purports in his writings to be the Dionysius who heard the Apostle Paul preach in the Areopagus in Athens. If, however, he were that Dionysius, he would have been over five hundred years old when he wrote his collection of works, including *Mystical Theology, The Ecclesiastical Hierarchy, The Celestial Hierarchy*, and *On the Divine Names*. These four works were translated into intelligible Latin in the ninth century by John Scotus Eriugena, and from that point on Pseudo-Dionysius made an immense impact in the Latinate worlds (his influence on Greek-speaking Christianity was important already in the early seventh-century work of Maximus the Confessor). That is about all we can say with certainty about Pseudo-Dionysius, yet his work undeniably reflects and presages important developments in the way Christians have spoken about God.

Two sets of theses in Dionysius's thought stand out as essential to negative theology: first, his reflections on hierarchy, and second, his distinction between *kataphasis* and *apophasis*. The most important point to be made about these theses is that you cannot have the latter without the former. Indeed, Dionysius's conception of hierarchy makes the distinction between *kataphasis* and *apophasis* possible (and, consequently, makes possible the negative way in theology). To see why, let us treat each set of theses in turn.

The word "hierarchy" does not appear in texts before it appears in Dionysius's work.[2] In contemporary usage we associate hierarchy with a vertical ordering of power relationships concentrated on top and more or less dispersed at the bottom (like Amway and the federal government, for example). Understandably, this makes many of Dionysius's readers uneasy.[3] But there are good reasons to pay close attention to Dionysius's view, since doing so reveals how his understanding of hierarchy differs from ours. In the first place, Dionysius links his account of hierarchy to the doctrine of creation. For Dionysius, all creation is directed toward and by God so that its structure reflects God's glory. Moreover, because God is the sole simple principle, no one aspect of created reality can adequately manifest God.[4] Creation, therefore, must display God's glory in a harmony of parts. Aspects of creation are divided and subdivided into parts that, when taken in concert, tell us something about what God is like.[5]

According to this understanding, one of theology's essential tasks is to reflect on the interconnections between objects in creation in order to see how God's glory surpasses the world's wonderful intricacy. In Dionysius's view, the life of stones is less revelatory of God than that of humans, but both are necessary—because we must reflect on how stones are like and unlike humans and vice versa—to approach fuller knowledge of God. This is to say that the importance of hierarchy for Dionysius lies not in the *ranking* of humans above stones, but in the way that the created hierarchy *as a whole* displays how creation is intrinsically ordered to reflect God.[6] To put it simply, for Dionysius hierarchy is less about what things are higher than others and more about the articulate and ordered account of creation needed to begin to show us what God is like.

For Dionysius, the ideal earthly hierarchy is found in the Church. Demonstrating Ignatius of Antioch's influence, Dionysius insists that ecclesial order mirrors the heavenly order.[7] But he develops Ignatius's theme by arguing that people have different charisms in the Church, and only by exercising them in concert with each other does the Church mirror heaven. In other words, Dionysius emphasizes that no charism places a person intrinsically closer to God than any other person.[8] And, as in the Church, so in the world. God acts at every level of the created hierarchy in an unmediated way. There is no distance between anything or anyone and God, even though there will always be relationships of distance, and proximity, between differing created things. God is infinitely close to each of us, closer than we are to ourselves, but in order to begin to see this, we must place ourselves in relationship to other things. That is what the word "hierarchy" does for Dionysius: It shows us that the relationship of immediacy between God and creatures is unbalanced.[9]

This asymmetrical relationship of immediacy between God and creatures drives Dionysius's account of theological language. And here we move to the discussion of *kataphasis* and *apophasis*. On the one hand, because every utterance has some part in manifesting God's glory in creation (since every utterance refers to created things), there is a theological need to build up and accumulate speech about God. Dionysius's account of how we talk about God thus relies on pleonasm; all language must work in harmony to reflect God's glory.[10] On the other hand, Dionysius recognizes that no speech about God can perfectly mirror God, since any speech is but a part of creation. In confessing God, humans are therefore caught in a double bind. Every time we attempt to make reference to God, we find ourselves needing to say what cannot be adequately said.

Kataphasis and *apophasis* are Dionysius's terms for how we talk about being caught in that double bind. *Kataphasis* is the attempt, in a rough and ready way, to say something positive about God, like "God is my rock" or "God is good."[11] Its rationale is quite straightforward: Because God is the cause of all things, which are ordered toward God's glory by their participation in the created hierarchies, "we should posit and ascribe to [God] all the affirmations we make in regard to beings."[12] *Apophatic* language is more difficult because it includes two moments. In the first place, *apophasis* involves learning to deny positive assertions about God, since every positive assertion about God is inadequate to its object. Because created harmony inadequately reflects divine simplicity, it is for Dionysius always more adequate to pick out one aspect of created reality and deny that God is like that than it is to attempt to assert how God in fact is. "God is not good" reminds us of the complexity of God's creation in a way that "God is good" does not. A crucial point, however, should not be missed: The negation of positive language about God is *not* more nearly true than positive language is in its own right. "God is not good" is *not* more nearly true than "God is good." Rather, the dissimilarity between our expectations about what God is like and the statement "God is not good" reminds us of the complexity of making adequate reference to God in a way that the statement "God is good" does not.[13]

The first moment of *apophasis*, then, lies in learning to negate positive assertions about God. In the second place, however, *apophasis* also involves learning to deny that denying things about God puts one in a more substantive position of knowledge about God than do positive assertions. Indeed, *apophasis* is precisely a lack of substantive knowledge; it is a "hidden silence" and a "brilliant darkness" beyond speech and illumination.[14] Denys Turner's approach in *The Darkness of God* is instructive. He argues that such "opaque utterances" as "brilliant darkness" are "deliberately paradoxical, but they are not merely artful." He continues:

> We must both affirm and deny all things of God; and then we must negate the contradiction between the affirmed and the denied. That is why we must say affirmatively that God is "light," and then say, deny-ing this, that God is "darkness"; and finally, we must "negate the nega-tion" between darkness and light, which we do by saying: "God is a brilliant darkness." For the negation of the negation is not a *third* utterance, additional to the affirmative and the negative. . . . It is not some intelligible *synthesis* of affirmation and negation; it is rather the collapse of our affirmation and denials into disorder, which we can only express, *a fortiori*, in bits of collapsed, disordered language, like the babble of a Jeremiah.[15]

There are two things to learn from these reflections. First, it is important to remember that speech about God in the Christian tradition characteristically depends upon a particular metaphysics. In the case of Dionysius's negative theology, speech about God depends upon the metaphysics of hierarchy, cos-mological order, and the "great chain of being." To the extent that we no longer share that metaphysics, we should be careful with attempts to annex for our own use spiritual insights based on it.[16]

Second, it needs to be reiterated that negative theology does not license one to say whatever one wishes about God. Negative theology disciplines theologi-cal speech, ultimately by denying the distinction in validity between positive and negative assertions about God. Negative theology emphatically does not imply, contrary to what seems the assumption of many theologians, that posi-tive assertions about God are only metaphorical, whereas negative assertions can be literally true. *All* speech about God fails to be adequate to its referent. So we are always awash and adrift in theology and prayer.

We are not, however, entirely without recourse. Like Irenaeus of Lyons, Dionysius thinks it takes Christ and God's long pedagogy of Israel recorded in Scripture to teach us how to speak well of God. Moreover, the issue for Dionysius is not how one comes to knowledge of God, but rather in what ways one's attentiveness to Christ will be shaped. That shaping comes primarily through reading Scripture in the context of the liturgy where Christ's body and blood are made present. Negative theology does not, therefore, cultivate prac-ticed agnosticism in the way many of Dionysius's later interpreters, including contemporary theologians, have claimed that it does.

Negative Theology and Contemporary Spirituality

In the second portion of this essay, I address, at least in part, how contemporary trends in Christian thought, and particularly certain uses of negative theology, separate spirituality from social ethics and thereby erode the centrality of discipleship to faith. I should say up front that this is not an issue of the contemplative life versus the active life. Cistercians are no more likely to be guilty of this than Anabaptists. Anabaptist theologians Scott Holland and James Reimer have both recently used tropes from negative theology to argue for the "violence" of God.[17] Yet, in doing so, they have turned the negative moment of theology into exactly the kind of practiced agnosticism that the Pseudo-Dionysius's reflections on theological speech are meant to rule out. What do Holland and Reimer argue?

Both Holland and Reimer contend against the taming of the Christian God by contemporary Christian pacifists. As Holland puts it, "There is a great temptation in any religion or spirituality to domesticate the Divine and thus make God our family, churchly, tribal or national deity."[18] That temptation to domesticate God takes the following form, according to Reimer: "Some . . . theologians have implied that if we take Jesus to be the full revelation of God, and if we understand the gospel of Jesus essentially as the rejection of all violence, then it follows that God is a pacifist."[19] This will not do, according to both theologians, because it fails to reckon with "the reality of violence in our lives and in our world" and gives no account of how we can "reconcile the apparent violence of the God of Abraham, Isaac, and Jacob, and the non-violence of Jesus as found in his teachings in the Sermon on the Mount and his death on the cross."[20]

The answer to the problem, they continue, is to point contemporary Christians to the doctrine of God, insisting "that such a confession returns us to the mystery of the Triune God, a God who is revealed but also hidden, transcendent and immanent, loving and terrifying."[21] Reimer elaborates:

> The basic claim behind the trinitarian confession is that God the Creator, God the Son, and God the Spirit are one, yet distinct. God the Creator is the invisible, absolutely transcendent, unknowable, mysterious source of all that is, both being and non-being. . . . This God is no . . . pacifist. This God is beyond all human ethical systems, beyond our rules of good and bad. . . . God is just, righteous, good, and loving, but in ways that are not fully transparent.[22]

Reimer's and Holland's arguments make clear use of tropes associated with negative theology, including the transcendence, unknowability, and mystery of God. On the Pseudo-Dionysius's terms, however, much of what they have to say about how the doctrine of God can help us resist domesticating God is badly misleading. And this is for two main reasons.

In the first place, for Dionysius, it is only on account of the triune God's creative activity that God is knowable at all. As we saw in our discussion of Dionysius's account of hierarchy, if and only if God is the creator of all that is— and for the "classical Christianity" Dionysius represents, the notion that God is the source of nonbeing is pure sophistry—can we begin to use creaturely language to speak of God. Dionysius argues that "the unnamed goodness . . . contains everything beforehand within itself . . . in an uncomplicated and boundless manner. . . . Hence the songs of praise and the names for it are fittingly derived from the sum total of creation."[23] Only because God boundlessly possesses that which God creates is it fitting to speak of God using the names of all things in creation.

Oddly then, any theology that attempts to speak of God solely by denying God's analogies with created reality domesticates God. Despite their talk of transcendence and mystery, Holland's and Reimer's use of theological grammar is insufficiently apophatic, because they associate unknowing primarily with the denial of positive claims about God. This produces a God who is sure to act contrary to the expectations of Reimer's and Holland's audiences—an important point, to be sure, and to the extent that they purpose to shock Christians out of an easy piety, it is entirely proper. Yet Holland and Reimer want to do more than shock otherwise complacent Christians, and here is where the negative way goes awry in their work. Reimer, for his part, hopes negative theology can make nonviolence responsible practice for Christians: "Our commitment to the way of the cross (reconciliation) is not premised on God's pacifism or non-pacifism. It is precisely because God has the prerogative to give and take life that we do not have that right. Vengeance we leave up to God."[24] Holland agrees with Reimer and furthermore thinks that such an "understanding of God is not only good classical theology but also good psychology and spirituality for the work of conflict transformation and peacemaking in a blessed but fallen world."[25]

The problem is that these positions still domesticate God by making particular ways of saying *who God is not* serve Reimer's and Holland's own agendas. Far from avoiding a tame, "golden and gleaming" God by denying positive assertions about God, Reimer's and Holland's misuse of the negative way makes God a stable referent for our speech. In other words, they miss what I earlier called the second moment of *apophasis*, the "negation of negation" in which we come to see that neither positive nor negative assertions make adequate reference to God. Properly theological speech relies on the instability generated by the sum total of assertions about God, both positive and negative, which, at least in Dionysius's view, are to be drawn from an articulate (i.e., hierarchical) account of creation. Consequently, properly theological speech must say *both* that God is and is not a rock, a stronghold, good, a pacifist, and so on *ad infinitum* without allowing either the assertion or its negation to outweigh the other. That is the only disciplined use of the negative way in theology, the only use that resists domesticating God in language. The archbishop of Canterbury, Rowan Williams, puts the point well in *Christ on Trial*, his recent reflection on the passion narratives:

> If we are really to have our language about the transcendence—the sheer, unimaginable *differentness*—of God recreated, it must be by the emptying out of all we thought we knew about it, the emptying out of practically all we normally mean by greatness. . . . God's "I am" can only be heard for what it really is when it has no trace of human power left to it; when it appears as something utterly different from human authority, even human liberty; when it is spoken by a captive under sentence of death.[26]

Williams's statement points to the second problem with Holland's and Reimer's uses of negative theology, namely, that they evidence an inadequate Christology. Given the Christian story, as well as the way theological speech works according to the Pseudo-Dionysius, God's transcendence is not absolute difference from created reality, nor is God's immanence pure sameness. Rather, what Christians proclaim is the mystery that God in Christ has acted to remake the world from within it. It is precisely God's closeness to us in Jesus Christ that is ultimately and unimaginably strange.

Christology and Spirituality according to Gregory of Nyssa

Gregory of Nyssa, the fourth-century Cappadocian father, understood the Christian spiritual life as a matter of the strangeness of God's closeness to humanity in Jesus Christ. I turn, then, in the final part of this essay to Nyssa's Christology and to a set of reflections on the interplay between Christology and negative theology. Having mentioned "strangeness," it will undoubtedly seem strange to suggest that we can profitably move backwards from the Pseudo-Dionysius to Gregory of Nyssa. Should we not rather move forward, perhaps to Maximus the Confessor, who is generally credited with articulating Dionysius's insights in a determinatively christological key? In moving from Dionysius back to Nyssa I do not aim to downplay the importance of later reflection on Dionysius's negative theology. Rather, I wish to insist that a reading of Dionysius, if it is to help reconnect spirituality and social justice, ought not to be considered separately from the sources on the basis of which it gains its immediate polemical and systematic contexts. More than any other theologian prior to Dionysius, Nyssa reflected on the negative aspects of Christian spirituality. I want only to suggest that his spirituality emerges from his Christology, in a way that helps us consider how Jesus' life as the incarnation of God's justice is itself a journey into the hiddenness of God.

Nyssa, as Mark McIntosh observes, took it to be the case that "whatever we might mean by Jesus' self-understanding . . . we ought to look not for propositional details of cognition, but for a pattern of self-giving action and love even in the face of seeming rejection."[27] For Nyssa, to know God is to participate in God's acts. It is not to have a cognitive grasp of what God is and is not. Indeed, Nyssa demonstrates, with a clarity that provides the basis for the Pseudo-Dionysius's negative theology, that God is not an object of any kind, not "part of the metaphysical furniture of the universe."[28]

Participation in God was a common way of speaking of the life of blessedness in the early Church. In attending to human participation in God's activity, as opposed to God's *being* in abstraction from activity, Nyssa shifts the terrain of negative theology to make participation, the vision of God, a positive ground for human perfection. Reflecting on Matt 5:8, "Blessed are the pure in heart, for they will see God," Nyssa writes:

> Seeing . . . that the manner of rejoicing . . . depend[s] upon purity of heart, once again my mind finds itself in a state of dizziness, in case purity of heart turns out to be something impossible and wholly beyond our reach. For if that is the way forward to see God, and Moses did not see him and Paul laid it down that neither he nor anybody else could see him, it would appear that there is something impossible lying before us in this beatitude. For what profit is there in knowing how God is seen if we lack the power to implement this promise?[29]

Later, Nyssa elaborates the problem: "The divine nature in and of itself . . . is unapproachable and inaccessible to human conjectures. . . . He who by nature is above every nature . . . , who is both beyond the senses and beyond the mind, is seen and grasped by some other method."[30]

Rowan Williams argues that the search for this "other method" led Nyssa to reflect on and develop Origen's picture of *epektasis*, "the Christian life as unceasing advance, 'straining forward to what lies ahead.'"[31] *Epektasis* involves the desire for God, which cannot be uncoupled from the pursuit of virtue. So, as with Dionysius's account of the created hierarchies, Nyssa shifts the inquiry from *being* to *activity*, from a static experience of the self to the arena of human action, the restless struggle toward lived—and therefore precarious—purity of heart after the pattern of Christ.

This restless struggle is the life of a community, eminently political, open to judgment, that we call the Church. Such communities are always marked by a lack of clarity, by the need for communal discernment, and by the risks attendant upon "straining toward what lies ahead." But in Nyssa's view, this sense of ambiguity does not differ radically from that which characterized Christ's own life. Rather, Gregory thinks that unknowing and lack of clarity are the effective marks of truthful knowledge of God, which Christ presumably had. This means, as McIntosh says, that the knowledge of God is not best conceived as "information in the mind but [as] a sharpening sense of mission and identity."[32]

In other words, "the vision of God is discipleship."[33] We imitate the incarnate Christ in his acts of love, poverty, and compassion. There is no more determinative knowledge of God than this, and just so, there is no more determinative account of the things God does, like hiding or executing justice. That is a hard pill to swallow, because it disrupts our attempts to find security— even a security that flies in the face of suburban pieties—in a doctrine of God. No guaranties, no security, no rest—just *epektasis*, unceasing advance. Negative theology is not finally useful as a "spiritual" technique for criticizing human patterns of knowing and doing. Negative theology is useful because it points out the resourcelessness of any Christian spirituality, ethics, or dogmatics abstracted from a tenacious following after Christ.

Notes

1. I refer to Buber's famous work *Between Man and Man* (trans. Ronald George Smith; New York: Macmillan, 1948).

2. Joseph Stiglmayr, "Über die Termini Hierarch und Hierarchie," *Zeitschrift für katholische Theologie* 22 (1898): 180–87.

3. Mark A. McIntosh, *Mystical Theology: The Integrity of Spirituality and Theology* (Oxford: Blackwell, 1998), 46.

4. Pseudo-Dionysius, *The Divine Names* (PG 3:641a), in *Pseudo-Dionysius: The Complete Works* (trans. Colm Luibheid and Paul Rorem; Mahwah, N.J.: Paulist Press, 1987), 61. All references to Dionysius are from this translation, giving the column references to the Greek text in J.-P. Migne, ed., Patrologia cursus completus, series graeca, vol. 3 (Paris: Migne, 1857), followed by the page number in the Luibheid-Rorem translation. Cf. McIntosh, *Mystical Theology*, 47–51.

5. See Andrew Louth, *Denys the Areopagite* (London: Geoffrey Chapman, 1989), 28. Cf. McIntosh, *Mystical Theology*, 50.

6. Pseudo-Dionysius, *Celestial Hierarchy* (PG 3:165a–b), 154.

7. Ibid. (PG 3:121c–d), 146; cf. idem, *Ecclesiastical Hierarchy* (PG 3:376b–c), 198–99.

8. Pseudo-Dionysius, *Ecclesiastical Hierarchy* (PG 3:401c–404b), 207.

9. Denys Turner, *The Darkness of God: Negativity in Christian Mysticism* (Cambridge: Cambridge University Press, 1995), 31.

10. Pseudo-Dionysius, *Divine Names* (PG 3: 593d–596a), 54.

11. As a movement in theological speech, *kataphasis* relies heavily, perhaps even exclusively, on Scripture. See Pseudo-Dionysius, *Divine Names* (PG 3:588a–b), 49; (PG 3:589d–592a), 51; idem, *Celestial Hierarchy* (PG 3:136d–144a), 147–51.

12. Pseudo-Dionysius, *The Mystical Theology* (PG 3:1000b–c), 136. Cf. Turner, *Darkness of God*, 23.

13. Cf. Turner, *Darkness of God*, 25: "A 'golden and gleaming' God is too like what we might choose to praise; a God 'enraged,' 'cursing' and 'drunk and hungover' might have greater power to shock us into a sense of the divine transcendence by the magnitude of the metaphorical deficiency."

14. Pseudo-Dionysius, *Mystical Theology* (PG 3:997a–b), 135.

15. Turner, *Darkness of God*, 22.

16. If we do not share Dionysius's metaphysical assumptions, we should have difficulty embracing his arguments about how language does and does not refer to God. This, of course, says nothing of whether Dionysius's metaphysical assumptions are good or bad, nor does it address the important question of how we could know we share (or no longer share) the metaphysical assumptions that inform his theology.

17. Scott Holland, "The Gospel of Peace and the Violence of God," *CrossCurrents* 51 (2002): 470–83; A. James Reimer, "God Is Love but Not a Pacifist," in *Mennonites and Classical Theology: Dogmatic Foundations for Christian Ethics* (Kitchener, Ont.: Pandora Press, 2001), 486–92. Both theologians adduce the influence of Miroslav Volf, *Exclusion and Embrace: A Theological Exploration of Identity* (Nashville: Abingdon, 1996).

18. Holland, "Gospel of Peace," 473.

19. Reimer, "God Is Love," 491.

20. Ibid.

21. Holland, "Gospel of Peace," 478.

22. Reimer, "God Is Love," 491–92. For present purposes I leave aside the question of Reimer's incipient Trinitarian modalism, which I addressed in a review of Reimer's book in the *Mennonite Quarterly Review* 74 (2002): 137–39.

23. Pseudo-Dionysius, *Divine Names* (PG 3:596d–597a), 56.

24. Reimer, "God Is Love," 492.

25. Holland, "Gospel of Peace," 479.

26. Rowan Williams, *Christ on Trial: How the Gospel Unsettles Our Judgement* (London: Fount, 2000), 7.

27. McIntosh, *Mystical Theology*, 202.

28. Stanley Hauerwas often puts the matter this way, most recently in his Gifford Lectures, published as *With the Grain of the Universe: The Church's Witness and Natural Theology* (Grand Rapids: Brazos, 2001), 28.

29. Gregory of Nyssa, "Homily 6: On the Beatitudes," in *Gregory of Nyssa* (ed. Anthony Meredith; London: Routledge, 1999), 93.

30. Ibid., 94.

31. Rowan Williams, *The Wound of Knowledge: Christian Spirituality from the New Testament to St. John of the Cross* (London: Darton, Longman & Todd, 1979), 54.

32. McIntosh, *Mystical Theology*, 201–2.

33. Williams, *Wound of Knowledge*, 61.

10

DECONSTRUCTION, MESSIANIC HOPE, AND JUST ACTION

— *Gerald J. Biesecker-Mast* —

Christians have long struggled with the question of how to be engaged with their cultural context without being overcome by those surroundings. This struggle is animated by the seemingly contradictory claim that arises from the confession of Jesus' incarnation: The reign of God has come among us and is yet on the way. Because Jesus became human and dwelt among us, we know that historical human cultures can reflect divinity; at the same time, we know that in Jesus' life, death, and resurrection the limits of history and death have been transgressed in a way that has not yet been fully revealed. We are both anticipating the kingdom and living in the kingdom. We are sinners and we are saved.

Living a life shaped by the way of Jesus and the kingdom he proclaimed thus requires a kind of alertness to both the limits of one's own habits and prejudices (sin) and the miraculous potential in everyday practices and exchanges (grace). Christian scholarship contains many resources for such a life of attentiveness and hope. At the same time, there has been a hesitation among Christian scholars to acknowledge the resources provided by contemporary social theory for people who seek to understand both the intractability of sinful social patterns and the conditions of possibility for transforming those patterns.[1]

Among the writers often viewed as posing the greatest threat to Christian understandings of truth is Jacques Derrida.[2] Considered by many to be the most significant and influential living philosopher in the Western world until his death in October 2004, Derrida spent much of his academic career moving between his post at the Ecole des Hautes Etudes en Sciences Sociales in Paris and various assignments at universities in the United States, including Johns Hopkins University, Yale University, New York University, and the University of California, Irvine. Much of Derrida's work consists of close readings of the classic texts of Western philosophy and religion through which he challenges that tradition's acceptance of the metaphysics of presence—that is, the assumption that textual meaning is based, however imperfectly, on the intention and consciousness of an author whose existence in turn is guaranteed by the presence of a transcendental Author. Derrida's greatest concern is how this Western metaphysics of presence has functioned to hide the social and political particularity of texts and thus to exercise unacknowledged power by making certain symbolic hierarchies appear natural and given.

While acknowledging the power exercised by the invocation of *presence*, [Slo]venian theorist Slavoj Žižek has argued that such an invocation is necessary [to] the successful pursuit of any meaningful political project, including the [for]ms of radical democracy to which he is committed. Born in Ljubljana, [infl]uenced as a student by such French scholars as Derrida, Jacques Lacan, and [Mic]hel Foucault, and shaped profoundly by the political struggles leading up [to] and following the breakup of communist Yugoslavia, Žižek's work has [foc]used on the psychic traumas and social dramas around which human sub[jec]ts articulate identity and find agency in the age of globalization and cyber[cul]ture. Žižek has spent much of his academic career at the Institute for Social [Re]search at the University of Ljubljana, and was active in the political struggle [for] a postcommunist Slovenia.

Both Derrida and Žižek seem to me to be concerned with some of the same [pr]oblems that Christians encounter as they seek to make the reign of God [pos]sible. Both are concerned with the question of what it means to act in the [t]ime of justice at a time when every such act or effort to act seems to be [ab]sorbed or deflected or subverted by the cultural politics of late capitalism. [A]nd both have increasingly engaged these questions by returning to the narra[ti]ves and desires associated with Christianity and its Jewish antecedents, especially the messianic expectations that shape these religious traditions. This essay provides an introductory comparison of the religious arguments advanced by Derrida and Žižek, with an eye toward how their work can help Christians act hopefully and justly in the world.

The comparison takes as its point of departure the differing assumptions about "the Other" that circulate in texts by Derrida and Žižek. The Other means many different things in contemporary social theory. In the Christian tradition, concerns about the Other can best be translated as questions about how to fulfill the greatest commandments: to love God with all our hearts and our neighbors as ourselves.

Derrida and Messianic Hope

For Derrida, the Other constitutes a horizon of obligation—a needy world beyond the self—that demands a response but, at the same time, makes all responses to the call of the Other problematic insofar as any particular response neglects or excludes some dimension of that call. The Other is that for which our words and practices inevitably fail to account, that which eludes representation, and that which disrupts the order and the meaning of speech and action. Following the work of Emmanuel Levinas, Derrida regards the Other as the one to whom I owe an infinite debt of responsibility—a debt that renders all particular and historical obligations as betrayals of that infinite responsibility.[3]

Derrida's accounting for such an Other begins with the particular reading strategy for which he has become known: deconstruction. Contrary to conventional wisdom, deconstruction, at least as practiced by Derrida, is not about textual destruction or symbolic relativism. To deconstruct a text is rather to expose the text to the fault lines and contradictions that are the conditions of its own possibility—to the *différance*, or the deferral of meaning that makes any particular meaning apparent. An example of such deconstruction is Derrida's analysis of the standard Western philosophical preference of speech over writing, going back at least as far as Plato. The claim that speech is to be preferred over writing because of the immediate presence of the speaker, the opportunity for the speaker to correct audience misperceptions, the identity between communication and context, and so on, is shown by Derrida to be based on an acknowledgment about the absence of the author/speaker in the written text that turns out also to be the case with the spoken text. Any frustrating interpersonal conflict that involves an argument about who said what, what was intended, what was heard, and what was misinterpreted demonstrates how the same absence that haunts written texts is already apparent in the spoken text. Yet this obvious absence of presence that occurs in very ordinary conversations must be excluded from consideration in order to make the priority of speech over writing an apparently natural hierarchy. At the same time, upon consideration, it seems that precisely the absence of human beings to one another is the condition of possibility for something like a text. We speak not because we are present to one another but because we are in some defining sense absent from one another.

It is precisely such exclusions upon which "common sense" claims rest that Derrida wishes to expose. Thus, rather than writing being an imperfect and secondary form of speech, Derrida shows how in fact speech can best be understood as a kind of writing, an inscription or marking that makes available a trace of the author/speaker, rather than his or her presence.

Derrida's assumption is that symbolic meaning does not simply reflect or provide an unproblematic access to the world outside of the text, but rather that the symbolic world—the world that appears to us by virtue of our ability to make meaning through speech and language and in the basic distinction between presence and absence—is as much a deflection of the "real" world as it is any sort of representation of that world. Speech and language and the movement of symbolic meaning are as much about human desire and social relationships and power structures as they are about description and explanation. To address another person or to describe a subject is at the same time to practice the maintaining of intersubjective relations or the building of institutions or the exercising of social power.

To expose symbolic practices to deconstruction, then, is to make visible the arrangements of power, convention, privilege, and exclusion that are the condition of possibility for any particular speech or text or sentence. As Derrida himself says, such exposure should not be seen primarily as an act of discrediting or disestablishing but rather of renewal and transformation. Speaking of the relationship between deconstruction and institutions, for example, he argues that deconstruction has "never, never opposed institutions as such." To the contrary, deconstruction "is affirmative in a way that is not simply positive, not simply conservative, not simply a way of repeating the given institution," but rather constitutes a way "to criticize, to transform, to open the institution to its own future."[4]

Here we can see how for Derrida deconstruction can best be understood as a kind of hospitality toward the future, toward what is to come, toward that which does not yet make sense within the present horizon of meaning. To deconstruct a text is to seek in that text a trace or a symptom of what is missing in the text, of what it could not say wittingly yet could not help but acknowledge unwittingly, of what must be excluded from the text in order for the text to have meaning for us. Deconstruction should be seen then as a practice of vigilance and attentiveness, analogous to the biblical injunction to watch and wait, for we know not at what hour the Lord may appear (Matt 25:13).

It is not surprising, then, that Derrida's work has taken a turn toward the religious, and especially toward those religious traditions and texts associated with messianic faiths: those that hope for and pray for an intervention from outside, those that long for the coming of an Other who will transform and remake the old ways, and those that anticipate a future that will outstrip present imaginations. For example, in a recent book that takes up the work of Czech dissident philosopher Jan Patočka, Derrida argues that the practice of religion—in particular, Christianity—is identified with the acceptance of responsibility associated with a free self that willingly subjects itself "to the wholly and infinite other that sees without being seen."[5] This hidden and all-seeing Other has been given the name of "God" in Judaism and Christianity, the mystery of which is the source of both terror and hope. We are terrified because we cannot see the One who sees us; we are in the gaze of we know not who or what. We have hope because the hidden One is associated with the infinite gift of love and with the coming of salvation.[6]

To live and to act within the context of such a terrifying hope is precisely to live within the logic of obedience, according to Derrida, to accept the orders of One whom we cannot address but who works his will in us and through us, even as we work out our "salvation with fear and trembling."[7] As Derrida puts it, "we fear and tremble before the inaccessible secret of a God who decides for us although we remain responsible, that is, free to decide, to work, to assume our life and death."[8] The responsibility demanded by this relationship to the all-seeing One is a responsibility that cannot be fulfilled, a responsibility that forces us to turn a blind eye to the call of *that* neighbor as we respond to the cry of *this* one.[9]

This experience of confronting an impossible obligation in the needs, injustices, and cries for help that confront us is surely the experience of all who seek to follow Jesus, to be obedient to the call of Christ. And it is an unfulfilled obligation that makes us yearn for the One who is to come, who is beyond us and thus can accomplish what is beyond us—that is, what we have been commanded to do, but cannot in our finitude get our minds or our bodies to take up. We hope, in short, for the impossible, for that which is on the way but has not yet arrived.

What sorts of actions or practices might such an experience of impossible obligation, of incommensurability, press upon us? In another recent work, *The Politics of Friendship*, Derrida has articulated a vision for friendship that would exceed the relationship of mutual exchange and fraternal regard that have motivated friendship throughout human history.[10] Among the features of such friendship is the opening to a love for enemies, to a community of those without community, and to an extension of friendship without calculation, without oaths of allegiance, and without limit.[11] Perhaps most significantly, however, the practice of friendship toward which Derrida points is one that is based in alterity rather than similarity.[12] The hope for such a friendship based in difference is derived partly through a deconstructive reading of conventional friendship to show how conventions of friendship are of necessity structured around the acknowledgment of difference or even of the impossibility of friendship, as in Aristotle's reputed claim: "My friends, there is no friend."[13] This sort of analysis is very typically Derridean; a careful reading of a conventional term and of its genealogy, in this case friendship, leads to a recognition that conventions of speech about that term carry with them both a recognition of the limits of those conventions and an opening toward what is absent or excluded in such conventions, and therefore what may yet be on the way—namely, an impossible friendship based on excess rather than exchange, and on gift rather than debt.

In addition to his work on friendship, Derrida has also explored forgiveness, using a deconstructive analysis to show how the term "forgiveness" and the expectations associated with it are dependent on a basic paradox: It is only possible to truly forgive that which is in fact unforgivable. That which can be forgiven, the forgivable, does not require forgiveness. If the harm you do me is something for which I am capable of accepting your repentance, then, in fact, forgiveness is not necessary. Only what is unforgivable requires forgiveness. Only the impossible makes forgiveness possible.[14]

Derrida observes that most of what falls under the category of forgiveness in human social and political life is in fact some sort of exchange: I will forgive you if you are truly sorry and repentant. I will forgive you if you promise never to do it again. You are forgiven if you make restitution. You are forgiven if you spend twenty years in prison or if you give your life in an electric chair or the executioner's gurney. All such transactions are not in fact acts of forgiveness, for they rest upon a logic of exchange, not of giving up to the other what he has taken. And in many instances, these transactions are undertaken by a third party—the state—rather than by the only person who in fact can forgive, namely, the victim.[15]

Yet, as Derrida points out, all of these acts of pseudoforgiveness are in fact given currency by the impossible act from which they all fall short: the pure and impossible act of forgiving that which cannot be forgiven, of forgiving even when forgiveness is not requested and when no repentance is forthcoming. Derrida observes that pure forgiveness and transactional forgiveness are both part of the biblical tradition. As he puts it, "Sometimes, forgiveness (given by God, or inspired by divine prescription) must be a gracious gift, without exchange and without condition; sometimes it requires, as its minimal condition, the repentance and transformation of the sinner."[16] Furthermore, he argues, "it is between these two poles, *irreconcilable but indissociable*, that decisions and responsibilities are to be taken."[17] In history, forgiveness takes the form of particular negotiations—of amnesty, for example, or of reparations and reconciliation. Yet, as he writes, "all of that refers to a certain idea of pure and unconditional forgiveness, without which this discourse would not have the least meaning."[18]

This brief summary of Derrida's analysis of the concept of forgiveness as it is articulated in the Western legal tradition and its Jewish and Christian antecedents is an instance par excellence of Derrida's account of human actions and responsibilities; they are only possible and meaningful against the backdrop of what in fact they cannot attain or that to which they cannot adequately respond. The possible is made possible by the impossible. Presence requires absence. And the absent impossible is just around the corner, on the way, yet to be seen and heard, if only we will attend to and subject ourselves to what we cannot see or hear.

Žižek and Just Action

Given Derrida's Jewish roots as well as his relationship to the Jewish ethicist Emmanuel Levinas, it is perhaps not surprising that Derridean deconstruction emphasizes that dimension of the Other for which we cannot account and to which we are nevertheless accountable. Slavoj Žižek, on the other hand, associates the Other not only with the unsymbolizable remainder of any system of signs (that which is left over when we try to make meaning) but also with the symbolic order itself that mediates between the remainder (which haunts us even though we cannot account for it in language) and the ordinary neighbor. Returning again and again to the psychoanalytic theories of Jacques Lacan, Žižek finds symptoms in both philosophical and popular texts of what in Lacanian psychoanalysis is referred to as the barred subject—the human subject whose condition of possibility for self-conscious existence is precisely that subject's inability to achieve any complete identity. In Lacanian psychoanalysis the intrusion of the Other into the consciousness of the developing child is identified with the imposition of the symbolic order that orders and organizes the social identity and self-understanding of humans.[19] But this order is always incomplete and never final; it always leaves something out that exceeds social order and personal identity. That which is left behind in the coming into language both prevents a final establishment of identity and is, in a sense, the difference that also drives the historical, provisional establishment of specific forms of social identity, incomplete though they may be.[20]

Thus, while Derrida is always concerned with what is excluded in conventions and reasoning practices of particular traditions of speech and writing, Žižek is more concerned with the particular formation of ideological subjects made possible through such particular traditions. If Derrida's focus is on the text, Žižek's is on the subject of those texts. If Derrida is attentive to what the text excludes, Žižek is interested in what the subject lacks. And while both Derrida and Žižek share much theoretical and ethical terrain, Derrida's greatest desire seems to be toward a radical hospitality toward what is to come, while Žižek's recurring impulse is toward a radical intervention into how things are.

To grasp Žižek's account of human action and intervention, it is necessary first of all to understand his description of the constraints on human action and behavior, constraints that arise directly from the interrelationship between the socialized subject and the symbolic order. Just as the subject itself organizes its social identity in a way that leaves a constitutive remainder (the undeniable and inescapable Thing that is left over when we struggle to make meaning through symbols), so is the social order within which the subject is granted consciousness also the result of a founding act that gave rise to a constitutive remainder. In other words, both subjects and the social order are predicated on what they of necessity cannot in their organizing principles account for. It is this constitutive remainder that is both the elusive Other of any given subject or society and, at the same time, the condition of possibility for the pleasure of transgression.

In Žižek's view there is an obscene underside to any civilizational order or law, an underside that is brought about precisely by the coming of that law and linked with the founding and sustaining violence associated with and prohibited by that civilizational order. In the United States, for example, the Revolutionary War established the American version of that order, and all struggles to maintain that American civilizational order are usually referred to that founding violence. Alongside the revolutionary violence, we know that other forms of authority and order—racism, for example—were also embedded in the founding of the American civilizational order. The violence associated with the Civil War, the Ku Klux Klan, and any number of incidents of racial violence represents an outbreak of that obscene underside into social consciousness. More recently, when Timothy McVeigh bombed the federal building in Oklahoma City, he was making visible the obscene underside of that revolutionary mythology, referring repeatedly to the need to water the tree of liberty with the blood of tyrants and describing the people he killed as collateral damage.

In this same respect, Žižek has written a pamphlet about the spectacular violence associated with the terrorist acts of September 11 in which he argues that global capitalism and terrorist networks such as Al Qaeda are both part of the same civilizational order of things, with Al Qaeda and Osama bin Laden representing the obscene effects of United States foreign policy, rather than outside enemies. Furthermore, rather than being the ugly intrusion of the real into a certain American naïve fantasy of safety and security, Žižek argues that the September 11 attacks were an "image that shattered our reality."[21] We were prepared for the power and persuasion of that image by the consumption of an endless series of Hollywood blockbusters that precisely constituted the Other of the American dream (i.e., that which cannot be accounted for in that dream, such as images of Muslim theocracy or angry environmentalists) through fantasies of spectacular violence and destruction arising from an encounter with that Other, blockbusters that at the same time provide the cultural capital for the extension of American power and hegemony throughout the world of global capitalism.

For Žižek, the symbolic structure and its obscene underside subsume practically all practices that seek to resist it. Again and again we are asked to make
a choice of identification that is really only an effect of the prior symbolic
order. The ultimatum proclaimed by President Bush in the aftermath of
September 11—you are either with us or you are with the terrorists—provides
us with two sides of the same symbolic coin. As Žižek puts it, "The fact that
global capitalism is a totality means that it is the dialectical unity of itself and of
its other, of the forces that resist it on 'fundamentalist' ideological grounds."[22]
For any real action to take place, such action would need to unplug from that
symbolic order by reorganizing the coordinates associated with that order. I
other words, it would need to find a different social symbolic order to plug

Such unplugging is not a simple matter, for it involves a psychologica
symbolic transformation that the subject cannot simply muster from w
In his book *The Fragile Absolute*, Žižek suggests that Christianity offers a n
by which such unplugging can take place:

> What if the split between the symbolic Law and the obscene shadow
> supplement of excessive violence that sustains it is *not* the ultima
> horizon of our experience? What if this entanglement of Law and i
> spectral double is precisely what, in the famous passage from Roman
> 7:7, Saint Paul denounces as that which the intervention of th
> Christian *agape* (love as charity) enables us to leave behind?[23]

For Žižek, it is apparent that the Christian tradition offers resources for
unplugging from what he calls "the vicious cycle of Law and its four
Transgression," namely, the work of the Christ as interpreted by Paul
offers a new model for social relations: radical charity.

Such radical charity involves at least two dimensions in Žižek's thou
First of all, Christianity as promoted by Paul effects a separation from
social order rather than harmony with it, so that the neighbor can be
apart from his or her function within that social order and thereby loved
brother or sister. Here Žižek quotes Paul's injunction to "regard no one fr
human point of view" since, "in Christ, there is a new creation: everythin,
has passed away; see, everything has become new!"[24] As Žižek makes clear, such
a renewed contemplation of our fellow human beings should not be mistaken
for a liberal humanist project of seeing people as individuals over against their
social signification within the present cultural system, or a New Age project of
inner peace amidst the present order, but rather a loving consideration of our
neighbors from within the context of a new order—the alternative community
of believers. For Žižek, "Christian 'unplugging' is *not* an inner contemplative
stance, but the active *work* of love which necessarily leads to the creation of an
alternative community."[25] In terms of the recent terrorist attacks, Žižek points

out that such a stance would enable an unqualified identification with all of the victims of the September 11 attacks, both those killed by the plane crashes and those killed subsequently by U.S. bombs.

Second, such a posture of radical Christian regard for the neighbor is related to the suspension of the law-sin dialectic as suggested by Paul. Žižek notes that in today's world, the most widely practiced form of resistance to the present order is the transgression of the law, whether it is right-wing national- ists promoting the pleasures of ethnic solidarity over polite multiculturalism, or whether it is New Agers promoting the enactment of personal desires over against cultural mores. In both these cases, it is assumed that the law's grip can be broken through identification with its obscene underside, that is, with transgression. Žižek argues that the truly Christian posture is to suspend "not so much the explicit laws but, rather, their implicit spectral obscene supple- ment."[26] In other words, rather than posing pleasure against duty, one should cut the symbolic knot that maintains the power of the law-sin dialectic. This is done, in Žižek's view, by renouncing what is most "precious to the self" in the same manner that we find Christ doing in the crucifixion.[27]

Indeed, only through such self-renunciation can the fear of the Other and the pleasure of self-preservation lose their mutually sustaining grip on our psyches in order to open the way to a new social world in which the law-sin dialectic has been suspended. The subject of such a new world is described by Žižek in his gloss on Paul's well-known ode to love in 1 Cor 13, where love is linked to knowing only in part: "Only a lacking, vulnerable being is capable of love: the ultimate mystery of love is therefore that incompleteness is in a way *higher than completion*."[28] In sum, rather than trying to solve the problem of incompleteness by seeking perfection or security or closure, the Christian sub- ject of Žižek's theory accepts this incompleteness as the condition of possibil- ity for acknowledging and identifying with the Other, even in the Other's terrifying dimension.

To fully understand this proposal, however, it is helpful to review the place of the Other in Žižek's work. For Žižek, the Other carries three dimensions that together create the conditions of possibility for action itself. The Other is (1) the ordinary neighbor to whom I relate according to the conventions of the social order, (2) the terrifying abyss that threatens the structure of meaning and selfhood, and (3) the symbolic order that mediates between the first two instances of the Other and that depends on those two instances for its own perpetuation.[29] For Žižek, Christian action acknowledges not only the neigh- bor whom I recognize and who is like me but also the radical Other that lurks within both self and neighbor, the remainder of the symbolic order that con- stitutes the self-neighbor relationship within conventional practices. The Christian who acts to unplug from the social order does so not only by acting in accord with that terrifying Other, but in some sense by precisely becoming that Other, by discovering that it is not I but someone or something else that works in me. Such identification with or becoming what cannot be integrated into the present social order is the condition of possibility of the new, of the constitution of a new set of symbolic coordinates, of the changing of the very "parameters of the possible."[30]

The Words and Deeds of Christian Hope

The contrasting works of Derrida and Žižek offer a compelling approach to the troublesome yet energizing tension described at the beginning of this essay. On the one hand, Jesus is the Messiah whom we believe has redeemed the world from sin and death through his death and resurrection on the cross. On the other hand, Jesus is the coming King whose reign has not been accepted by the powers and establishments of the world. On the one hand, we are called to live as if the social and symbolic coordinates have been reordered. On the other hand, we cannot help but notice that they have not. If Žižek helps us remember what it would mean to live according to a new set of coordinates, Derrida helps us remember how our efforts to do so tend to produce old habits of exclusion and violence.

This tension, to my way of thinking, is the location of genuinely Christian speech and action in the world. The tension can be described in existential or philosophical terms, and it can be associated with contemplated mysteries or doctrinal paradoxes. But to be a Christian is to live that tension, to allow Christ to act in us while inhabiting a world that is without Christ. As should be clear, there is no place for selfhood or identity outside of the symbolic world. Thus, it is not a question of being governed by a social order, but it is rather a question of which order will shape our practices. The tension between action and expectation then can only be kept alive through identification with Christ's body—the Church—which, when it is faithful, constitutes one version of the Other of the social order. To identify with Christ's body is to make visible the new creation that is struggling to be born within us and around us.

Such a christological identification goes beyond Derridean deconstruction of texts and Žižek's reconstruction of "unplugged" coordinates. Through identification with Jesus, Christians recognize that brokenness and crucifixion are conditions associated with redemption, not simply expectation. At the same time, Christians insist that this redemption does not come from human action that somehow reorders the social coordinates by violent intervention on the part of individuals. Christians do not need to intervene because Christ has already intervened. Christian action does not seek so much to reorder the social world as it does to accept the coordinates of an alternative social world. It is less concerned, for example, with transforming global capitalism than in being transformed by the reign of God. It is not so much interested in effectiveness as it is in faithfulness.

We can compare Christian action with the actions of suicide bombers and of the U.S. military in this way. The Christian horror at suicide attacks or military missions should not be preoccupied with the willingness of people to risk their lives or blow themselves up on behalf of a spiritual or political cause. The Christian opposition to suicide bombing stems rather from the vengeance and calculation associated with it, the hope to make history move through self-sacrifice and killing, a hope associated with all missions that include weapons and bombs and the intent to kill. The Christian way is to renounce such calculated and violent interventions without giving up either hope for justice or actions of mercy. What if all those suicide bombers who are willing to relinquish their lives were also able to give up the desire to destroy the lives of their enemies? By the same token, what if all the idealistic Americans who have joined the armed forces as an act of patriotism were willing not only to die but also to renounce killing on behalf of their neighbors?

Such a renouncing of not only one's own life but also of all control over the world of causes and effects, of retaliation and of retribution—*that* would truly be radical action, truly redemptive action. Yet that is the kind of action to which Christians are called because that is the work that Christ has done for us, is doing in us, and will complete one day in the whole creation. What is Christian spirituality but attentiveness to that work?

Notes

1. Christian scholarship has tended either to simply privilege social theory over theology or to pose theology against social theory. A notable exception to these tendencies is John Milbank's work and the emerging school of radical orthodoxy associated with him. See especially John Milbank, *Theology and Social Theory: Beyond Secular Reason* (Oxford: Blackwell, 1990). Milbank shows how it is possible to use the insights of modern and postmodern social theory without simply assimilating Christian theology to social theory. A more sympathetic account of postmodern theory, with particular attention to Derridean deconstruction, is found in John Caputo, *The Prayers and Tears of Jacques Derrida* (Bloomington: Indiana University Press, 1997).

2. A theological critique of Derridean deconstruction that typifies negative evaluations of Derrida but with an unusually rigorous argument is Brian Ingraffia, *Postmodern Theory and Biblical Theology* (Cambridge: Cambridge University Press, 1995), 167–241.

3. Jacques Derrida, *Writing and Difference* (Chicago: University of Chicago Press, 1978), 83–84; Emmanuel Levinas, *Totality and Infinity* (Pittsburgh: Duquesne University Press, 1961), 212–16; and Emmanuel Levinas, "Ethics as First Philosophy," in *The Levinas Reader* (ed. Seán Hand; Oxford: Blackwell, 1989), 82–84.

4. Jacques Derrida and John Caputo, *Deconstruction in a Nutshell* (New York: Fordham University Press, 1997), 5–6.

5. Jacques Derrida, *The Gift of Death* (Chicago: University of Chicago Press, 1995), 2; see also Jan Patočka, *Essais hérétiques sur la philosophie de l'historie* (trans. Erika Adams; Lagrasse: Verdier, 1981).

6. Derrida, *Gift of Death*, 55–56.

7. Ibid., 56.

8. Ibid.

9. Ibid., 68.

10. Jacques Derrida, *The Politics of Friendship* (New York: Verso Books, 1997), 138–67.

11. Ibid., 26–45.

12. I am indebted to Chris Huebner's analysis of Derrida's *The Politics of Friendship* and especially of how Derrida's account contrasts with that of John Milbank's radical orthodoxy. See Chris Huebner, "Christian Pacifism as Friendship with God," in *Anabaptists and Postmodernity* (ed. Susan Biesecker-Mast and Gerald Biesecker-Mast; Telford, Pa.: Pandora Press U.S., 2000), 343–53.

13. Derrida, *Politics of Friendship*, 124.

14. Jacques Derrida, *On Cosmopolitanism and Forgiveness* (New York: Routledge, 2001), 32–33.

15. Ibid., 34–44.

16. Ibid., 44.

17. Ibid., 45.

18. Ibid.

19. Jacques Lacan, *Écrits: A Selection* (New York: W. W. Norton & Co., 1977), 1–7.

20. Slavoj Žižek, *Tarrying with the Negative* (Durham, N.C.: Duke University Press, 1993), 9–44.

21. Slavoj Žižek, *Welcome to the Desert of the Real* (New York: Wooster Press, 2001), 18.

22. Ibid., 57.

23. Slavoj Žižek, *The Fragile Absolute* (New York: Verso Books, 2000), 99–100.

24. Ibid., 126–27; the Pauline quotation is from 2 Cor 5:16–17.

25. Ibid., 129–30.

26. Ibid., 130.

27. Ibid., 157–58.

28. Ibid., 147.

29. Slavoj Žižek, *Did Somebody Say Totalitarianism?* (New York: Verso Books, 2001), 163.

30. Ibid., 169.

PART IV

CONNECTING SPIRITUALITY
AND SOCIAL JUSTICE
IN PRACTICE

11

Prayer

JUST PRAYING, ACTING JUSTLY: CONTEMPLATION AND MANIFESTATION

— *Kent Ira Groff* —

To clasp the hands in prayer is the beginning of an uprising against the disorder of the world.

Karl Barth, *The Christian Life: Church Dogmatics* IV.4

At a conference I recently attended, one leader punctuated his lengthy prayer with the repeated refrain, "Lord, we *just* pray for . . . and we *just* ask that . . . God, we *just* pray now . . ." A friend beside me listened for a while, then leaned over and whispered, "Ah, we're getting another 'just prayer.'"

I have pondered my friend's humorous remark about this overworked evangelical litany. What if all praying were really "just prayer"—only in the deeper sense of being integrally connected to a concern for justice in the world? How would prayer, in both its corporate and solitary forms, look different? "Prayer means turning to Reality," wrote Evelyn Underhill in her classic work, *The Spiritual Life*.[1] And in Hebrew the word for repent (*shuv*) means "turn." So how would our lives, directed and sustained by our prayers, turn in different directions? In contrast to many popular spiritualities that advocate prayer as a means to escape from the world and its gritty complexities, real prayer—just prayer—begins by turning and returning to God in the attempt to see the world through God's eyes.

Much of this essay is devoted to reframing prayer practices that, in various times and places, have assisted Christians in their return to what Underhill calls "Reality": seeing the world through God's eyes. Before considering them, however, I want to propose two concepts for understanding Christian spirituality that create a proper context for praying justly: *incarnational spirituality* and *primodern spirituality*. Each functions to define the notion of just prayer (since not everything that goes by the name of prayer can be considered just prayer). At the same time, these concepts function to free twenty-first-century Christians in the Western world from the constraints of Enlightenment thinking that have sometimes been counterproductive to the practice of prayer. Taken together, these concepts provide a framework for rethinking prayer, its place in the lives of Christians, and its role in establishing God's kingdom "on earth as it is in heaven."

Incarnational Spirituality

Spirituality unhooked from Reality denies the incarnation of Jesus Christ. In John's gospel we read, "The Word became flesh and lived among us"—sharing humanity's pain and promise—"for the life of the world" (John 1:14; 6:51). Jesus' life and ministry teach us that authentic spirituality needs the messy membrane of human community to be complete. The Apostle Paul's theology affirms that fact. While contemporary theologians have sometimes accused Paul of splitting body from spirit, he in fact extended the notion of incarnational spirituality by choosing the metaphor "the body of Christ" to refer to the community of Christian believers. Even as Christ's body continues to be incarnate in the messy membrane known as the Church, so too authentic spirituality today is incarnational, attuned to the fleshly needs of the body and the world.

The Lord's Prayer exemplifies this incarnational spirituality, and thus serves as a foundation and guide for praying justly (Matt 6:9–13). Two elements of this prayer deserve particular note. First, the Lord's Prayer begins as a prayer for earthly global awareness: "Your kingdom come, your will be done, *on earth* as it is in heaven." Second, Jesus casts this model prayer in the plural: "*Our* Father . . . Give *us* this day *our* daily bread. . . . Forgive *us* our debts as *we* also have forgiven. . . ." While we in Western culture tend to think individualistically, Christians in other places and times have been much less apt to do this. The medieval Christian mystic Meister Eckhart would stretch our vision of Reality: "There is no such thing as 'my' bread. All bread is *ours*."[2] Bread is God's gift of life, given to us through each other. Whatever awakens us to our personal giftedness and global indebtedness can rightly be called prayer.

But what exactly does this mean, to give priority to *us* over *me* in an incarnational spirituality? I was forced to consider this question when I was asked to lecture in India, at Morningstar Theological College during the worldwide Week of Prayer for Christian Unity. As I pondered the question "What divides us?" in light of my Indian context, the widening gap between rich and poor came quickly to mind. This gap, of course, is not limited to comparisons between Calcutta and, say, central Pennsylvania, where I live. Indeed, a national U.S. magazine recently devoted its cover article to the question "Whatever happened to America's middle class?" From fights over water rights to the big divide between high-tech medical care and mere survival, economic lines are drawn between wealthier Northern and poorer Southern Hemisphere nations, within nations, and even within churches.[3]

These divisions are only exacerbated by the human tendency to defend them or attack them by violent means. Even before September 11, 2001, we inhabited a world in which people killed each other (and sometimes themselves) in response to divisions and injustices. In such a world, where a pluralism of viewpoints abounds, an authentic, incarnational spirituality attests to Christ's uniqueness and his universality, even as it repents of the ways his uniqueness and universality have frequently been expressed by those who call themselves Christians. Only through such a turning to Reality can followers of Jesus pursue an authentic Christian existence that demonstrates the congruence of spirituality and action.[4] To split any of these categories—spirit from body, individual from community, spirituality from action—is to forsake the integrity of the gospel and the communal mission of Jesus' disciples.

Primodern Spirituality: Primal and Modern

Ever since the Enlightenment, René Descartes' maxim "I think, therefore I am" has provided a simple and convenient summary of the West's bias toward objective data and empirically verifiable knowledge. There is much to be said for this individual, cognitive approach to the world, not least its considerable problem-solving potential. Nonetheless, this highly empirical approach requires the checks and balances offered by primal cultures, which frequently pursue truth through other means—through dreams, gestures, drama, dance, and myth. I therefore advocate what I call "primodern spirituality," that is, spiritual practices that link our primal ways of knowing with modern forms of knowledge secured through modern technology, critical thinking, and logical analysis.

Primal people are not "primitive" in the worn-out, anthropological sense of the term, but rather are persons who, even today, offer treasures that have been lost, obscured, or otherwise ignored in large portions of the West. For instance, instead of Descartes' notion of human identity rooted in the thinking processes of solitary persons, traditional African cultures offer this communal counterpoint: "I am, because we are" (*ubuntu ungumuntu ngabantu*, in Zulu), which can be translated, "A person is a person because of others."[5]

Anticipating what some postmodern philosophers and theologians have recently "discovered," most Africans have long valued community over the individual, knowing that without community no individuals could *be*, let alone survive.[6]

Just praying seeks to honor *both* our primal yearnings *and* our modern learnings, an approach to prayer that is illumined by the holistic lens of educator Howard Gardner. According to Gardner, there is not one "intelligent" way of approaching the world and its complexity. Rather, there are "multiple intelligences" that human beings exhibit and that, depending on the context, serve the actors best.[7] While Gardner did not develop his intelligences theory with a specifically Christian frame of mind, it is nonetheless readily applicable to issues of spirituality and justice (see figure 11.1). I use Gardner's work as a lens for integrating primal and modern concerns, as well as for integrating the needs for personal and social transformation.

Five Practices for Just Prayer

Throughout this essay I offer varied images and definitions of prayer. Just prayer is any practice that *nurtures wakefulness to God and God's action in the world*. In light of this view of prayer as wakefulness, many forms of prayer and other spiritual practices work in concert with each other. Such prayer ultimately means more than simply awaking to God; it means offering the "what is" of our lives and the world to the "what is possible" of divine life at the heart of the universe. But unless we first become aware—of God's love and desires, along with our own gifts and wounds—we cannot truly offer our whole lives to God and the world God has made.

The five prayerful practices outlined below move beyond the most common Westernized conception of prayer as primarily a verbal activity, conducted with bowed heads and closed eyes. Prayer defined as wakefulness often occurs with eyes wide open, with pen and paper in hand, or with feet in motion and arms held out to other human beings. In any case, each of the practices identified below has both contemplative and active aspects.

The ancient metaphor of the tree illustrates well this unity of contemplation and action.[9] We can think of the underground, hidden life of the tree—with its roots, stretching deep, drawing vigor from the source of life—as the contemplative, hidden, and often silent aspects of prayer. Similarly, we can think of the tree's branches, leaves, and fruit as the manifest aspects of prayer, as in the process of photosynthesis, interacting with the needs of the world. Both contemplation and manifestation can occur in solitude or in community. That is, we can contemplate divine love in the world's pain alone or with others. Similarly, we can manifest the fruit of such love alone or with others.

FIGURE 11.1

Spiritual–Social Justice Perspectives on Multiple Intelligences: A Glossary

The nine multiple intelligences as developed by Howard Gardner's Harvard Project Zero provide a frame to integrate primal and modern experience, and personal and social transformation. Incarnational theology means spiritual intelligence is integrated throughout, not a separate mode.

1. *Linguistic/verbal.* Language in the service of prayer and justice: "the pen is mightier than the sword," "poetic justice" (poetry and humor as protest); language as basic to community.
2. *Logical/mathematical.* Thinking theologically; statistical and analytical studies in the cause of justice, health, and welfare; political and religious debating.
3. *Spatial/visual.* Cross-cultural travel as mission and spiritual learning; holy spaces as respite for activist burnout; visual arts as social witness; place and architecture as witness.
4. *Musical/rhythmic.* Music and song as social spiritual witness; union of political *and* spiritual themes in African-American "sorrow songs" such as "Swing Low, Sweet Chariot."[8]
5. *Kinesthetic/bodily.* Hospitality to one's own body as prayer; walking for hunger; marching for peace; offering one's body in nonviolent protest; fasting as action-prayer.
6. *Interpersonal.* Encountering the sacred in community, in small groups or one-to-one relationships; correspondence as spiritual support and communal witness.
7. *Intrapersonal.* Silence in the cause of justice, as in monastic and Quaker traditions; solitude as respite for prophetic clearness and courage.
8. *Naturalist.* Causes for environmental justice; beauty as an aspect of justice; nature's rhythms of devastation and renewal as a paradigm of hope regarding social justice causes.
9. *Existentialist.* Persistent need for meaning and purpose in the face of violence and injustice.

What follows, then, are five prayerful practices, disciplined ways to stay awake to God's presence in the world: (1) awareness: listening to God's love in order to love (the Hebrew *Shema*); (2) discerning how best to live and love; (3) seeing one's life as part of the divine story; (4) cultivating silence and simplicity; and (5) practicing hospitality as a way of meeting God.

Prayer as Awareness: "Listen to Love, to Love" (the *Shema*)

Incarnational prayer practices beckon us to listen simultaneously to the cry of God's love and the cries of the world. Just prayer begins with awareness and ends in love; the *Shema* forms the essential "trunk" on the tree of Hebrew daily prayer: "*Hear*, O Israel: The Lord our God, the Lord is one; and you shall *love*"—God, neighbor, and self with one's whole being, body and soul.[10] The *Shema* calls out, "Listen to how deeply you are loved by God in order to love": pay attention to God and the world at once. Even a failed attempt to love neighbors may be the window for knowing and accepting one's own self, and hence for knowing and accepting God's love. Listen to Love, to love—God, world, and self.

Practicing a daily examen. The *examen*, or inventory of consciousness, has a long, venerable tradition, dating back to the Psalms: "O LORD, you have searched me and known me" (Ps 139:1). Personal prayer is a primal call to know oneself this day in light of God's love. Ignatius of Loyola created a practical *examen* in *The Spiritual Exercises* in the sixteenth century.[11] In its most basic form, the *examen* asks participants to take inventory and notice of three things: the *gifts* of the past day ("Where have I experienced being loved or loving?"), the *struggles* of the past day ("Where has it been difficult to love or allow myself to be loved?"), and the *possibilities* for wholeness that God offers ("What grace do I need to name and claim to be more whole this day?").

The *examen* is typically practiced in solitude, often at the beginning or end of the day, yet it can also be used with an eye toward one's community. How is my life gifting a particular group and being gifted by it? What are the barriers to my loving and being loved in this community? And what is God's invitation through these gifts and struggles? If, for instance, I find others rejecting my gifts, what is the invitation? It may be to listen to some primal unrest in mind or body, to listen more closely to those at the margins of the community, or perhaps to listen more deeply to my own passion and gifts. Do I offer my gifts here, or is this an invitation to a call elsewhere? Such questions are difficult, and they need to be answered in a balance of solitude with community. *Examen* is one way to assess God's work in the world and in one's life in order to connect deeply with others.

Praying with the body. Paul reminds us to present our bodies as worship and so discern God's will (Rom 12:1–3). We need to honor the need for rest and exercise: to sit in quiet, walk, or jog. Psalmlike gestures of kneeling or bowing remind us of humility; folding hands, of the offering of the work of our hands; lifting hands heavenward, of our dignity. Gestures bear social witness. Rabbi Abraham Joshua Heschel, professor of "mysticism and ethics," aptly said of marching for civil rights, "I prayed with my legs as I walked."[12]

Praying the news. In the wake of September 11, I found myself sucked into the media blitz almost to the point of obsession. Recognizing this tendency in myself, other times I would flip in the opposite direction, walling off the media from my consciousness. Either way I was becoming hypercynical, unhelpful to myself or others. One morning it struck me: Many people whose images I saw on television did not have the luxury of being still. I thus resolved (again!) to carve out twenty minutes a day for silence as intercessory prayer on behalf of the world's victims of violence. In that context, I have found "prayers of the heart"—short, repetitive prayers like "Lord Jesus Christ, have mercy . . ." or "Be still . . ." or "*Maranatha*" ("Our Lord come"[13])—to be particularly apt. With few exceptions, I now start each day with a brief radio news summary (while brewing my fair-trade coffee[14]) and then turn the radio off. Then, using an ancient prayer of the heart, I devote my tiny one-third hour of quiet emptiness for lives so emptied of hope, or perhaps so filled with fear and noise, that they have lost their purpose. Being present to God's love is essential to discern how to be present for others.

Prayer as Discernment

One of prayer's central purposes is to discern clues of God's vision for the world. Sometimes this vision is primarily for a community. However, glimpsing God's vision for the world also directly affects the way we live our particular lives. Thus, personal discernment may be assisted in community through liturgical prayers, hearing sermons, sacramental actions, involvement in cross-cultural mission—in which participants are reminded of God's love and God's lordship. Prayers of discernment awaken us to our particular ministry in this universe that God loves.

Developing a mission statement. "The person who has a *why* to live can endure almost any *how*." Victor Frankl, a Nazi concentration camp survivor, expressed this thought in his work *Man's Search for Meaning*.[15] Centuries earlier, Jesus expressed the same idea: "If your eye is single, your whole body will be full of light" (Matt 6:22; my translation). A clear life focus can create a healing of purpose that enables one to experience hope in the face of obstacles, and even to use suffering creatively. "The surf that distresses the ordinary swimmer produces in the surf-rider the super-joy of going clean through it," wrote Oswald Chambers, an early YMCA leader, providing an image of the aptitude for rising to the challenge of life's stresses, using resistances to develop an even deeper passion.[16] Such passion is needed for social justice work, for the needs of the world can quickly become debilitating. For this reason, mystic, scholar, and activist Howard Thurman advised his listeners to focus not on what "the world needs." Rather, "ask yourself what makes you come alive, and then go do that. Because what the world needs is the people who have come alive."[17]

Listening to dreams. Everyone dreams, though many do not recall their dreams, largely because we inhabit a culture that does not value them. This is true not only of empirically oriented scientists but also of most formally educated church leaders. Such disregard for dreams has been much to our spiritual detriment, for dreams provide ways to listen to our primal longings, warnings, and callings. I find it helpful to record my dreams in my journal, leaving space at the end to ponder their significance, and so that I can share them with trusted persons. In such ways, one can participate in a venerable biblical tradition, in which dreams provided individuals with warnings, messages of reassurance, and vocational invitations.[18] Disturbing visions, such as Peter's vision in Acts 10, or those of Julia Esquivel, a teacher turned activist in Guatemala, could redirect a whole community's life.[19]

Assembling a "Clearness Committee." Developed by Quakers for discerning the appropriateness of marriage, Clearness Committees can be adapted for a variety of discernment issues, including ones pertaining to works of justice. The focus person (the one seeking "clearness") writes up concerns in advance and circulates them to a small group of trusted persons, usually four to seven, inviting them to participate in the clearness process. One is asked in advance to serve as convener, another as note taker. The convener opens the group meeting with silence, and then invites a fresh statement of issues from the focus person. This is followed by silence, then by discerning questions ("Have you considered . . . ?") and gentle observations ("I'm hearing four possible routes of action."). All of this happens in a meditative tone devoid of fix-it advice, and may end with a spoken or physical blessing, such as holding hands beneath the presenter's open hands.[20]

Prayer as Storying

I frequently use the word "story" as a verb. We need to story our conversations, our worship, our committee work, our speaking, and our writing with the fresh traces of grace that come through stories. And we need to story our prayers, drawing spiritual resources from the narratives that enliven the Scriptures and reveal our own lives. Creative stories are primal ways to participate in all nine multiple learning modes in modern settings; that is why so many stories are recast as musicals, ballads, dances, or dramas.[21]

Praying the stories of Scripture. Just prayer brings to life the gospel's stories of unconditional love that touch "the least of these"—or the least parts of one's own soul. In acts of social justice we re-story Jesus' parables, such as the Good Samaritan, the Rich Man and Lazarus, or the Sheep and the Goats. The Benedictine fourfold method of *lectio divina* (literally, "divine reading") provides a useful practice: read, reflect, respond, and rest. For example, in a group setting, one might begin with a question such as: Where have we seen the Good Samaritan at work since we last met together?

Keeping a spiritual journal. Journaling can be understood as a contemplative practice to relate God's story-journey with our own. Taking the time and effort to write about dreams, Scripture readings, conversations, art, and various other life experiences enables one to connect one's own story with the greater narrative of God's work of liberation. The eighteenth-century Quaker John Woolman offers a classic example, particularly with respect to his passionate mission to abolish slavery. As one later observer wrote, "Woolman's social consciousness concerning the poor and the enslaved arose not in spite of, but *because* of, his rich life of devotion."[22] Key to this lonely man's mission was his practice of keeping a journal, in which he recorded not only his interactions with other people but also his visitations by and conversations with God. We are fortunate this journal remains in print, for more than merely expressing one man's spiritual practices, it continues to give life to the Christian story of justice and mercy, encouraging disciples in all times and places.[23]

Prayer as Silence and Simplicity

"Be still, and know that I am God!" writes the psalmist (Ps 46:10). "Silence" means an inner fasting from words or images that distract; "simplicity" means fasting from things and possessions. Discussions and arguments, even those within ourselves, the Internet, the media, shopping malls—all can distract us from being awake to the Spirit and compromise our social witness.

Silence as fasting from words. While silence typically has no agenda beyond openness to God, surprisingly, it can also be a form of activism on behalf of justice. Jesus' silence before Pilate was a political statement (John 19:9). Likewise, John Woolman recounts in his journal how, in the course of visiting Quaker meetings in the Carolinas, sometimes "I found no engagement to speak concerning [slaves] and therefore kept silence, finding by experience that to keep pace with the gentle motions of Truth, and never move but as that opens the way, is necessary for the true servants of Christ."[24] So effective was Woolman's discernment when to abstain from words that by the end of the eighteenth century—more than sixty years before the Civil War—all the Quakers in North and South Carolina had emancipated their once numerous slaves, an occurrence that many historians attribute largely to Woolman's exemplary influence.[25]

Simplicity as fasting from things. Pursuing simplicity of life—including fasting in various ways from the goods of this earth—can be done for a host of reasons. With respect to prayer, its primary purpose is to encounter God and listen to God's voice, something that an excess of goods and food often undermines. It can become an intercessory prayer in solidarity with hurting people. One way to encourage fasting in a congregational setting is to hold a simple soup-and-bread meal on Ash Wednesday, and then encourage individuals and families to continue fasting on the Wednesdays throughout Lent, using the mealtime to share concerns, readings, and prayers. It follows that people

acquainted with fasting from food, fashion, and entertainment are more likely
to connect their small-scale deprivations with larger issues of deprivation in
the world—hunger, inadequate housing, and the lack of basic human rights.

In certain instances, entering into more severe deprivations in a spirit of
humility can actually serve the cause of justice. In the 1990s, U.S. Congressman
Tony Hall was informed that the House of Representatives' Select Committee
on Hunger, a committee he chaired, was being terminated for budgetary reasons. "Why don't you go on a hunger fast?" asked his wife. Two weeks into the
fast, as Hall felt the misgivings of being misunderstood, college and university
campuses joined him in his fast. In his fast's third week, the U.S. Secretary of
Agriculture invited the thinning congressman to help convene national and
regional summits on the issue of hunger in America. Soon after, House
Majority Leader Richard Gephardt admitted to Hall, "I feel ashamed. You've
embarrassed us in the right way."[26]

Prayer as Hospitality

The English word "hospitality" comes from the Latin *hospis*, which can
mean either guest or host. The Scriptures abound with such reversals.
Abraham and Sarah, for instance, extended hospitality to three strangers
whom Abraham addressed as "Lord." In hosting the three strangers, however,
the aging couple was mysteriously hosted by the Lord of the universe, who
extended to them a promise of cosmic generativity greater than the stars of the
sky and the sand of the sea (Gen 18:1–18). Andrei Rublev's icon The Holy
Trinity, which is based on this vision of three visitors at Abraham and Sarah's
table, wonderfully captures the symmetry of human and divine hospitality
(see figure 12.1).

Extending hospitality to self. Here is an essential connection between inner
and outer hospitality: Embracing the least parts of one's soul is absolutely vital
to becoming awake to God and to those who have been marginalized by our
society. Unawake to our own neediness, we put those we serve in an inferior
position. Making time for rest, retreat, and worship is a biblically sanctioned,
concrete form of self-compassion. It not only provides space for attentiveness
to God, it forges a link between contemplation and manifestation. Turning our
minds (*metanoia*) toward the exiled parts of ourselves manifests itself in an
outer posture toward social exiles who inhabit places where Jesus still hangs out.

Practicing hospitality with others. Both Luke and Matthew tell dramatic stories about Jesus as stranger. On Easter evening, Luke recounts, as two disciples
walk along a rural road, a stranger joins them. Their anonymous guest
becomes their host; in the breaking of bread, they recognize the risen Christ
(Luke 24:13–35). As for Matthew, he records Jesus' parable of the Sheep and
the Goats (Matt 25:31–46), which tells of hungry, naked, and lonely persons,
and includes Jesus' stunning announcement: "Just as you did it to one of the

least of these . . . you did it to me." All this should lead us to wonder: When Jesus said, "No one comes to the Father except through me" (John 14:6), who exactly was the "me" he had in mind? Might this be the upside-down way of the cross, that we encounter Jesus Christ today in the people our society has deemed the least significant?

And who is less significant, less valued, than those we consider our enemies? Desmond Tutu has recounted numerous stories of brutality during South Africa's era of apartheid, for example, killers who cooked their enemies alive at one end of a campsite while enjoying a barbecue at the other end. In the Truth and Reconciliation Commission hearings that followed apartheid's demise, Tutu observed that perpetrators of these brutal acts often confessed regret without emotion, staring aimlessly across the courtroom or perhaps looking at their shoes. But if a victim's family member said, "Turn to me; now say what you just said," confessors would be deeply moved, hardly able to gasp the deeply felt words of repentance. Here we see the incarnation of spirituality, of hospitality, in which the simple human act of turning *embodies* spiritual power. Just repentance begins with a posture of turning one's thoughts toward the least, and ends in turning one's body and whole being toward them.[27]

Welcoming novel ideas and projects. Christians can practice justice by entertaining surprising ideas—as in the early Church's opening to Gentiles and as in affirming leadership of excluded people. Social causes are often born from people's nonconformist lives and spiritual experiences. Dorothy Day and others who befriended her out-of-wedlock child spawned the Catholic Worker movement. One can glimpse a sort of "poetic justice" in Toyohiko Kagawa, an orphaned Japanese Christian activist, and Julia Esquivel, an ordinary Guatemalan schoolteacher turned prophet.[28] Their prophetic witness for justice was embodied in prayerful poetry that countered the injustices they each found embedded in both Church and state.

Just Prayer: Contemplation and Manifestation

In his *Letters and Papers from Prison*, Dietrich Bonhoeffer wrote, "Our being Christians today will be limited to two things: prayer and righteous action among humanity. All Christian thinking, speaking, and organizing must be born anew out of this prayer and action."[29] Bonhoeffer's words, written under the shadow of Hitler's Third Reich, demonstrate that the goal of Christian maturity is not a spiritual seesaw between prayer and action. Rather, the goal is for the spaces between prayer and action to grow ever narrower until we find a paradoxical union of contemplation and manifestation.

Seeking such a union is not unique to Bonhoeffer's Lutheran tradition. John Calvin's emblem of the flaming heart in an outstretched hand expressed the same truth, as did John Wesley's enjoining works of piety and works of mercy. For these renowned Christian leaders, as well as for many other Christians throughout the Church's history, loving God meant loving neighbor, which in turn meant working for justice. "There is a point," wrote Quaker Douglas Steere, "where, blasphemous as it may sound, the contemplator is always at prayer, and where he is free to carry his action into the contemplation and the contemplation into the action. . . . It is, in short, *an abiding disposition*, and out of this the works come."[30] In other words, being mindful of God and wakeful to God's ways creates the essential posture for taking steps in the world of action, but the reverse is also true: The world of action paves the way for wakefulness to God.[31] So even as prayer answers the call of sacred love, it must also pay heed to the cries of the world.

Notes

1. Evelyn Underhill, *The Spiritual Life* (Harrisburg, Pa.: Morehouse Publishing, 1955), 55.

2. As quoted in Matthew Fox, *Original Blessing* (Santa Fe: Bear & Co., 1983), 265.

3. This gap is still widening. The June 14, 2003, cover of the *Christian Century* reads, "The Widening Gap: Income and Inequality." Inside, Harlan Beckley reviews four recent books on the subject: Douglas A. Hicks, *Inequality and Christian Ethics* (Cambridge: Cambridge University Press, 2000); David Hollenbach, *The Common Good and Christian Ethics* (Cambridge: Cambridge University Press, 2002); Benjamin I. Page and James R. Simmons, *What Government Can Do: Dealing with Poverty and Inequality* (Chicago: University of Chicago Press, 2002); and Rebecca M. Blank and Ron Haskins, eds., *The New World of Welfare* (Washington, D.C.: Brookings Institution Press, 2001).

4. For more on these divisions, see Kent Ira Groff, "Listening: Unity in Prayer and Action," *Sampriti: News Bulletin of Commission for Ecumenism* 2 (1999): 3–4; and Groff, *The Soul of Tomorrow's Church* (Nashville: Upper Room Books, 2000), 132–39.

5. For these ideas I am indebted to South African pastor-theologian Thulani Ndlazi, as well as to Graham Cyster, a South African living in the United States. See also John S. Mbiti, *An Introduction to African Religions and Philosophy* (Oxford: Heinemann International, 1989).

6. For more on primodern spirituality, see chapter 6 of Kent Ira Groff, *What Would I Believe if I Didn't Believe Anything? A Handbook for Spiritual Orphans* (San Francisco: Jossey-Bass, 2004).

7. See Howard Gardner, *Frames of Mind: The Theory of Multiple Intelligences* (New York: Basic Books, 1983); and Gardner, *Multiple Intelligences: The Theory in Practice* (New York: Basic Books, 1993).

8. In *The Souls of Black Folk* (New York: Signet Classic, 1995), W. E. B. Du Bois speaks of sorrow as energy for justice and hope (274).

9. For the Hebrew metaphor of tree, see Ps 1:1–3. For other religions traditions, see "The Tree of Life," a feature issue of *Parabola: A Magazine of Myth and Tradition*, published in 1989. See also Roland E. Murphy, *The Tree of Life: An Exploration of Biblical Wisdom Literature* (New York: Doubleday, 1990).

10. Mark 12:29–30; see Deut 6:4. God is sometimes referred to as "the One," beckoning us to loving at-one-ment with God, neighbor, self, and the cosmos.

11. For a version of Ignatius's form of *examen*, see David L. Fleming, S.J., *Draw Me into Your Friendship: The Spiritual Exercises* (St. Louis: Institute of Jesuit Sources, 1996), 33.

12. Quoted in Robert Greenleaf, *Servant Leadership* (New York: Paulist Press, 1977), 253.

13. *Maranatha* is preserved in Aramaic in 1 Cor 16:22.

14. Fair-trade coffee aims to give coffee growers fair wages in a global economy that works against them. Having visited with coffee workers, I have made this simple act a part of my morning prayers of world awareness.

15. Victor Frankl, *Man's Search for Meaning: An Introduction to Logotherapy* (Boston: Beacon, 1992), 9 (adapted for inclusiveness). Frankl was fond of the statement based on Nietzsche.

16. Oswald Chambers, *My Utmost for His Highest* (New York: Dodd, Mead & Co., 1961), 67.

17. Quoted in a sidebar to Jeremy Hajdu-Paulen, "Dwelling More Fully in God," *Candler Connection* (Spring 2001).

18. For more on dreams, see Morton T. Kelsey, *Dreams: A Way to Listen to God* (New York: Paulist Press, 1978); and Robert A. Johnson, *Inner Work: Using Dreams and Creative Imagination for Personal Growth and Integration* (San Francisco: HarperSanFrancisco, 1989).

19. See Julia Esquivel, *Threatened with Resurrection: Prayers and Poems from an Exiled Guatemalan* (Elgin, Ill.: Bethany, 1982); and Esquivel, *The Certainty of Spring: Poems by a Guatemalan in Exile* (Washington, D.C.: Ecumenical Program on Central America and the Caribbean, 1993).

20. See Parker Palmer, "The Clearness Committee," *Weavings*, November-December 1988, 37–40.

21. The movie *O Brother, Where Art Thou?* provides a powerful example of Homer's primal myth of Odysseus, recast in the American South, highlighting poor people, injustice, prison conditions, and beauty. It is exactly the kind of thing Christians ought to be doing with the gospel of Christ.

22. Elton Trueblood, *The New Man for Our Time* (New York: Harper & Row, 1970), 49.

23. John Woolman, *The Journal and Major Essays of John Woolman* (ed. Phillips P. Moulton; Richmond, Ind.: Friends United Press, 1989).

24. Woolman, *Journal*, 70.

25. Woolman's prophetic silence is attested to elsewhere. In 1758, after speaking against slavery in London Grove, Pa., Woolman was invited for dinner at the home of Thomas Woodward. Upon entering Woodward's home, Woolman observed Negro servants and learned they were slaves. With neither words nor ill will, he quietly left. When guests gathered at the dinner table, everyone understood the gesture of Woolman's absence. The next morning Woodward freed all of his slaves, unwilling to maintain a household where a man as good as Woolman did not feel free to be present. Two years later the local Quaker meeting recorded an official minute that the discontinuance of slavery in the area "hath been visibly blessed with Success." Trueblood, *New Man for Our Time*, 48.

26. Tony Hall's story can be found in Jim Wallis, *The Soul of Politics* (New York: Harcourt Brace, 1995), 252–55.

27. This information is from a public lecture given by Archbishop Desmond Tutu at Elizabethtown College, Elizabethtown, Pa., March 17, 2000.

28. See Robert Mikio Fukada, "Toyohiko Kagawa: A Mosiac Artist for God," *Princeton Seminary Bulletin* 10, no. 1 (1989): 23–41; and Toyohiko Kagawa, *Song from the Slums: Poems* (Nashville: Cokesbury, 1935). For Esquivel's writings, see n. 19 above.

29. Dietrich Bonhoeffer, *Letters and Papers from Prison* (ed. Eberhard Bethge; trans. Reginald Fuller; New York: Macmillan, 1972), 300 (adapted for inclusive language).

30. Douglas Van Steere, *Work and Contemplation* (New York: Harper & Brothers, 1957), 57.

31. In this vein, United Nations Secretary General Dag Hammarskjöld wrote, "The road to holiness necessarily passes through the world of action." Dag Hammarskjöld, *Markings* (trans. Leif Sjöberg and W. H. Auden; New York: Alfred A. Knopf, 1964), 122.

12

Iconography

LEARNING TO SEE:
THE SACRALIZED VISION OF
BYZANTINE ICONOGRAPHY

— Randi Sider-Rose —

The soul is overwhelmed and excited upon seeing beauty, writes Plotinus, the ardent student of Plato. Recognizing something of itself in the beauty of the world, the soul returns to itself in delight. "These experiences must occur whenever there is contact with any sort of beautiful thing," Plotinus continues, "wonder and a shock of delight and longing and passion and a happy excitement."[1] The beauty of Byzantine iconography, formed in part by the Neoplatonic tradition, contains some of this ability to shock with delight. Some have identified an eye-catching, "primitive" appeal in their polychromatic colors laid side by side in stark simplicity. Others are drawn in by the steady gaze of the iconographic face, giving viewers the sense that they are not the only ones doing the looking. But lingering questions stifle many people's appreciation for these sacred works of art. Does the beauty have anything to do with this world? Or do icons lead the viewer into self-absorption and mystical escapism, as some similarly accuse Neoplatonism?

A deeper look into the context and practices of iconography sheds more light on the nature of their beauty. They are crafted in a process of contemplation and fasting, in which every brush stroke represents a prayer. Upon being blessed as a mediator of divine presence and healing, icons fill churches or what is called the "beautiful corner" of a house. Candles are lit in front of them, they are kissed, and they are prayed before with eyes open or closed. Clearly, the beauty of iconography is not apprehended in the manner of museum art; their devoted consideration is even further removed from the passive viewing cultivated by the advertising and entertainment industries. One notices that many icons are not even particularly beautiful, at least according to contemporary habits of viewing. The iconographer seemed to have little conception of perspective and space, anatomical accuracy, or light.

Yet herein lies the key to the nature of the icon's beauty. The source of the beauty is based in, but not identical to, the empirical world. Instead, the beauty of the icon is symbolically represented as originating in God, who can be named Beauty according to early patristic writers. The process of coming to see icons as beautiful is the same as coming to see God's world as beautiful, thereby expanding our periphery of concern. As recent studies of beauty and justice have shown, "seeing as beautiful" facilitates a kind of spontaneous generosity that can exceed ethical calculations, Plotinus's "happy excitement" directed toward fellow creatures.[2] This process of learning to see with a sacralized vision serves the biblical image of radical hope and generous compassion.

This essay argues that iconography enables such a sacralized vision of the world, a vision that helps to nurture and nourish compassionate action. While any number of aesthetic analyses of iconography could illustrate the relationship between seeing and acting, from the prayerful production of icons to their effect on viewers in the liturgical environment, this essay concentrates on the aesthetic properties of icons as material artifacts. More specifically, the techniques of portraying inverse distance perspective, an underlying geometric order, and a stylized naturalism illustrate the false dichotomy between spirituality and the quotidian affairs of earthly existence. Though many and conflicting readings of visual artifacts are often possible, the particular history of theological reflection on icons, especially as it developed in response to the early iconoclastic controversy, suggests that the aesthetic characteristics of icons are in fact intended to symbolically unite material and spiritual worlds. In the process of depicting this vision, icons train the eye in the practice of sacralized viewing. Taken from the sanctuary to the street, this way of seeing enables one to act in the world with caring and concern.

Historical Context: Icons as Material Pointers

During the major iconoclastic controversy of the eighth and ninth centuries, many Christians came to an explicit awareness that humanity's relationship with the things of this world do in fact relate to spirituality. The theologians at the Seventh Ecumenical Council, held in Nicea in 787, and those of the next generation both exemplified and articulated this development. During this time, iconodule (icon-venerating) thought moved from the reluctant acceptance of the crafted materiality of icons to the realization that this very quality affirmed God's creation and the incarnation in addition to protecting the icon from charges of idolatry. In other words, icons are not so much transparent windows as *material pointers* to the divine. Material symbols, such as icons, are not God, but neither can they be divorced from the human experience of God, which necessarily entails embodied existence. On the level of practice, a particular iconographic style of painting developed that reflected this awareness of the icon as a mediating object.

In the *Three Apologies*, written beginning in about 730, John of Damascus describes the icon as a window transparent to divinity, albeit "through a glass darkly."[3] The ecumenical council appropriated this concept, describing the icon's transparency in terms of the longstanding notion of a "likeness" between the icon and the subject depicted, the "prototype."[4] The concept of likeness ensured that icons served to draw attention away from themselves and toward the divine, evoking a memory of and zeal for the prototype.[5] At the same time, the council appropriated John of Damascus's affirmation of the material nature of icons. Although matter can be used for improper purposes, argued the Damascene, it cannot be considered evil in and of itself. God's involvement in the world, according to the doctrines of creation and the incarnation, establishes matter as a suitable object of veneration (though never of worship). "Never will I cease honoring the matter which wrought my salvation!" exclaimed John of Damascus. "I honor it, but not as God."[6] This enthusiasm for matter was theologically sound, but it seemed to stand in tension with the argument that icons are valuable only because they show forth a likeness to the prototype, as if transparent.

After the victory of the iconodules at the council, theologians continued to hammer out how the dual emphases on likeness and materiality could be reconciled. On the one hand, the icon must be similar to the prototype. It must have a "likeness" in order to allow the viewer to venerate the person, not the portrayal itself. On the other hand, the icon must be understood as distinct from the prototype so the two are not equated in the viewer's mind. Only the divinity *beyond* the icon is to be venerated, not a divinity contained *within*.

The patriarch Nikephoros, who probably wrote in the 780s, realized that the key lay in rejecting the notion of icons as transparent windows altogether. The notion of transparency falsely suggests a kind of objective honesty, an ability to disappear in order to let the viewer gaze directly upon divinity. Even though the iconographer should strive for likeness, the result will always be a concrete pointer, a mediating object. An icon, wrote the patriarch, is an "artifact (*technes apotelesma*) shaped in imitation of a pattern but differing in essence and subject (*to hypokeimeno*); for if it does not differ in some respect, it is not an image, nor an object different from the model."[7] The icon's very materiality is a declaration of its honesty, so obviously declaring itself to be different from the prototype.

This solution allowed the materiality of the icon to be valued without encroaching upon idolatry. For Nikephoros and others pursuing this same theme, writes art historian Charles Barber, the very crafted, artifactual nature of the icon both distinguished it from the prototype and made it valuable as a mediating object.[8] This concept was compatible with continuing to assert the sanctification of matter through creation and the incarnation, affirming icons as suitable for veneration. Popular piety confirmed that engaging with the prototypical subjects of icons properly involved ritual interaction with objects rather than abstract, cognitive speculation.

Artistic practices, in turn, attempted to come to terms with the biblical affirmation and qualification of matter. Things of the earth, whether bodies, objects, or humanly crafted art, have been sanctified by God, went this argument. Matter is not therefore "worthless and dead," as the iconoclasts claimed.[9] But neither are material objects ends unto themselves, a perspective that would improperly imply a closed-circuit world that exists autonomous from God. Instead, all aspects of material existence become the means by which humanity is invited to commune with God. Working from this theological standpoint, iconographers were compelled to find ways to symbolically indicate the balance between the limited, material nature of their craft and God's involvement in embodied existence, selectively choosing artistic techniques that facilitated a sacralized vision. Among these, the aesthetic characteristics of inverse perspective, geometric ordering, and stylized naturalism eventually came to distinguish iconography from other forms of art.

Aesthetic Characteristics of a Sacralized Vision

Inverse Perspective

The inverse perspective of Byzantine iconography can best be understood in contrast to the realist perspective of most Western art. In much of the post-Renaissance West, perspective has been achieved by depicting distant objects as increasingly small until they disappear into a vanishing point somewhere real or imagined in the image. This realistic method of depicting space transforms the panel into a virtual window through which the viewer imagines he or she can see the scene. As Erwin Panofsky observes of this perspectival view of space, "The material surface upon which the individual figures or objects are drawn or painted or carved is thus negated, and instead reinterpreted as a mere 'picture plane.'"[10] Art historian John Berger points out that everything in realist perspective takes the eye of the beholder as its center. The result is that the "visible world is arranged for the spectator as the universe was once thought to be arranged for God."[11]

In contrast, one of the perspectival techniques of Byzantine icons, often called *inverse perspective*, depicts figures that seem to come out from the icon rather than receding into the distance. The background is often curved forward as if in sphere, moving out inversely toward the spectator. In the fifteenth-century icon of the Holy Trinity by Andrei Rublev, the pedestals beneath the angels' feet demonstrate inverse perspective particularly clearly (see figure 12.1). The parts of the pedestals that are farthest from the viewer are the widest, rather than disappearing into a small distant point. The same is also true for the table, as is especially apparent with the legs. In the most masterful icons, the space between the figures is also beautifully executed, drawing attention to the surface of the icon. In Rublev's icon, the interior outlines of the angels on the left and right form the shape of a chalice, suggesting that the

Figure 12.1. Inverse perspective in Andrei Rublev's fifteenth-century icon, the Holy Trinity. Tretyakov Gallery, Moscow, Russia. Scala / Art Resource, N.Y.

human community of bread and wine is as important as the space delineated for individuals.

The experience of viewing a panel depicting inverse perspective with an emphasis on foreground differs from experiencing realistic perspectival space in two important respects. First, attention to the surface alerts the viewer to the material nature of the icon with which they are interacting. It cannot be mistaken for a mere picture plane, an emphasis that accords nicely with Nikephoros's notion of the icon's value as a mediating object rather than a transparent window. Second, the vision of inverse perspective connects the spiritual reality represented to the world outside the icon. This linkage is achieved because the so-called vanishing point is not within the depth of a fictional picture plane, but extends in the form of multiple points in front of the panel. With the perspective thus oriented from within the picture, the viewer is displaced as the determiner of the vision. Instead, a larger, more universal perspective is assumed. Nicholas of Cusa's response to an omnivoyant icon might well have been said in response to inverse perspective. Addressing the divinity beyond the painting, Cusa wrote, "Since your seeing is your being, therefore, because you regard me, I am, and if you remove your face from me, I will cease to be."[12]

In Rublev's icon of the Trinity, for example, inverse perspective makes demands on the viewer by including him or her within the event depicted. Because neither the Trinity nor God can be pictorially represented, the icon is based on another event in the Bible often thought to foreshadow the doctrine of the Trinity: the visitation of three strangers to Abraham beneath the oaks of Mamre in Gen 18. In representations of this event preceding Rublev, Abraham is often shown exhibiting his hospitality, sometimes with Sarah laughing from the house nearby. In Rublev's iconographic adaptation, however, the patriarch is missing and the icon extends out to the viewer. The ones standing before the panel have the opportunity to exhibit Abraham's hospitality, inviting the divine guests into the embodied world. Whether it is accepted or rejected, the opportunity to exhibit hospitality has been presented. There can be no neutral response. In consequence, the vision portrayed becomes relevant and demanding as it spills out into the world. As in Cusa's response, the viewer must become responsible for his actions before the divine vision.

Geometric Ordering

Among the characteristics of the sacralized vision spilling out into the world is the affirmation of a divine order, ensured by the doctrines of creation and the incarnation. Medieval theologians based their vision of an ordered world on a verse from the Wisdom of Solomon: "But you have arranged all things by measure and number and weight."[13] They also cited Gen 1:31—"God saw everything that he had made, and indeed, it was very good"—to argue that

the beauty of the universe was integrally greater than any of its parts in isolation.[14] Subsequently, according to Greek patristic doctrine, the incarnation
recreated the divine order that was established from the beginning. In sending
the divine Word and ordering principle, or Logos, to dwell among us, God
sanctified all matter. In his work *On the Incarnation*, Athanasius explored this
theme, writing that Christ alone, "being Word of the Father and above all, was
in consequence both able to recreate all, and worthy to suffer on behalf of all."[15]

From an aesthetic standpoint, iconography communicates divine order
through the characteristic of an underlying, unifying geometry. As in ancient
Greek and Egyptian art, a visual harmony is ensured on the level of technique
by simple proportions executed with lines and arcs drawn in a similar pattern
for each icon-type. For example, the underlying geometry on a twelfth-century
icon of the Holy Face dates back to antiquity, irrespective of the dimensions
of the board or church wall (see figure 12.2). As with many facial icons, the

Figure 12.2. Geometric orderings, illustrated by a twelfth-century icon of the
Holy Face. Tretyakov Gallery, Moscow, Russia. Scala / Art Resource, N.Y.

measurements are based on the length of the nose which, when doubled, reaches the top of the head. When the arc formed by this circle is itself doubled, it corresponds with the halo. Dividing the rest of the icon into simple quadrants and triangles reveal a corresponding order in the shape of the beard, the placement of the ears, and so on. This method of creating a geometric ordering for iconic types visually links images of Jesus throughout the history of Byzantine art, while allowing for geographical and cultural adaptation. The same technique also unifies more complex icons, such as scenes including animals, trees, buildings, and rock formations. Regardless of the subject matter, geometric ordering creates a sense of interconnected harmony among different elements of the painting.

For the purposes of this essay, envisioning the divine interconnectedness of the world within itself and with God corresponds to Christ's incarnate ministry. What has been thoroughly documented in the social and ecological sciences is true for the sacralized vision as well: The plight of the poor and degraded affects us all and has everything to do with our relationship with God. As Jesus states in Matt 25:40, "Truly I tell you, just as you did it to one of the least of these who are members of my family, you did it to me." The Christian vision that recognizes an interconnected order of creation presents a strong counterargument to the perception that Christianity has always been world hating. As commentator Ananda Coomaraswamy observes, disdain for the world is not cultivated in the Christian speculative intellect but only in "an empirical vision of the world as made up of independently self-subsistent parts."[16]

The etymology of "devil" (or that which is "diabolical") and "symbol" have the same root in Greek: -*bolos*, which literally means "throwing." The difference is that the slanderer "throws apart" (*dia-bolos*) what the symbol "throws together" (*sym-bolos*). In other words, the divine perspective and human reality are thrown together in the symbolic world of the icon, which makes it possible to learn to see earthly and transcendent interpenetration. As Pope John Paul II expressed so well in his "Letter to Artists," every genuine artistic intuition "springs from the depths of the human soul, where the desire to give meaning to one's own life is joined by the fleeting vision of beauty and of the mysterious unity of all things."[17]

Stylized Naturalism

Not everything in the iconographic vision is subordinated to abstract schemas of perspective and geometry. Individual persons and events are depicted as well, in all their embodied particularity. This tradition contrasts with Plotinus's rejection of portraiture on account of the notion that the pure idea of the absolute would be obscured in such physicality.[18] Iconographic figures are recognizable from their appearance during their earthly existence or, if this knowledge was lost, a tradition of portraying them in a particular

manner. For example, the twelfth-century icon known as the Virgin of
Vladimir (see figure 12.3) stands in a long tradition of depicting the Mother of
God in a red cloak and blue undergarment, the colors thought to symbolize
her human and divine aspects. The stars on her shoulders and forehead represent her virginity before, during, and after the birth of Christ. Jesus, on the

Figure 12.3. Stylized naturalism in the twelfth-century icon, the Virgin of
Vladimir. Note the Christ child's small head, and Mary's minimized ears, nose,
and mouth. Tretyakov Gallery, Moscow, Russia. Scala /Art Resource, N.Y.

other hand, often manifests noticeably uneven eyes, the result of iconographers' efforts to avoid representing, by virtue of a geometrically defined face, *only* his divinity. For less commonly known saints, viewers are forced to rely more heavily upon particulars of color, clothing, hair, and facial characteristics, although a particular saint's name usually appears on icons as well. The net effect of all this is the sense that discrete individuals, not just humanity in general, image forth divine presence. Standing in a sanctuary filled with icons, one has the sense of being surrounded by an individuated cloud of witnesses even as one's own particular sainthood is called to mind—an experience that dovetails nicely with the ethical demand made upon the viewer by inverse perspective.

Even as icons portray individuals, they also appear abstract, or stylized. Icons are not realistic in the manner of photography, much less in the manner of the Renaissance's exaggerated naturalism. To be sure, the concept of stylization is a contemporary one, and can only be superficially imposed upon the Byzantine iconographic vision; from their point of view, Byzantium Christians would have simply identified images as having a "likeness." Coomaraswamy describes the modern inability to see ancient art as accurate as arising from the scientific, empirical, and rational assumption that the "signs" of art physically resemble what is supposedly signified, when in fact much of art is properly thought of as symbolic.[19] Nevertheless, given our contemporary aesthetic lenses, the category of stylization is helpful for explaining a distinct characteristic of icons. If the aesthetic techniques of perspective and geometry draw attention to *materiality* by emphasizing the icon's surface and *spirituality* through the depiction of the divine perspective interpenetrating and ordering the world, the icon's human figures communicate these qualities through holding the naturalism of individual portraiture in tension with stylization.

Two stylistic devices stand out to the modern Western viewer: a distinct anatomy and an inner light source. The former characteristic is exemplified in icons of Mary such as the Virgin of Vladimir. The adult proportion of Christ's small head with respect to his body, for example, is not due to a lack of understanding of the anatomy of children on the part of the iconographer. Rather, the portrayal of the child-man represents the eternal wisdom of Christ, who has existed since before the creation of the world even though he was born fully human. As with all Byzantine icons of saints, the nose of Mary is thinned and her ears and mouth minimized to indicate the final transfiguration of the senses, now used for their proper purposes. Her eyes, on the other hand, are enlarged, engaging the viewer directly and contemplatively. In a corresponding fashion, iconographers used stylized gestures to communicate relationships between the figures in the icon or dispositions toward the viewer or God. Although strong emotions were not typically shown, since they were seen as distracting from contemplation, the dramas evoked were often highly emotive.

In this particular example, Mary looks knowingly out into the world, while Jesus is portrayed as responding to her sadness with wisdom and compassion.

Similarly, the absence of light shining from a natural source locatable within the scene suggests that the divine source of all creation is being symbolically represented. In the icon of the Virgin, Mary's face is evenly lighted on both of its sides, the brightest spots generally coinciding with those that would be closest to the viewer. Technically speaking, iconographers achieve this effect by beginning with the darkest layer and gradually adding thin layers of lighter pigment. This method of painting from dark colors up to bright creates the sense that the light source issues from within the figure, rather than reflecting off the figure from the sun or another source. Since Christ and the saints are intended to be represented in a postmortem, divinized state, Orthodox theologians have described this depiction of an inner light source as representing the saints' transfiguration. In sum, iconographers not only depicted saints with the particular physical characteristics they had on earth (if they were known) but also with the illumined flesh of their perfected state, symbolically shining forth the eternal truth that these individuals embodied.

The concept of divine light is nothing new, of course, in art, philosophy, and theology.[20] The significance of luminosity for the iconographic tradition, however, lies in the suggestion that the material world is not denied, but rather shown in its optimal state. Christ's bodily incarnation and resurrection affirm the importance of incarnate existence, approached with an eye toward its telos of divine transfiguration. His ministry of healing demonstrates that incompleteness and decay are not the last word for earthly existence. The obvious effect of Christ's birth, ministry, death, and resurrection on the Christian's relation to the world is the expansion of concern from the "purely" spiritual or material to a more integrated dynamic. Christians are called to image forth Christ's luminous mission in the material world, the medium of the contemplative life.

None of these stylistic techniques amount to a magical transformation of the viewer, however. Whatever has been made possible through the icon is attributed to God in the ethos of iconography. Traditional icons are not signed by the iconographer for this reason. As Pope John Paul II suggests in his "Letter to Artists," God is the Creator, forming the world and everything in it *ex nihilo*; humans are only craftspeople, using something that already exists and attempting to give it form and meaning.[21] Even though Christ's existence inaugurated the possibility of icons in the Church (as articulated in the Seventh Ecumenical Council), true artists recognize their own limitations and the limitations of that which they create. In other words, they adhere to Paul's warning in Acts 17:29 that "we ought not to think that the deity is like gold, or silver, or stone, an image formed by the art and imagination of mortals."

The Ethical Mandate of a Sacralized Vision

Even as iconography insists on waiting, watching, and listening for the move-ment of the Holy Spirit in history, it forms disciples able to imagine the audacity of co-laboring with God in the messy edifice of our material world. The tension of recognizing that God is the primal actor, even while heeding the divine imperative to act in the world, characterizes human attempts to create not only icons but social change as well. God has called humans to co-labor in the building of the kingdom of God. But it is God who has laid the foundation and enables our sacralized vision of the building that needs to be done. Iconographers and activists alike must be able to see themselves, their work, and all of creation with eyes that can contemplate and give thanks and praise to God.

Not all are called to be iconographers, but all are called to craft lives that cultivate visions of the sacred. This cannot be done by passively accepting all the images of our respective cultures. Living in a culture of superficially shock-ing and sexually explicit visual bombardment, many contemporary Americans, including many Christians, have lost the tools for analyzing and discriminating between images. But what we choose to direct our attention toward forms not only our viewing practices but also the kind of persons we become. This is the ancient wisdom of Neoplatonism and other philosophical systems, wisdom accepted as common sense by early Christians. Plotinus wrote, "Different souls look at different things and are and become what they look at."[22] This close connection between what one perceives and one's inner life is similarly recorded in Luke 11:34, where Jesus says, "Your eye is the lamp of your body. If your eye is healthy, your whole body is full of light; but if it is not healthy, your body is full of darkness." Centuries earlier, the psalmist declared, "I will not set before my eyes anything that is base"(Ps 101:3).

The icon testifies to an age-old Christian discipline of contemplative, form-ative, and compassionate perception. As historical theologian Margaret Miles puts it, we must rediscover disciplined viewing, developing "a trained and con-centrated seeing that overcomes conceptual barriers between the visible and the spiritual worlds."[23] The salient aesthetic attributes of icons—their inverse perspective, geometric ordering, and stylized naturalism—serve to demon-strate the false dichotomy not only between what is seen and what is known but also between spiritual contemplation and embodied action. By visually demonstrating God's involvement in the world, one's perception of beauty and therefore one's periphery of concern is widened to all creation. We will see with a sacralized vision not as the result of straining our eyes but as the natural outpouring of generosity and delight that comes from seeing the world's source in beauty. Different from a rational appeal to human willpower, Byzantine iconography enflames the heart and activates the imagination with an authentically Christian vision—a vision that, above all else, reveals to us that Christ was the image-event that created new possibilities of who we can be as seers and doers.

Notes

1. Plotinus, *Enneads* (trans. A. H. Armstrong; Cambridge, Mass.: Harvard University Press, 1966), 245.

2. See, for example, Margaret R. Miles, *Plotinus on Body and Beauty: Society, Philosophy, and Religion in Third-Century Rome* (Malden, Mass.: Blackwell Publishers, 1999); and Elaine Scarry, *On Beauty and Being Just* (Princeton, N.J.: Princeton University Press, 1999).

3. John of Damascus, *On the Divine Images: Three Apologies against Those Who Attack the Divine Images* (trans. David Anderson; Crestwood, N.Y.: St. Vladimir's Seminary Press, 2000), 53. John quotes here from 1 Cor 13:12.

4. The preference for realistic over symbolic depictions was articulated in the eighty-second canon of the Quintesext Council of 692. See Daniel J. Sahas, *Icon and Logos: Sources in Eighth-Century Iconoclasm* (Toronto: University of Toronto Press, 1986), 220D.

5. Ibid., 225A.

6. John of Damascus, *On the Divine Images*, 23; see also pp. 17, 61.

7. Nikephoros, *Antir.* 277, quoted in John Travis, *In Defense of the Faith: The Theology of Patriarch Nikephoros of Constantinople* (Brookline, Mass.: Hellenic College Press, 1984), 49–50.

8. Charles Barber, *Figure and Likeness: On the Limits of Representation in Byzantine Iconoclasm* (Princeton, N.J.: Princeton University Press, 2002), 115.

9. Sahas, *Icon and Logos*, 277D.

10. Erwin Panofsky, *Perspective as Symbolic Form* (trans. Christopher S. Wood; New York: Zone Books, 1997), 27.

11. John Berger, *Ways of Seeing* (London: British Broadcasting Corporation and Penguin Books, 1972), 16.

12. Nicholas of Cusa, "On the Vision of God," in *Selected Spiritual Writings* (trans. H. Lawrence Bond; New York: Paulist Press, 1977), 240.

13. Wis 11:20b, quoted in Umberto Eco, *The Aesthetics of Thomas Aquinas* (trans. Hugh Bredin; Cambridge, Mass.: Harvard University Press, 1988), 23.

14. See, for example, Augustine, *Confessions* (trans. R. S. Pine-Coffin; New York: Penguin Books, 1961), 340.

15. Athanasius, *On the Incarnation* (trans. and ed. by a religious of C.S.M.V.; London: Mowbray, 1982), 33.

16. Ananda K. Coomaraswamy, "Mediaeval Aesthetic: Dionysius the Pseudo-Aeropagite, and Ulrich Engelberti of Strassburg," *Art Bulletin* 17 (1935): 46 n. 28.

17. Pope John Paul II, "Letter of His Holiness Pope John Paul II to Artists," *L'Osservatore Romano*, Weekly Edition in English, April 17, 1999, 2.

18. Hans Belting, *Likeness and Presence: A History of the Image before the Era of Art* (trans. Edmund Jephcott; Chicago: University of Chicago Press, 1994), 132.

19. Coomaraswamy, "Mediaeval Aesthetic," 37 n. 10.

20. Umberto Eco traces its history, for example, in *Art and Beauty in the Middle Ages* (trans. Hugh Bredlin; New Haven, Conn.: Yale University Press, 1986), 47.

21. Pope John Paul II, "Letter to Artists," 1.

22. Plotinus, *Enneads*, 57.

23. Margaret R. Miles, *Image as Insight: Visual Understanding in Western Christianity and Secular Culture* (Boston: Beacon, 1985), 150–51.

13

Singing

LUKE'S SONGS AS MELODIES
OF THE MARGINALIZED

— Rick L. Williamson —

The Church in every age has sung of God and what God has done for the redeemed. From the Psalter's lofty yet life-related poetry to Paul's enjoinder to "sing psalms and hymns and spiritual songs" (Eph 5:19), biblical faith sings. Christians in myriad times and places have extended this tradition, gifting the Church with classics such as "All Creatures of Our God and King" (Francis of Assisi), "A Mighty Fortress Is Our God" (Martin Luther), and "To God Be the Glory" (Fanny Crosby). For their part, eighteenth-century Anglicans John and Charles Wesley provided guidance to the emerging Methodist movement through the production of over 6,500 hymns. In these and other hymn writers, we find evidence that the Church of Jesus Christ has been a singing Church.

In addition to being venerable, the Christian hymn tradition has been full and varied. Whereas some hymns sing to and about *God*, praising the person and activity of the divine, others choose the voice of *personal testimony*, celebrating God's transforming work in the lives of women and men. From a musical standpoint, Christian musicians and songwriters have succeeded in producing hymns and choruses in a wide variety of styles—from classical to jazz, from reggae to rock. The recent explosion of music in the arena of so-called contemporary worship has added to this variety, providing new avenues for Christians and seekers to honor God and voice their spiritual yearnings. It is arguable that the variety of musical expression in the Church has never been as wide as it is today in contemporary North America.

Despite this variety, however, many ecclesiastical traditions in North American Christianity continue to exhibit a gap in their hymnody. For even as North American churchgoers sing of God and of God's work in transforming *individuals*, many of these same worshipers rarely encounter hymns about God's transforming work in *society*. There are some exceptions, to be sure (for instance, Harry Emerson Fosdick's "God of Grace and God of Glory," which condemns materialism and "warring madness," and, more recently, Fred Kaan's "For the Healing of the Nations," which decries "all that kills abundant living" and sings of our "common quest for justice"). Nevertheless, Christian hymns and choruses that sing a faith that addresses crushing poverty, gnawing hunger, and imprisoning systems are relatively few. It is not a stretch to suggest that some Christians *never* voice those concerns in the course of their singing. And given that many North American Christians deem musical experiences to be fundamental to their "spirituality," it is little wonder that spirituality and justice often lack an integral connection in our churches.

This disconnection, of course, runs counter to an authentic biblical faith and those who have sought to incarnate that faith. The Hebrew prophets knew no religion that did not have implications for justice. Amos represents the spirit prevalent in the prophets of Israel: "Hate evil and love good, and establish justice. . . . Let justice roll down like waters, and righteousness like an ever-flowing stream" (Amos 5:15, 24). Some 2,500 years later, John Wesley argued that spiritual formation both buttressed and enabled ministry to the poor; indeed, ministry to and with the poor was integrally linked in Wesley's mind to the sanctified life. For him, such a ministry was not simply a duty, but a gracious means God provided to help persons become the holy people God intended.[1] John's brother Charles wrote that only in listening to the cries of the suffering, the widow, and the orphan, and then giving "my life, my all for them," does one "show the Spirit within."[2]

The gospel writer Luke would have agreed with that assessment. Not only does Luke, more than any other gospel writer, convey a deep concern for the way Christian faith becomes incarnate in action, he also provides the Church with compelling models for singing about God's passion for justice. In four brief hymns, best known according to their Latin designations as the *Magnificat* (1:46–55), the *Benedictus* (1:67–79), *Gloria in Excelsis Deo* (2:13–14), and *Nunc Dimittis* (2:28–35), Luke records the reality of social and political systems at odds with God's purposes, as well as God's desires for setting these systems aright. More than that, these four Lukan hymns affirm God's love, often expressed through God's people, for persons who are *marginalized*—that is, those who by various measures lack social and political power and sometimes even voice. The infancy songs of Luke need to be "sung" more robustly in the Christian Church, for they give increased voice to the marginalized. Moreover, those capable of creating music and lyrics must follow Luke's example, enabling their fellow Christians to sing of God's love for, and their responsibility to, the poor.

Luke, Poverty, and Social Justice

More than the other gospel narratives, Luke's story of Jesus (and its continuation in Acts) emphasizes the connections between spirituality and the use of one's possessions.[3] Simply put, how one possesses and shares material goods provide a measure of God's activity in a person's life. Correspondingly, the language of rich and poor permeates Luke's account of the Christian life. The words for "rich" and "riches" appear fifteen times in Luke compared to only nine times in Matthew and Mark, with no occurrences whatsoever in John. Similarly, the word "poor" appears nine times in Luke compared to five each in Matthew and Mark and four in John. Of course, the word "poor" designates for Luke more than simply a dearth of material goods. Rather, it reflects a way of being in the world, an orientation to life by those who understand their need, receive the gospel, and seek God's consolation.[4] In that very regard Luke's first beatitude reads, "Blessed are you who are poor, for yours is the kingdom of God" (6:20).

In addition to this emphasis on poverty, Luke's gospel reflects an abiding concern for marginalized persons and groups. This concern is most clearly demonstrated at the beginning of Jesus' public ministry (4:18–19), when Jesus quotes Isa 61:1–2 to underscore his passion for the poor, the captives, the blind, and the downtrodden. Jesus' concern for marginalized persons appears elsewhere in Luke's gospel (e.g., 7:22; 14:13), further illustrating the kingdom significance of those who are deemed by their fellow human beings to be unworthy of full participation in society and the life of God's people.[5] In a closely related vein, Luke records for his readers the struggle in the developing Christian movement over matters of race and culture (e.g., Jew-Gentile tensions), the place of women in the faith community, and the Christian's relationship to the state. In all these ways, Luke makes it clear that the gospel made visible in the life, teachings, death, and resurrection of Jesus Christ has profound social implications.

Of course, the gospel for Luke is more than mere humanitarianism, for along with these prominent social themes, no gospel writer depicts the spirit of God operating in people's lives more effectively than does Luke.[6] Similarly, Luke finds ways to emphasize prayer more frequently than any of the other evangelists; for instance, only in Luke does Jesus pray at his baptism (3:21) and on the Mount of Transfiguration (9:29). For the purposes of this essay, we simply wish to note the close Lukan interplay of spiritual practices—

whether private prayer or corporate worship—with a concern for social justice. Neither Luke nor his cast of characters can think of a spirituality that is divorced from a social conscience. Or, to approach this issue from the other direction, neither Luke nor his characters can imagine social justice expressions that are not grounded firmly in the rich soil of vital faith and practice. That is, the gospel is not gospel unless it offers both eternal and this-worldly redemption.[7]

In sum, the combination of social concern with vital piety, of life-giving compassion with spiritual practices, characterizes for Luke an authentic Christian faith. And although we can question the degree to which this combination is incarnated in contemporary North American churches, it is nonetheless true that most churches do, in fact, address both of these aspects of the Christian life. Along with clear calls to engage in various spiritual practices (and to convey the importance of the spiritual life to others), most denominational manuals of discipline encourage members to feed the hungry, clothe the naked, visit the sick, and minister to the needy. Again, the degree to which North American churches respond to this call is sometimes less than praiseworthy. But the call is usually there, at least on paper.

What is not so apparent, however, is the place of music and hymnody in the formation of the Church's social conscience. We will return to that question at the end of this essay. First, however, we will consider the songs of Luke as sung by Mary, Zechariah, the angels and shepherds, and Simeon, for the contexts and themes of their songs offer resources for making contemporary worship authentically Christian.

The Songs of Luke

The Magnificat (Luke 1:46–55)
The Magnificat, sung by Mary upon learning of her role in God's salvation, emerges from a well-known though disquieting context: Betrothed to Joseph, a humble young woman will bear the holy child ("Jesus . . . the Son of the Most High," 1:31–32) without engaging in sexual intercourse. In the Christian Scriptures, fertility is usually viewed as a sign of God's grace, and while Mary's experience is no exception to this rule, it nonetheless places her in a humiliating and perhaps even dangerous social situation. Unmarried yet betrothed, she is certain to be viewed by her Jewish neighbors as violating well-established standards of morality. At the very least, she would be set aside, much discussed in her village, and socially ostracized. At worst, she could lose her life (see Lev 20:10). In the language of twenty-first-century America, she is a young, single female with a problem pregnancy and unclear family support.

In response to this startling call, Mary describes her condition as one of "lowliness" (1:48). The Greek word Luke uses here is not *ptoxoi*, but *tapeinoi*, a term that emphasizes the lowly or humble aspects of poverty and is used in the Septuagint together with *ptoxoi* to describe the oppressed and downtrodden.[8] More than being lowly, however, Mary is also God's servant, God's *doulē* (1:38, 48). *Doulē* appears in the Septuagint as a translation of the Hebrew *nabi*, which is often used to denote prophetic roles (e.g., with Moses and Isaiah). As a servant of the Lord, Mary functions here as a prophet in anticipation of Peter's declaration at Pentecost that God's spirit would soon be poured out, enabling "sons and daughters [to] prophesy." In these "last days," says Peter, "young men shall see visions," "old men shall dream dreams," and "both men [*doulous*] and women [*doulas*] . . . shall prophesy" (Acts 2:17–18).

The thematic lines in Mary's Magnificat confirm this prophetic role as they resound with a deep concern for justice. To be sure, much of this concern is cast in nationalistic terms (e.g., references to God's "servant Israel" and God's promises to "our ancestors, to Abraham, and to his descendants forever"). Israel was, after all, an oppressed nation, suffering at the hands of its Roman occupiers. Still, Mary's voice conveys wider concerns not necessarily tied to her situation or to the fortunes of the people Israel. The language of the Magnificat cannot help but be heard as calling for a radical overturning of society, a rearrangement of societal hierarchies in which the proud are "scattered," the powerful are "brought down . . . from their thrones," and the rich are "sent . . . away empty" (Luke 1:51–53).[9]

In these refrains, then, the melodies of the marginalized sing. Mary, herself a poor and lowly woman, elevates the condition of the humble, the weak, and the poor through her song. Moreover, the social reversal that she anticipates is deemed to be nothing less than the result of God's saving activity: the sending of a sovereign who "will reign over the house of Jacob forever" and whose kingdom will never end (1:33). In both of these respects, the Magnificat can be heard as a song of both personal and social liberation, wherein God is characterized as one who acts on behalf of the lowly, the oppressed, and the suffering.[10] The melody line of mercy to one woman has been written into a majestic chorus. By acting on behalf of a humble woman, God signifies and sanctions a social revolution for the world.[11] Moreover, God's gracious activity is said to find special expression through people who are rightly devoted to God, and the mercy of the Lord is tied to "those who fear him" (1:50): the poor, the humble, the lowly.

The Benedictus (Luke 1:67–79)

The song of Zechariah continues Luke's focus on marginalized persons. Although Zechariah and Elizabeth are described as "righteous before God, living blamelessly according to all the commandments and regulations of the Lord" (1:6), they nonetheless have no children, and time is getting away from them. Their childlessness finds ready identification with persons in every age whose yearning for children goes unfulfilled. In a culture where offspring were viewed as a gift from the Lord, Zechariah and Elizabeth stand on the margins of society, wounded and silent, lacking a lullaby.

Exacerbating this marginality are Zechariah's physical limitations. Due to his meager belief in the message spoken by God's angel (that Elizabeth would bear a son, "great in the sight of the Lord"), he is rendered speechless. Unable to pronounce the priestly blessing for which the people were waiting, nothing remains for this righteous man but to go home. He remains silenced for the entirety of Elizabeth's pregnancy and until the eighth day of their son's life, when his written insistence that the child shall be named John frees his tongue (1:63–64). At least temporarily, however, Zechariah stood with the physically challenged of the world.

Emerging from this context of marginality, Zechariah sings his prophecy, the Benedictus. For Zechariah, God is "the Lord God of Israel" who raises up a savior from "the house of his servant David," thus ratifying the covenant that God "swore to our ancestor Abraham" centuries earlier (1:68–69, 73). In these ways, Zechariah's nationalistic orientation is made clear. Still, the covenant that God pledged to Abraham was for "all the families of the earth" (Gen 12:3). "Those who sit in darkness" will receive "light," says Zechariah, "by the tender mercy of our God" (Luke 1:78–79). God's interests, expressed in measure by Zechariah's words that closely echo Isaiah, include a mission to all people. Moreover, as we discover in the course of this narrative, the God of Zechariah is one who mercifully translates deep inner yearnings into tangible acts of care. To feel with another impels expressions in behalf of those in need. Mercy always moves to make a difference.

Gloria in Excelsis Deo (Luke 2:13–14)

The angels' announcement to the shepherds sustains the Lukan theme of God's initiatives to the lowly. In later rabbinic tradition, shepherds are regarded as thieves.[12] Thus, much like Mary in Luke 1, the shepherds function in Luke 2 as the lowly who are exalted by the Most High.

The shepherds' exaltation by the Most High derives from their role as the recipients of a grand announcement. Delivered to them by angels, this heavenly message has profound implications for the earth, for it announces that peace has come "among those whom [God] favors" (2:14). The shepherds, who are initially cast as rapt listeners, quickly become messengers in their own right, making known "what had been told them about this child" and "glorifying and praising God for all they had heard and seen" (2:17, 20). Once again, as we saw in Mary's experience, God has chosen the lowly of the earth to bear his message of salvation to the world.

While this yet-to-be-realized peace on earth derives from God's good favor, the role of *persons* in extending the favor of God is nonetheless manifest in Luke nd later in Acts.[13] Luke frequently reports the expectations for compassionate ervice by Jesus' disciples. The Sermon on the Plain (Luke 6:17–49) highlights angible acts of compassion, speaking of hunger, lending, and "doing good." "he Spirit-filled community in Acts attends to food distribution (Acts 6:1–7) nd collections for the relief of the poor (Acts 11:27–30). In these ways and nany more, Luke makes it abundantly clear that God's graciousness is inte- rally connected to ordinary acts of justice and compassion.

Nunc Dimittis (Luke 2:28–35)

The story of Simeon is well known: A "righteous and devout" man is "look- ng forward to the consolation of Israel" (2:25), assured by the Holy Spirit that he would not see death before he had seen the Lord's Messiah" (2:26). Luke's eaders are thus prepared for the fulfillment of this promise, which occurs vhen Mary and Joseph bring Jesus to the temple for his dedication to God. "here they encounter Simeon, who takes the Christ child into his arms and egins to praise God.

Simeon's song, Nunc Dimittis, sets the stage for Luke's larger message of an nclusive gospel. Echoing two of Isaiah's Servant Songs (42:6; 49:6), Simeon lescribes the "salvation" he holds in his arms as both "a light for revelation to the ientiles" and "glory to your people Israel" (Luke 2:32). This notion that God's urposes include all people ("the nations," according to Isaiah) argues forcefully or the elimination of racial and cultural antagonism as well as hostilities that rise from geographical boundaries. That this was Luke's intention unfolds learly in Acts, where we see the gospel embracing ever-widening people groups, xpanding both geographically and culturally. Acts 1:8 sets the direction for the "hurch's story, moving the narrative from Jerusalem/Judea to Samaria, and, argely through Paul's travels, to "the ends of the earth." At the same time, the ;ospel embraces not only Jews but also Samaritans (the first revival outside of udea, recorded in Acts 8:5–14, takes place in Samaria), God-fearing Romans Cornelius in Acts 10:1–33), and eventually Gentiles of every description. The :ingdom of God knows no lines drawn on a map, no barriers of race and culture.

Not only are geographical and cultural boundaries transcended by the ;ospel, but socioeconomic distinctions are also redefined. Luke's reference to 'imeon's anticipation of "the consolation of Israel" (2:25) finds an ironic, neg- tive fulfillment in the first woe of Luke's beatitudes: "But woe to you who are ich, for you have received your consolation" (6:24). In other words, although 'imeon received his consolation in the person of Jesus, the rich do not await uch a consolation because they already have one of their own. The rich do not aunger and sorrow as do the poor; rather, they are satisfied and laugh with uperior self-regard. According to Luke, this present good fortune of the rich vill eventually collapse into hunger and weeping.[14]

Given the manner in which, according to Luke's songs, the Messiah will turn the world upside down, it is hardly surprising to hear Simeon conclude his prophecy with the warning that Jesus will "be a sign that will be opposed" (2:34), and that Mary, in witnessing this opposition, will have her own soul pierced (2:35). In this way, Mary represents all who suffer through their identification with Jesus. Even so, Simeon is able to declare that, in the incarnation of Jesus, he has now found "peace" (2:29). In this passage, then, we see both the promise of finding security in Jesus and the continuing reality of determined opposition to Jesus. In sum, Simeon's song speaks to racial and cultural issues, matters of poverty and wealth, and the confrontation of political and economic power represented by Jesus and the values that he represented.

The Songs of Luke and Worship Today

One finds in Luke a distinct tension between the eschatological call of Jesus and the Christian's responsibility to the world.[15] As we have noted, however, the Lukan themes pertaining to the poor and marginalized have frequently been absent from the North American Church's hymnody. How shall we retain our mission to the poor, so apparent in Jesus' ministry and in the early Church, if we do not include this refrain in our music traditions?

Perhaps, however, we should not dismiss so quickly the witness of North America's churches. For over two hundred and fifty years, African-American Christians have been singing from faith about social justice issues. Music as a deeply cultural expression—creating community within and expressing resistance to oppression from without—has been an essential component of the African-American experience.[16] Historians have long noted the way in which African-American slaves likened their bondage to that of the Israelites, a conviction they expressed in spirituals such as "Go Down, Moses," which called on slaveholders to "let my people go." More recently, African-American activists and their white allies accompanied and advanced the civil rights movement with song, transforming old spirituals into contemporary songs of protest and hope. According to Kerran Sauger, these activists found their "voice" for social protest in the company of others.[17] As they sang for the transformation of society, they found transformation themselves, sensing that they were working in concert with God and God's purposes. Individually and corporately, those who sang perceived of a new world, recreated in measure by their melodies from the margins.[18]

Owing in part to the witness of the civil rights movement, some churches and denominations have begun to devote more attention to social justice themes in their hymnals. Some of these hymnals, including the United Church of Christ's *New Century Hymnal*, the Christian Reformed Church's *Psalter*

Hymnal, the *United Methodist Hymnal*, and the nondenominational hymnal *The Worshiping Church* include topical sections on justice, peace, and social holiness.[19] Scotland's Iona Community, which practices what it sings in this respect, has been particularly imaginative in wedding musical expression to social justice concerns. For instance, Iona's *Innkeepers and Light Sleepers* is a collection of original Advent music that includes "He Became Poor" and "Justice in the Womb" among its many selections. Iona's musicians have also produced *Blessed Be Our Table*, a booklet of graces and reflections for meal-time that integrate thankfulness with a passion for justice.[20] Still another example are some recent hymns by Constance Cherry, which express social justice concerns in profound and specific ways, touching on substance abuse and peacemaking, among other issues.[21]

Of course, the biblical theme of justice can be "sung" in other ways, reminding worshipers about the implications of Christ's incarnation for the poor and lowly. Even churches indisposed to the liturgical calendar turn to Luke's infancy narratives during Advent, affording them numerous opportunities to underscore social justice themes. For instance, when Christian churches are celebrating the birth of Jesus, community agencies would gladly provide representatives to tell how their work incarnates God's love and care. A congregation could easily couple these readings from Luke with information about specific local ministries, transposing Luke's concerns into dollars for food, clothing, and shelter.

Similarly, Luke's songs lend themselves to dramatic presentations (perhaps set best in contemporary contexts) that illustrate the incarnation's significance for the poor and the weak. A young teen, pregnant and afraid, could speak of societal prejudice against persons like her. A vignette portraying poor workers being visited by God's messengers would remind worshipers that Advent is not about fanfare and God's visitation to the rich. North American cultural biases against the elderly, wholly absent from Luke's narrative about Simeon and Anna, could be addressed by asking if our own communities honor the aged in ways that were customary in the first century.

Indeed, the social justice concerns central to Luke's songs and his Advent narratives merit some of the Church's best creative expression, for these melodies of the marginalized are songs that all of God's people must sing. With Mary we must sing of the God who lifts the lowly and fills the hungry. In a war-torn world where prejudice abounds, the angel's proclamation of "peace on earth" offers a word of hope that needs to ring loud and clear. And with Zechariah we must sing of rescue from enemies so that we "might serve [God] without fear, in holiness and righteousness before him all our days" (Luke 1:74–75). By making Luke's melodies our own, we not only learn about God's concerns, we also begin to embrace God's concerns as our own.

Notes

1. Randy L. Maddox, "'Visit the Poor': John Wesley, the Poor, and the Sanctification of Believers," in *The Poor and the People Called Methodists* (ed. Richard P. Heitzenrater; Nashville: Kingswood Books, 2002), 81.

2. Charles Wesley, "Jesus, the Gift Divine I Know," in *Wesley Hymns* (comp. Ken Bible; Kansas City, Mo.: Lillenas Publishing Co., 1982).

3. Luke Timothy Johnson, *The Literary Function of Possessions in Luke-Acts* (Missoula, Mont.: Scholars Press, 1997).

4. Ibid., 132.

5. Ibid., 133–34.

6. Joseph A. Fitzmyer, *The Gospel according to Luke I–IX* (Garden City, N.Y.: Doubleday, 1981), 227–31.

7. Philip Francis Esler, *Community and Gospel in Luke-Acts* (Cambridge: Cambridge University Press, 1987), 199.

8. Walter Grundmann, "*tapeinos*," in *Theological Dictionary of the New Testament* (ed. Gerhard Kittel; trans. Geoffrey W. Bromiley; Grand Rapids: Eerdmans, 1972), 8:1–11.

9. Robert C. Tannehill, "The Magnificat as Poem," *Journal of Biblical Literature* 93 (1974): 267.

10. Jane Schaberg, *The Illegitimacy of Jesus* (San Francisco: Harper & Row, 1987), 92.

11. Tannehill, "Magnificat as Poem," 274.

12. Herman L. Strack and Paul Billerbeck, *Kommentar zum Neuen Testament* (Munich: Beck, 1975), 2:113–14.

13. See the brief discussion in Joseph A. Fitzmyer, "Peace upon Earth among Men of His Good Will (Lk 2:14)," *Theological Studies* 19 (1958): 225–27.

14. Johnson, *Literary Function of Possessions*, 135.

15. Ibid., 129.

16. See Angela P. Dodson and A'Leila P. Bundles, "Jubilee," *Black Issues Book Review* 5, no. 3 (2003): 17–22.

17. Kerran L. Sauger, *When the Spirit Says Sing: The Role of Freedom Songs in the Civil Rights Movement* (New York: Garland, 1995), 9–10. See also Pete Seeger and Bob Reiser, *Everybody Says Freedom* (New York: W. W. Norton & Co., 1989).

18. Sauger, *When the Spirit Says Sing*, 100. In a different land, though along similar lines, South African pastor Allan Boesak saw the power of biblical poetry to serve as refrains for reform. For Boesak, who was fighting apartheid in the 1980s, the praises around the heavenly throne (Rev 4–5) became powerful, joyful songs of freedom that foreshadowed the demise of a corrupt political system. See Allan A. Boesak, *Comfort and Protest* (Philadelphia: Westminster, 1987).

19. *The New Century Hymnal* (Cleveland: Pilgrim, 1995); *Psalter Hymnal* (Grand Rapids: CRC Publications, 1988); *United Methodist Hymnal* (Nashville: United Methodist Publishing House, 1989); and *The Worshiping Church: A Hymnal* (Carol Stream, Ill.: Hope Publishing Co., 1990).

20. For more information, visit http://www.iona.org.uk.

21. Constance M. Cherry, *Proclaim New Hope* (Carol Stream, Ill.: Hope Publishing Co., 2001).

14

The Lord's Supper

FOOD FOR THE JOURNEY: WESLEYAN EUCHARISTIC PIETY AND THE INTEGRATED CHRISTIAN LIFE

— *Aaron Kerr* —

The term "Eucharist" derives from the Greek word *eucharistia*, meaning "thanksgiving." More commonly, it refers to the ritual in which Christians are fed by Christ's body and blood in order that they might feed others. Jesus, who asks his followers to visit those in prison and those who are sick, who asks them to feed the hungry, has also commanded them to "do this in remembrance of me" (Luke 22:19). But why do this? And what has this to do with the search for justice? More to the point, what has this ritual to do with right relationships between persons and between persons and God?

Because giving thanks has always been central to the Church's worship life, the Eucharist has long comprised both the functional and the theological center of many ecclesiastical traditions. Moreover, as the New Testament well attests, this ritual has long wielded power both to sever and unite (see 1 Cor 11:17–34). Part of its volatility stems from the fact that the Lord's Supper is beyond human ability to understand; it is a "mystery" in Christ.[1] At the same time, the Eucharist carries a "super abundance of meaning," touching all facets of human personhood—the intellect, the affections, and the will.[2] As an embodied experience of Christian doctrine, the Eucharist facilitates the expression of theological convictions, interior longings, and public commitments. All this makes the Eucharist a theologically potent—and explosive—element of corporate Christianity.

For our purposes, reflection on this ritual enables us to clarify the content of spirituality and social justice, as well as probe the relationship between them. At the very least, examining the Eucharist (in this particular case, through the theological lenses of John and Charles Wesley) helps us to grasp the possibility that our worship rituals have some abiding connection to our moral commitments and social actions. This, in turn, should assist us in the work of living integrated lives that can be made whole and holy through worship and service.

Eucharist and Social Change

Although the Eucharist has functioned in different ways at different times, examples abound that illustrate its connections to discipleship, church renewal, and social change. Most of these examples derive from the Roman Catholic tradition, which generally speaking has awarded a more prominent role to the Eucharist than has Protestantism. For instance, the Franciscan movement, named for Francis of Assisi (1181–1226) and known for its ministry among the poor, has been deemed by some historians to have been a "eucharistic crusade."[3] Similarly, the now beatified Catherine of Genoa (1447–1510) attended mass daily even as she cared for the sick and dying, making her home in the Hospital of the Pammotone.[4] More recently, Roman Catholics who suffered under Chile's oppressive Pinochet regime became the body of Christ through worship and service. After large segments of the Chilean church went underground for fear of state torture, the Eucharist served to weave the body of Christ back together. In this more recent example, writes William Cavanaugh, the Eucharist became nothing less than the counterpolitics to the politics of power and terror.[5]

While these examples of eucharistic practice and social engagement point to an integral relationship between the sacrament and Christian discipleship, such connections have been far less prominent in the Protestant tradition. In some branches of Protestantism, which relies mainly on "the Word" to convict believers' hearts, sacramental awakenings have been rare, perhaps even theologically unthinkable. Not so, however, with the Wesleyan movement. In the early Wesleyan movement we find a Protestant example of a passionate mission to the poor that was both evangelical and sacramental. For both John and Charles Wesley, the Eucharist comprised the connective tissue that effectively integrated the Christian life, linking works of mercy to the practice of piety, connecting orthopraxis to orthodoxy.[6]

Our concern, then, is a practical one. How can regularly attending to the Eucharist gather up the fragments of our lives and help us focus on the primary mission of the Church, a mission to the poor? For Christians, living an integrated life is at once a spiritual gift and a spiritual challenge, and part of that challenge involves the temptation to link justice, worship, and spirituality *programmatically*. That is, we are tempted to assume that if only we could write a more justice-oriented liturgy, or use worship as a polemical tool for justice and peace, the Church would be a stronger voice for justice in the world. To the contrary (and as John Wesley argued), the only thing eucharistic worship is "good for" is to praise the living God.[7] The ultimate purpose of our lives is doxological; we are to be a people of praise and thanksgiving.

Of course, the implications of that spiritual fact are profound, especially with respect to social action and public witness. This returns us to our central question: How can a heritage that is both evangelical and sacramental deepen Christian faith and strengthen Christian social witness? We will first consider this question by examining one of the ways the Eucharist challenged the early Methodist movement. We will then consider the Wesleys' notion of salvation (and how this "lived spirituality" evoked the desire for consistent eucharistic practice) before finally tracing some concrete connections between the Eucharist and Wesleyan social concern.

The Challenge of Eucharistic Piety: A Historical Precedent

Throughout their lives as Anglican priests and leaders in the Methodist renewal movement, John and Charles Wesley encouraged weekly reception of the Eucharist. This was a regular component of a comprehensive spiritual vision that, above all, included an abiding commitment to build strong relationships with the poor.[8] The Wesleys' shared vision of sacramental theology was best expressed in their 1745 publication, *Hymns on the Lord's Supper*, a collection of 166 eucharistic hymns, mostly written by Charles. In addition to Charles's poetry, *Hymns on the Lord's Supper* contained an abridgment of Anglican theologian Daniel Brevint's *Christian Sacrament and Sacrifice*, a theological summary that corresponds roughly to Charles's eucharistic hymns.[9] According to Brevint, the significance of the Eucharist was fivefold; it was a memorial of the sufferings and death of Christ, a means of grace, a pledge of heaven, a sacrifice, and, most significant for our purposes, a sacrifice of our persons.[10] Brevint's theology and the Wesleys' hymnody manifest a clear correspondence. In the Wesleys' hymns, Brevint's eucharistic teaching was given tangible, poetic expression in order to be embodied and sung in a lived spirituality.

Given the state of eucharistic practice in mid-eighteenth-century England, the Wesleys believed this teaching necessary. Few Anglicans at the time were having the Lord's Supper weekly. In fact, Anglican churches in rural areas celebrated the Eucharist only three or four times a year, and while urban churches celebrated it more frequently, many of them did so only monthly.[11] Why then would the Wesleys publish so many hymns specific to the Lord's Supper?

That *Hymns on the Lord's Supper* was penned at the "very height of the Methodist revival" offers a significant clue.[12] Although the historical record is less than clear at this point, one may reasonably envision hundred of peoples waiting before and after reception of the Eucharist in a state of collective song and prayer. Indeed, the very existence of the Wesley's eucharistic hymnal points to the fact that the Methodist movement was driven by a sacramental, no less than an evangelical, revival within the Anglican Communion. In sum, the Wesleys' logic seems to have been that if people were not attending to the word and sacrament within their mainstream churches, they would instigate a ministry of engagement in which word and sacrament would be conveyed to the people. The Wesleys encouraged Methodists to receive the sacrament from the hands of Anglican priests, even as they encouraged Anglican priests to provide it more consistently.

For the Wesleys, then, sacramental practice was the expression of evangelistic joy, even as evangelism "fed" the desire for communion with the Lord. Soon, however, their advocacy of the sacrament placed them at the center of an evolving ecclesiastical conflict. This conflict, which was closely connected to the larger question of whether Methodist societies should split from the Anglican communion, stemmed from the widespread Methodist belief that the Anglican priesthood did not have the requisite moral rectitude to preside over the kind of Communion Methodists deemed fitting.[13] The moral rectitude question raised by some Methodists was further complicated by the problem of frequency. As Methodist leaders, both John and Charles Wesley had encouraged the reception of weekly Communion at an Anglican parish, but since the Anglican Church's Book of Common Prayer dictated that Communion only had to be received three times a year, parishes that had weekly Communion were few and far between.[14] The Wesley brothers thus found themselves at odds with both Methodist followers and Anglican leaders, albeit for different reasons: The Methodists wanted the Wesleys to advocate weekly Communion outside the walls of the Anglican churches, and Anglican leaders wanted the Wesleys to rest content with less frequent Communion administered by Anglican priests.

Ultimately, John Wesley, in concert with his brother Charles, decided that the Church of England should maintain its grip on Christ's ordinances, and that Methodists should not ordain "separate" priests to serve their purposes.[15] Wesley may have agreed with his Methodist followers that the Anglican priesthood was unfit to serve the Eucharist, but in Britain at least, he was not willing to forgo the unity of Christ's body.[16] It was in Christ's body, Wesley maintained, where the possibility of full incorporation existed, a coming together of rich and poor, of High Church Anglicans and Calvinistic Methodists. John Wesley knew that maintaining relationships between different classes of people was a difficult task, even more so in the midst of ecclesiastical conflict. Thus, his insistence upon regular attendance at the eucharistic celebration, in addition to being an expression of discipleship, was a theological affirmation of a social vision of unity in Christ. According to Wesley, respect for the Eucharist as a meal of solidarity and unity contradicted—and therefore overruled—the notion of a separate Communion.

In sum, the Wesley brothers' eucharistic advocacy was not about restructuring ecclesiastical boundaries. Rather, their insistence upon consistent eucharistic practice was an effort to increase awareness of and participation in God's grace. Furthermore, it was a challenge to Methodists to embody an abundant life that would both demonstrate and contribute to Christian unity. And, of course, this effort was integrally connected to their view of salvation.

Wesleyan Eucharistic Piety: Experience of Salvation

For the Wesleys, the Christian life was an integrated life, one that could not be easily compartmentalized. To be sure, John Wesley's understanding of Christian "experience" meant first and foremost the experience of sanctification, an experience that involved "personal assurance of God's justifying, pardoning grace."[17] Still, Wesley understood the Christian life as an ongoing process toward wholeness, weaving "an organic continuum" of repentance, reconciliation, regeneration, and sanctification into all experience.[18]

The organic nature of Wesleyan soteriology is most clearly represented by the notion of renewal and restoration. According to John Wesley, human beings are invited by and through the Holy Spirit to participate with God so that they will be "renewed after the image of God in righteousness and true holiness."[19] Corresponding to this emphasis on restoration, Albert Outler has noted that in Wesley's soteriological reflections, "therapeutic metaphors tend to outweigh the forensic ones that dominated Western traditions since Anselm."[20] Of course, John Wesley cannot claim originality in this regard. To the contrary, John and Charles both imbibed during their Oxford days from "the fountain head of Eastern Orthodox Spirituality," nourishing themselves on the works of Clement of Alexandria, Marcarius, and the Cappadocians.[21] It was here, in the works of these Eastern theologians, that the Wesleys discovered their theology of spiritual renewal, in particular, their notion of life lived in "the likeness of God."

The Wesleys sought to express this soteriological notion via their eucharistic practices. Furthermore, John's writings on the Eucharist aptly "sacramentalized" their synergistic, soteriological vision that stressed the interplay of human freedom and God's grace. In a tract entitled "The Duty of Constant Communion," Wesley defined the Eucharist in two ways: as a mercy and as a command. By focusing on the Eucharist as a mercy, Wesley characterized it as something for which Christians can only be *grateful*. In the same tract, however, he also explained that the Eucharist was a command ("Do this in remembrance of me"), that is, it is something that Christians *do*.[22] For Wesley, understanding the Eucharist as both mercy and command effectively integrated the two dimensions of all Christian experiences of grace: giving and receiving. When Christians bring themselves to Christ's table, he argued, they are a people who do. They act in a very particular way, and by doing this particular thing, they demonstrate their response to God's gift in Christ, giving themselves back to God. At the same time, they receive nourishment, taking in the mercy God has in store in the Son. They receive that which they neither earned nor deserve. They give because they have received, but they only can give back what God has given to them in Christ.

Theologian Theodore Jennings has extended this Wesleyan notion of Eucharist as both mercy and command, arguing that the sacraments are, in a sense, the epitome of all Christian action.[23] When Christians experience the reality of God's grace in public worship, says Jennings, they learn the fundamental fact about all Christian action: They are a people who are taken up into the mercy of God, blessed by this God's love in Christ, broken for the world Jesus loves, and shared for the benefit of others. Theologian Don Saliers offers a similar perspective, suggesting that "the four actions at the table—take, bless, break and share—are what we are to become."[24]

The Wesleys knew well what we must also recognize: Learning to be receivers and givers is difficult, perhaps impossible, without an awareness of God's initiative of mercy and justice. Fortunately, the Eucharist can be our tutor in that regard. When Christians gather to share the bread and the wine, awe and action merge. Gratitude for grace results in the action of receiving. Even more, in the reception of the Eucharist our claim that we are a grateful people willing to share sacrificially is made *public*. As an expression of our life together, the practice of the Eucharist reminds us to seek balance in our corporate life as well—a balance of works of piety and works of mercy, contemplation and action, reception and doing. While this balance will always pose a challenge to Christians, regular participation in the Eucharist helps to form participants into people who have learned how to be receivers and givers.

The Meaning of "Constant" in "The Duty of Constant Communion"

Wesleyan eucharistic piety maintains that irregular eucharistic practice stifles the awareness of God's grace. Just as other means of grace—prayer, Scripture reading, and the like—are not useful if rarely practiced, so too the Eucharist ceases to develop an awareness of God's work when Christians refrain from participating in it. Similarly, just as the visitation of the sick and poor serves to draw Christians into deeper communion with Christ, so too does the reception of eucharistic grace deepen Christian awareness of God's goodness poured out to all.

In support of their call for frequent eucharistic participation, both Wesleys pointed to the early Church. "Let everyone . . . who has either any desire to please God, or any love of his own soul, obey God . . . by communicating every time he can," wrote John in "The Duty of Constant Communion," adding that to do so would place eighteenth-century Christians in line with "the first Christians, with whom the Christian Sacrifice was a constant part of the Lord's day service."[25] Charles shared his brother's convictions on this issue, suggesting in one of his eucharistic hymns that the early Church received the Eucharist every day. "Nor would [they] from the commandment move," wrote Charles, "But every joyful day receive / The tokens of expiring love." This particular hymn continued by criticizing the laxity of eighteenth-century Anglican eucharistic practice and concluded with the stinging observation that "charity flees" when eucharistic practice subsides:

> Why is the faithful seed decreased,
> The life of God extinct and dead?
> The daily sacrifice is ceased,
> And charity to heaven is fled.[26]

In the Wesleys' eyes, then, to remain faithful to a gospel that does justice, the Church must remember the sacrificial love that initiated the gospel, a memory best served by the Eucharist. Indeed, they warned, when the "faithful seed" is decreased, love of neighbor inevitably subsides.[27]

Thus, in addition to having historical support from the early Church, the Wesleyan insistence upon weekly Communion held great theological significance. According to the Wesleys, the rehearsal of God's self-sacrificial love signaled and recalled the restoration of the image of God within human beings and society as a whole. That being the case, it infused all of life with the means to achieve personal and social holiness. Wesleyan eucharistic piety is thus consistent with the Wesleyan understanding of sanctification whereby Christian holiness is contingent upon certain formative experiences. Similarly, Communion must be "constant." Neither aiming to measure up to some objective standard, nor relying upon the Church as a conduit of grace, Wesleyan eucharistic practice nonetheless seeks to raise participants' awareness of being constantly fed by the spirit of God.[28] God is the constant presence of mercy, and the task of Christians is to participate in that presence. Just as the poor and Scripture are objective facts regardless of one's attention to them, so too is the Eucharist. As an experience of God's comprehensive grace, it should not be neglected.

Strengthened Connections: Eucharist and Social Concern

From the standpoint of Christian spirituality, the Wesleys are perhaps most renowned for their emphasis on "responsible grace," a synthesis of the Protestant insistence on grace alone and the Catholic affirmation of cooperation with God's grace.[29] This synthesis meant that the Oxford Methodists engaged in a wide variety of Christian spiritual practices. In addition to Bible reading, journaling, and meditating "upon the riches of the divine mystery," the early Methodists demonstrated a keen interest in caring for the sick, visiting the imprisoned, and giving aid to the poor.[30] Through these practices of mercy they learned that God's presence could be found in all arenas of life. John Wesley often encouraged his Methodist societies to *deliver* rather than *send* aid to the poor, a practical bias rooted in his conviction that face-to-face encounters with the poor evoked a deeper sense of Christian compassion and God's grace.[31] "How much better it is . . . to carry relief to the poor than to send it!" wrote Wesley in 1760. "And that both for our own sake and theirs. For theirs, as it is so much more comfortable to them, and as we may then assist them in spirituals as well as temporals; and for our own, as it is far more apt to soften our heart, and to make us naturally care for each other."[32]

Clearly, then, the early Methodists devoted themselves to works of mercy and justice. But just how did they conceive of the link between softened hearts, works of mercy, and eucharistic practice? Simply put, all these things beheld for them a genuine encounter with the otherness of Jesus Christ. John Wesley himself often pointed to "the Prayer of humble access" ("that we may evermore dwell in him and he in us") that characterized every eucharistic celebration as the promise of an encounter with Jesus Christ in and through the Lord's Supper.[33] For him, Communion meant nothing less than the *communication of Christ* to those who participated in the eucharistic meal.[34] At the same time, Wesley was well aware that the New Testament spoke of encountering Christ in other ways. For instance, in Matt 25, Jesus tells his listeners that, when they minister to the sick, the hungry, and the prisoner, they are in actuality encountering Jesus. In other words, the living Christ is *communicated* in and through vulnerable people. Similarly, the gospel writers tell of Jesus celebrating table fellowship with both rich and poor, once again denoting the possibility of an intimate encounter with the living Christ. Near the end of Luke's gospel, this notion of fellowship with Christ—now the risen Christ—comes full circle: "When [Jesus] was at table with them, he took bread, blessed and broke it, and gave it to them. Then their eyes were opened, and they recognized him" (Luke 24:30–31).

John Wesley underscored the scriptural notion that communion with Christ is founded upon two different sorts of actions: caring for vulnerable people (i.e., doing works of justice and mercy), and eating and drinking through the Holy Spirit (i.e., doing the work of worship). These actions, while temporally distinct and conceptually distinguishable, are not disconnected from one another. Rather, they are works that, when practiced constantly, deepen and sustain each other. According to John Wesley, Communion constitutes an intensification of the lived experience of forgiveness, conveying forgiveness, strength, and refreshment—gifts that correspond to the healing grace of the Spirit.[35] Moreover, the Christian's ability to perform works of mercy and justice springs from an abiding awareness of the saving work initiated and completed in Christ, an awareness that the Eucharist effectively promotes. Even as the Eucharist spawns works of mercy, however, these same works return us to participation with Christ. The presence of Christ and communion with him can be found "always and everywhere."[36]

Wesleyan eucharistic piety, then, leaves no room for passivity. Rather, it challenges believers to engage in eucharistic practice fully attuned to God's self-sacrificial action, a spiritual attentiveness that necessarily leads participants to become living sacrifices that participate with God in works of mercy and justice. At the Lord's table, Christians not only give thanks (*eucharistia*) for the gift of grace, they aver the following about the Son: "He healed the sick, fed the hungry, and ate with sinners." This prayer's meaning is deepened when we too keep the commandments of Jesus.

Conclusion

The Wesleyan tradition calls Christians to nothing less than *sacramental justice*. In its call for a holistic faith that integrates worship and service, it echoes Jesus' desire that his followers remember him in two ways. First, they are to remember him by rehearsing the entire drama of salvation in the eucharistic celebration. Second, they are to recall his engagement with those for whom God's heart breaks: the poor and the vulnerable.[37] More generally, Christian spirituality rightly practiced helps to balance the power of these memories, producing robust Christian disciples and communities characterized by joyful receiving and generous giving. Living sacramentally means that Christians place not only their minds and words in the service of justice, but their bodies too, including their corporate bodies. A church that does justice—that is, a church that goes to the point of human need, encounters others, and incorporates "the least of these" into the mercy of the Creator—is the body of Christ.

To be sure, frequent eucharistic practice does not ensure the formation of robust Christian communities that give generously and receive joyfully. The Wesley brothers would no doubt admit as much. Still, they would insist that regular participation in the eucharistic meal consistently deepens the awareness of Christ's presence in daily living. And in response to the objection, voiced so often in some Protestant circles, that frequent Communion would make it an "ordinary" event, the Wesleys might ask, "Is there not something ordinary about God's grace?" Is not this ordinariness the scandal of the Christian vision of reality? To perceive the wondrous love of God in Christ in the course of family dinners, in the faces of the poor, in the handshakes of strangers, is to become attuned to the glory of a God who never sleeps. Christians are those who can see in these everyday occurrences the mercies of a loving God. They are those for whom life is "constant communion" with the living Christ, encountered both in worship and in service.

Notes

1. Hoyt Hickman, "The Theology of the Lord's Supper in the New United Methodist Ritual," *Quarterly Review* 17 (1997): 362.

2. David F. Ford, *Self and Salvation: Being Transformed* (Cambridge: Cambridge University Press, 1999), 144–45.

3. Regis J. Armstrong and Ignatius C. Brady, introduction to *Francis and Clare: The Complete Works* (ed. Regis J. Armstrong and Ignatius C. Brady; New York: Paulist Press, 1982), 15.

4. Friedrich Von Hugel, *The Mystical Element of Religion: As Studied in Saint Catherine of Genoa and Her Friends* (New York: Crossroad, 1999), 113.

5. William T. Cavanaugh, *Torture and Eucharist: Theology, Politics, and the Body of Christ* (Malden, Mass.: Blackwell, 1998), 253.

6. Joerg Rieger, "The Means of Grace, John Wesley, and the Theological Dilemma of the Church Today," *Quarterly Review* 17 (1997): 377–93.

7. John Wesley, "The Circumcision of the Heart," in *The Works of John Wesley* (Grand Rapids: Zondervan, 1958), 5:207–8.

8. Task Force for the Bishops' Initiative on Children and Poverty, *Community with Children and the Poor: A Guide for Congregational Study: Based on the United Methodist Bishops' Letter "Community with Children and the Poor"* (Nashville: Cokesbury, 2003), 17.

9. Frank Whaling, introduction to *John and Charles Wesley: Selected Prayers, Hymns, Journal Notes, Sermons, Letters, and Treatises* (ed. Frank Whaling; New York: Paulist Press, 1981), 28; and Ole Borgen, *John Wesley on the Sacraments: A Theological Study* (Nashville: Abingdon, 1972), 28.

10. *John and Charles Wesley: Selected Prayers*, 28–29.

11. Henry D. Rack, *Reasonable Enthusiast: John Wesley and the Rise of Methodism* (Nashville: Abingdon, 1992), 19.

12. J. Ernest Rattenbury, *The Eucharistic Hymns of John and Charles Wesley* (2nd ed.; Akron, Ohio: OSL Publications, 1996), 11.

13. Richard P. Heitzenrater, *Wesley and the People Called Methodists* (Nashville: Abingdon, 1995), 191–93.

14. Rack, *Reasonable Enthusiast*, 418.

15. Heitzenrater, *Wesley and the People Called Methodists*, 192–93.

16. Wesley's argument for not ordaining Methodists can be found in John Wesley, "On Attending the Church Service," in *The Works of John Wesley* (Grand Rapids: Zondervan, 1958), 7:174–86.

17. Albert Outler, introduction to *The Works of John Wesley: The Bicentennial Edition* (ed. Albert Outler et al.; Nashville: Abingdon, 1984), 1:57.

18. Ibid., 1:80.

19. John Wesley, "The New Birth," in *The Works of John Wesley* (Grand Rapids: Zondervan, 1958), 6:71.

20. Outler, introduction to *The Works of John Wesley*, 1:80.

21. Albert C. Outler, preface to *John and Charles Wesley: Selected Prayers*, xiv.

22. John Wesley, "The Duty of Constant Communion," in *The Works of John Wesley* (Grand Rapids: Zondervan, 1958), 7:149.

23. Theodore W. Jennings, "On Ritual Knowledge," *Journal of Religion* 62 (1982): 118.

24. Don E. Saliers, *Worship and Spirituality* (Philadelphia: Westminster, 1984), 76.

25. Wesley, "Duty of Constant Communion," in *Works of John Wesley*, 7:148.

26. Rattenbury, *Eucharistic Hymns*, 202–3.

27. The Wesleys were correct about the early Church's eucharistic practice. Moreover, as David Ford argues, early Christian consciousness of salvation was largely conveyed through the eucharistic liturgy. Since the doctrine of salvation had not yet been formalized in creeds, the eucharistic liturgy provided continuity for shared meanings about the death of Christ and the forgiveness of human sin. See Ford, *Self and Salvation*, 137–39.

28. Richard R. Gaillardetz, *Transforming Our Days: Spirituality, Community, and Liturgy in a Technological Culture* (New York: Crossroad, 2000), 109.

29. Randy L. Maddox, *Responsible Grace: John Wesley's Practical Theology* (Nashville: Kingswood, 1994).

30. David Trickett, "The Early Wesleyan Movement," in *Christian Spirituality: Post-Reformation and Modern* (ed. Louis Dupré and Don E. Saliers; New York: Crossroad, 1989), 359.

31. Manfred Marquardt, *John Wesley's Social Ethics: Praxis and Principles* (Nashville: Abingdon, 1992), 27–33.

32. John Wesley, "Journal, Monday, November 24, 1760," in *Works of John Wesley*, 3:28.

33. Albert Outler, introduction to *The Works of John Wesley, Bicentennial Edition*, 1:56.

34. Borgen, *John Wesley on the Sacraments*, 184.

35. John Wesley, "Duty of Constant Communion," in *Works of John Wesley*, 7:148.

36. Here then we see the Wesleyan emphasis on orthodoxy and orthopraxis. John Wesley wrote that the former without the latter was not really a saving faith, a contention he tied directly to eucharistic participation. "For all that you profess at the Lord's table," wrote Wesley, "you must both profess and keep, or you cannot be saved. For you profess nothing there but this: that you will diligently keep [God's] commandments." Ibid., 7:153.

37. For a similar point, see Xavier Leon-Dufour, *Sharing the Eucharistic Bread: The Witness of the New Testament* (New York: Paulist Press, 1987), 283–84.

15

Table Fellowship

THE SPIRITUALITY OF EATING TOGETHER

— *Reta Halteman Finger* —

Although the title of this essay is "the spirituality of eating together," it is equally useful to think in terms of "the social implications of the Eucharist." Whether High Church or Low Church, Orthodox, Catholic, or Protestant, most North American Christians have partaken of the Lord's Supper many times. It is likely that few, however, are well acquainted with the social implications of this venerable Christian practice. Given what happens in most North American churches, this is hardly surprising. Yes, participants eat bread and drink wine together as a church body, but rarely do they interact with one another in the course of their eating and drinking. In many churches, individuals are directed simply to reflect on their relationship with Christ and his suffering for them. In some instances they are even urged to "leave behind earthly distractions" and "forget about" their neighbors as they ponder these "things above."

It is easier, of course, to identify the social implications of our other meals—with family, friends, and coworkers—though even then we sometimes miss the mark. I teach a course on the General Epistles, and when we get to James and its insistence that "faith without works is dead" (Jas 2:26), I require my students to participate in at least one act of social service. The last time I taught the course, I saw in the campus dining hall one evening two students who had been scheduled to go to a local soup kitchen that same evening. Since they were eating their dinner, I asked them if they had indeed gone to the soup kitchen. "Oh, yes, we went and served the meal." "But you didn't eat there?" I asked. "Well, no, we didn't think we should eat donated food." An honest response perhaps, though I wonder whether a more honest response would have been, "We wouldn't have felt comfortable eating with those people."

Where is the spirituality of eating together in the examples above? In most enactments of the Lord's Supper, we can no doubt find some "spirituality," but rarely is there much "eating together," since the actual "communion" is deemed only to be between individual believers and Christ. And while the soup kitchen example reveals a modicum of well-intentioned service, the gulf between educated, middle-class young people and those less privileged resulted in two different meals in two different dining halls. In this case, the poor became "the needy" we sometimes try to help but do not wish to associate with.

In order to overcome these gaps between spirituality and eating together, this essay considers several New Testament texts, each of which testifies to the ways the early Church integrated into its meal practices worship, the Lord's Supper, social interaction between different classes of believers, and care for the poor. Translating these ancient meal practices into contemporary American life is no easy task. Nevertheless, in the endeavor to connect its worship life and its justice work, the contemporary North American Church would be well served to consider these daily communal meals and pay heed to their boundary-breaking messages.

Class Divisions in Ancient Corinth

In 1 Cor 11:17–30, Paul chastises the Corinthians about their meal practices: "When you come together it is not for the better but for the worse" (v. 17). He then identifies his more specific concerns with this mostly Gentile church, the worst of which appears to be an inconsiderate competition between factions:

> When you come together as a church, I hear that there are divisions among you; and to some extent I believe it. . . . When you come together, it is not really to eat the Lord's supper. For when the time comes to eat, each of you goes ahead with your own supper, and one goes hungry and another becomes drunk. (vv. 18–21)

After recounting Jesus' last supper with his disciples (vv. 23–26), Paul continues with some strong words of admonishment:

> Whoever, therefore, eats the bread or drinks the cup of the Lord in an unworthy manner will be answerable for the body and blood of the Lord. Examine yourselves, and only then eat of the bread and drink of

the cup. For all who eat and drink without discerning the body, eat and drink judgment against themselves. (vv. 27–29)

The sociohistorical background of the early Church's meal practices helps to illumine Paul's indignation and admonishment. Churches met in homes in those days, probably every day, and the consecration of bread and wine always took place in the context of a full meal.[1] Apparently some of the Corinthian believers were wealthy enough not to have to work from sunrise to sunset, as did the manual laborers and the slaves. It was customary for such people to socialize by bringing food to each others' homes, sharing it in potluck fashion, or eating their own meals with one other.[2] Only the richest people had homes or first-floor apartments; ninety percent of the population was jammed into tiny one-room apartments on upper floors of tenement buildings.[3] The majority of Christians, that is, the poorer ones, would have joined the wealthy in their homes only after their workdays were done, and likely would not have had time or money to provide much food for the gathering.

Paul's reprimand, then, is due to class divisions. Because upper-class Christians in Corinth did not wait for their fellow Christians to arrive before eating, they tended to overeat or become drunk while the late arrivals went hungry. Paul insists that such eating is not the *Lord's* Supper, but "your own supper" (v. 21). Moreover, he says, those who eat in that way are eating and drinking judgment against themselves because they are not "discerning the body" (v. 29), a Pauline wordplay that underscores the symbolism of the bread, which stands in this case for the body of believers as well as the physical body of Christ.

This wordplay, when considered in light of the social context delineated above, helps explain an otherwise mystifying verse: Paul's claim that, for lack of discerning the body, "many of you are weak and ill, and some have died" (v. 30). On the surface, this verse appears to be saying that individuals who ate first, before others had the opportunity, became ill and even died due to their selfishness. While this interpretation parallels a common theory of suffering in the ancient world—that one's illness, hardship, or death was a sign of one's sin—other Pauline texts do not support this reading.[4] It is more likely that illness and death were afflicting working-class Christians who arrived late. If one main purpose of the daily communal meal was to nourish bodies as well as spirits, sharing food together was essential. The Lord's "judgment" against the entire community may have been the illness and occasional death of poorer believers who, living at or below subsistence level, did not receive enough calories at this primary daily meal. Their immune systems weakened, some became ill, and some even died, signaling God's judgment against a community that failed to eat the *Lord's* Supper together as one body.[5]

Understanding the social context of this text challenges the common assumption that the Lord's Supper is about the individual believer's "vertical" relationship with Christ. To the contrary, says Paul, this meal is not really the *Lord's* Supper unless all believers from every social strata are eating the same food together at the same time. Although this may sound less than earthshaking, it is important to remember that Roman society was highly stratified, and people only related socially with those of their class (house slaves did not even sit down to meals, but picked up leftovers or kitchen scraps on the run). A house church composed of rich and poor was a radical proposition to begin with, and now Paul is asking these early Christians to go one step further. Given our own tendency to resist the work of building relationships across race and class, it is little wonder that the Corinthian believers tended to fall back into their old habits.

A Common Purse and Common Meals

Acts 2:42–47 provides another account of early Church meal practices, this time from the very beginning of the church in Jerusalem:

> They [Christian believers] devoted themselves to the apostles' teaching and fellowship, to the breaking of bread and the prayers. Awe came upon everyone, because many wonders and signs were being done by the apostles. All who believed were together and had all things in common; they would sell their possessions and goods and distribute the proceeds to all, as any had need. Day by day, as they spent much time together in the temple, they broke bread at home and ate their food with glad and generous hearts, praising God and having the goodwill of all the people. And day by day the Lord added to their number those who were being saved.

Here we see eating and worship wholly integrated. Believers broke bread and ate together by households every day in the context of joyful worship!

Two quite contrasting interpretive approaches have been used to dismiss the authority of this account. On the one hand, many commentators have hedged about its historicity.[6] The author of Luke-Acts wrote these words fifty years after the fact, they say, and he was clearly idealizing the origins of the Church. Therefore, the notion of communal goods and communal meals is best understood as a symbol of the early Church's spiritual unity.[7] Other, more conservative commentators have taken a different approach, albeit equally dismissive. According to these commentators, Acts 2 is historically accurate, but the radical sharing it describes reflects the excitement of the moment and is therefore not practical today. The community of goods was practiced because early Christians expected Jesus' imminent return. After the famine discussed in Acts 11:28, the practice was rejected and we never hear of it again. Instead, alms were sent from one church to another as needs arose (e.g., 2 Cor 8:1–9:5).[8]

Both of these interpretive approaches manifest hermeneutical flaws, for they project modern, individualist, capitalist values onto an ancient, agrarian society in which 90 percent of the population lived at or below subsistence level. Our understanding of this passage is better served by asking this question: How did the underclass manage to survive exploitation by the upper classes and overtaxation by the Romans at a time when there was no state-sponsored welfare system?

The social safety net for the vast majority of such people was the kin-group.[9] People lived where their relatives lived, usually in small houses surrounding a common courtyard. Within kin-groups of siblings, cousins, aunts, and uncles, people could trust each other enough to share resources and otherwise compensate for each other when someone broke a leg or was widowed or the inevitable drought struck. These people knew what we often overlook as we peer through our lenses of individualism and nuclear families, namely, that fewer materials are needed when tools and utensils are shared and meals are eaten together.

Of course, Jesus' call to leave home and family to follow him disrupted this kin-group sharing. Therefore, the gospels tell us, Jesus organized a "fictive" kin-group around himself, fictive because it was composed of people not necessarily related biologically.[10] This group of male and female disciples acted like a biological kin-group, eating communal meals and sharing resources. It was an open group, and any persons could join who were willing to share everything they had. The poor in this case were not "the other." Rather, all were poor together, so that, at the basic level, "there was not a needy person among them" (Acts 4:34).

It was only natural that the growing group of post-Pentecost disciples would organize themselves similarly, following Jesus' pattern of table fellowship. Probably only a few of these early Christians were wealthy, such as Barnabas, who sold a field and contributed the proceeds (Acts 4:37), thus laying aside not only his wealth but also his higher-class status as a property owner. Ananias and Sapphira (Acts 5:1–11) must also have been among the community's wealthiest members. What brought about their downfall was their lying to the Holy Spirit, who initiated this movement (Acts 5:4). For a kin-group to survive and share life together, all members needed to be open and truthful with each other. Clearly this deceitful couple could not belong, and their deaths served to remind the others of this particular kin-group's high standards (Acts 5:11).

Widows at the Communal Meals

Acts 6:1–4 further testifies to the daily communal meals of the Jerusalem community, in this case opening a door to a gender-sensitive understanding of early Church life:

> Now during those days, when the disciples were increasing in number, the Hellenists complained against the Hebrews because their widows were being neglected in the daily table service.[11] And the twelve called together the whole community of the disciples and said, "It is not right that we should neglect the word of God in order to wait on tables. Therefore, friends, select from among yourselves seven men of good standing, full of the Spirit and of wisdom, whom we may appoint to this task, while we, for our part, will devote ourselves to prayer and to serving the word."

This text, like the Acts 2 text, has been variously interpreted. Conservative scholars who affirm the historicity of the Lukan community of goods interpret this food fight as the beginning of its breakdown. Communal sharing just does not work, they conclude, because some people cannot appreciate what they have been given.[12] For their part, redaction critics, who assume that the community of goods never really happened, suggest that Luke's storytelling in Acts 6 masks more significant divisions in the Jerusalem community. A disagreement among women simply would not have engaged the attention of the entire group and caused this sort of reorganization. Luke, they suggest, employed this relatively trivial disagreement as a smoke screen to cover up the real issues that divided Hebrews and Hellenists.[13]

While the redaction critics' suspicions must be taken seriously, they nonetheless fail to account for the significance of gender roles in this culture. In the ancient world, men operated in the public sphere (which included the realms of religious and political authority) and women operated in the private sphere of home and family. Since writing itself was part of the public sphere, women rarely appeared in the literature from this period unless they were exceptional or had become problems for men.[14] That being the case, Luke would hardly have made up this conflict to cover up a deeper one; this *was* the problem! Moreover, Luke would have been disinclined to detract from his positive portrayal of the community unless an actual issue lay behind this food fight among women.

How then shall we understand the events recounted in Acts 6:1–4? First, we must clarify the scene that Luke delineates in verse 1. Because most translators of Acts do not envision daily common meals eaten together in extended households, they often translate the Greek word *diakonia* as "distribution of food" (NRSV, RSV, NIV, NAB), thereby creating a picture of destitute, solitary widows receiving handouts each day. But *diakonia*, when used in the context of tables (see v. 2), always refers to table service.[15] What Luke is describing here, then, are common meals served on tables at which people sit and eat together. Somehow Hellenist women were being overlooked or neglected in this service.

This neglect had become a seriously divisive matter, for two reasons. First, the meal constituted the very heart of the community's life. With its sacred and ritual overtones and its joyful spirituality, it was the one time of day when all believers could worship and share their lives together. Second, the meal placed women at the center of communal life. It was women's work to prepare food, serve the meal, and clean up afterward—in the private sphere, yes, but now in a public sphere as well.[16] In other words, in Acts 6 we see the women's sphere enlarging to embrace nonrelatives as well as to bring worship of the risen Jesus into the warmth of communal fellowship. Or to put it differently, the public sphere of worship, traditionally performed in the temple (where women could not go beyond the Women's Court), was now moving into the private sphere of the household.

Given what we have already noted about this new fictive kin-group—that "there was not a needy person among them," a characterization we must assume applied even to widows—it makes more sense to see these women in Acts 6:1 as participating in the honorable female role of *serving* meals, rather than *being served*, as most interpretations of 6:1 imagine.[17] Perhaps the Aramaic-speaking Hebrew women were Galilean disciples of Jesus, who now may have been claiming more honor because of their past experiences with Jesus. The Hellenist women, who would have moved to Jerusalem from other parts of the Mediterranean world (and who likely would have only spoken Greek), may have felt sidelined because of the language barrier and because the Hebrew women were choosing the more honorable meal-related tasks. In any case, the kin-group tension was profound enough that the apostles themselves "called together the whole community of the disciples" and suggested a solution (v. 2). They would continue with their ministry of the word, while others would be appointed to supervise the ministry of the table. The larger community was pleased by this solution and chose seven Hellenist men (as their names reveal in v. 5) for this service.

Why choose men for this supervisory role, if indeed table service was women's work? There are two possible explanations. First, this may be Luke's way of suggesting the need for gender role reversals within the community. It is more likely, however, that since the supervisory role was in the public sphere, it was culturally expedient to choose men for this role. That two of these men immediately go out and adopt a preaching ministry similar to the Galilean apostles suggests that the actual meal organization continued to be overseen by women.

Essenes and Agape Meals

In addition to these extended scriptural treatments of early Church table fellowship, two other streams of evidence confirm the Jerusalem community's practice of daily commensality in the context of a shared economic life. The first stream flows from what we know about the Jewish ascetic community known as the Essenes. The Essenes also lived in fictive kin-groups and ate daily sacramental meals together. According to both Josephus and Philo, there were at least four thousand celibate male Essenes scattered throughout Palestine,[18] and archaeological excavations have demonstrated the likelihood of an Essene community living in the same part of Jerusalem as the traditional site of the Upper Room, that is, where many in the Jesus community may have lived.[19]

In fact, recent research by Brian Capper outlines the social impact of these small groups of communal Essenes living in villages throughout Judea. "Only *three* thousand celibate males," he says, "would have been enough to provide a fully viable group of fifteen celibate Essene males in each village and town."[20] Josephus also reports that there was an order of married Essenes (no doubt more common than the celibates) who likely were connected to the male communities.[21] Essenes saw themselves under a "new covenant," just as the early Christian believers did, characterized by a communal lifestyle of the righteous poor. Philo's description of their shared life makes it clear that there were day-laborers and artisans, not landed peasants or the elite, organizing a lifestyle that enabled them to survive in a subsistence economy that was heavily taxed and exploited by the wealthy elite.[22] It also enabled them to help other destitute people. Josephus reports that the male Essenes often adopted children, no doubt of the many who were abandoned because families could not support them.[23] In addition, the *Damascus Document* explains the way of life of the marrying Essenes. Communal life in their local villages centered on a "community house" that cared for those who had fallen through the kinship safety net.[24] These sources, coupled with clues in the Dead Sea Scrolls, make it clear that Essene social practices would have been obvious models for early Church organization.[25]

A second stream of evidence flows from the Christian *agape* meal tradition, a tradition that spread far beyond Jerusalem and lasted in the Church for hundreds of years. These "love feasts," which appear in a number of New Testament texts (e.g., Jude 12; John 13:1; and 2 Thess 3:6–11) as well as in the *Didache*, the letters of Ignatius, and other early Church writings, followed Greco-Roman and Jewish meal customs of the time.[26] According to general custom, these ritual meals began with bread-breaking and prayer to the deity in whose honor the meal was being conducted; then, after the main course, participants mixed drinks and poured out libations to this same god.[27] For Christians specifically, this practice entailed recognizing the risen Christ through the broken bread at the beginning of the meal and the cup of wine at the end—and ideally by the equal inclusion of Jew and Gentile, slave and free, male and female. For those who subsisted on these daily meals, Jesus literally became the bread of life to them. They gained strength to work another day, to survive the next plague, to witness to other slaves or beggars that this bread of life was for them as well. Thus, the Church grew, not just by prayer but also by chicken soup.

The Supper of the Lord in Contemporary Context

Although North American Christians now live far removed from the agrarian, precapitalist society of the early Church, our meals continue to reveal deep symbolic significance. Rarely do we eat with people who are not like us; most of us solemnly swallow our bread and wine on Sunday mornings, then quickly retreat to our homes for Sunday dinners with family and friends who inhabit our own social classes. If Paul were here today, would he find us eating the *Lord's* Supper, or our *own*? Are we, in fact, eating and drinking judgment against ourselves?

Moreover, our stripped-down Lord's Supper fractures the original, close connection of the ritual's sacramental aspects to the work of food preparation. We would be remiss to ignore the gender significance of this disconnection. Many North American Christians attend churches in which men serve the bread and wine from an altar while women prepare the Sunday potluck in the fellowship hall. An *agape* meal that integrates both of these elements of the Christian life would serve to remind us that women and their work are at the heart of the most sacred ritual of the Christian Church.

Might there be a way, even today, to bring together the Eucharist of the sanctuary with the Sunday potluck or, better yet, with the Wednesday soup kitchen? Here Protestant and Orthodox Christians would be well served to consider the witness of the Catholic Worker movement. Inspired by Dorothy Day's vision of Jesus' commitment to the poor, many Catholic Worker houses in this country can be found in low-income, often multiracial areas of cities, where workers live with and share meals with transient, transitional guests. The rationale for this sort of work is simple, straightforward, and biblically based: "Jesus is in the poor," says Jeremy Wind, a worker in the Houston, Texas, Casa Juan Diego Catholic Worker house. He continues: "When we serve and live with the poor, we are doing it for Jesus"—a theological claim rooted in

Jesus' parable of the Sheep and the Goats in Matt 25. Accordingly, this parable is often read in the worship liturgy at Casa Juan Diego.[28]

Another such house can be found in East Oakland, California, an area teeming with immigrants from Mexico and Central and South America. Begun in 1986 to provide sanctuary for refugees fleeing the violence in El Salvador and Guatemala, the house now serves as a community center and transitional shelter that welcomes its Latino guests for up to two months as they seek jobs and permanent housing. Each weekday, staff members and guests take turns preparing and serving a communal dinner. Both staff and guests share responsibility for cleaning and maintaining the household. In this way the guests, especially women who are used to serving others, come to see that there are no superior or inferior roles. Rather, everyone operates on an equal level.[29]

Although Catholic Worker programs and personnel vary from city to city, their houses invariably reflect the spirituality of eating together. For instance, the sixteen or so people who live in the Denver, Colorado, Catholic Worker house share a common meal together every evening.[30] Houston's Casa Juan Diego Catholic Worker house is quite a bit larger, with space for fifty men and forty women and children, but it too serves common meals once a day, with mass once a week. Of course, in light of the New Testament reflections above, the true supper of the Lord may actually be occurring each evening as all eat together around one table.

Table fellowship of this type is not limited to Catholic Workers. The Witmer Heights Mennonite Church, located in Lancaster County, Pennsylvania, likewise ministers through meals, though in a slightly different way. Each Sunday a Witmer Heights member plans to be a host family, preparing a meal for unknown guests. When Miriam Eberly's Sunday comes around, she sets her table for twelve and tries her best to fill it. One Sunday her table companions included the visiting pastor and her husband; a Seventh-Day Adventist neighbor who does not attend church; a couple who recently experienced a house fire, and their daughter, who resides in a community for mentally-challenged adults; two government employees from Washington, D.C.; and the son of a local Presbyterian minister. Since Miriam needed one more person to fill the table, she invited a young, disabled African-American man from her church. "When we sat down to eat," she recalls, "I suddenly had a moment of anxiety about how this was going to work with such a mix of people. After the blessing and before food was passed, I asked each person to tell their name and tell us something interesting about themselves. That took care of everything! I no longer was concerned about keeping conversation going; it just happened."[31]

A few hundred miles to the south, in Harrisonburg, Virginia, an unusual restaurant called the Little Grill provides table fellowship in yet another way. A collectively owned business that focuses on healthful cuisine, the Little Grill closes each Monday in order to prepare and serve free meals to anyone who wants to come. Diners are invited to come early to help prepare the food, or to stay late to clean up. The mix of people at the tables often includes a wide variety of people, from those lacking basic necessities to ordinary working people to college students and professors. Jason Wagner, one of the collective's members, delights in the variety of people who come, as well as the abundance of food that seems to appear. From gardens, from unsolicited contributions, from leftovers, and from shopping with a mere thirty dollars, participants create a wonderful meal for fifty people.[32]

Ron Copeland and his wife originally owned the Little Grill, but they have now sold it to people who work there. Although a practicing collective for some years, since June 2004 it has been organized legally as a worker-owned collective. According to Copeland, his vision for the Little Grill is rooted in his "understanding of the Way as articulated by Jesus." Writes Copeland, "I see Christ renouncing the ideas of exclusive ownership and collecting material wealth for one's own self. In fact, the early church, as described in the book of Acts, held all possessions in common and had no destitute people among them."[33] In view of expanding its table ministry beyond the table itself, the collective is now renovating a nearby building (to be called Our Community Place) that will host events aimed at attracting people from different classes and arenas of life.[34]

One final example of a shared, worshipful life across economic and racial divides is the Open Door Community in Atlanta. Begun by two Presbyterian couples and influenced by the Catholic Worker model, members of the Open Door Community currently share living quarters in an old apartment building in what used to be a rough urban neighborhood. Through their common life and work, the Open Door Community endeavors to "perform the Scriptures" in a contemporary urban context, seeking to incarnate the biblical text in much the way vocalists sing musical scores. In this respect, the Open Door Community serves nearly 100,000 meals per year to Atlanta's homeless community. More than simply providing food, however, the Open Door Community offers a variety of compassionate, humanizing services: showers, changes of clothing, telephone access, mail delivery to people without mailing addresses, and restroom facilities. Recognizing that homelessness is not only a personal issue but also a political one, the community also engages in various forms of public advocacy work.[35]

While drawing on the Catholic Worker model, the Open Door Community departs from that model in its efforts to train committed Christian leaders from the people who come to them and who are then supported by the community. This practice has not only fostered shared leadership across lines of race and class, but it also has enabled the core community to fully integrate worship into its common life.[36] This core community worships together regularly, twice a week at lunchtime and at each evening meal. On Sunday, community members celebrate the Lord's Supper around a table in the center of their circle.[37] In all these ways, this contemporary equivalent to an ancient house church meets Paul's stipulations for eating the Lord's Supper: gathering together across race and class, with everyone being fully and equally fed.

To be sure, even the Open Door Community does not constitute an exact parallel to early Christian house churches. Nevertheless, the meal traditions of the early Jesus movement, the Apostle Paul's censure of mealtime divisions and factions, and the powerful example of creative, committed communities like Open Door should challenge us to consider the racial and economic divisions that so casually and maliciously structure our lives. Similarly, they should help us see the Lord's Supper as more than a device to nurture one's "vertical" relationship with God. Luke's gospel tells us that the disciples who met the risen Jesus on the road to Emmaus did not recognize him until they broke bread together (Luke 24:30–31). We too may not recognize Jesus until we break bread with those with whom he most closely identifies, those our society has deemed to be of least value.

Notes

1. Acts 2:46 and 6:1 describe communal meals as a daily occurrence, while 1 Thess 4:12 and 2 Thess 3:10 imply that all workers in the Christian community are, or should be, fed regularly so that none are in want. First Corinthians 11 clarifies the embedded nature of the bread and wine rituals in a full meal.

2. For long workday of slaves and the lower classes, see James S. Jeffers, *The Greco-Roman World of the New Testament: Exploring the Background of Early Christianity* (Downers Grove, Ill.: InterVarsity Press, 1999), 61. Many wealthy people did not work for a living. Inherited wealth, property rentals, and money lent at high interest protected the rich from labor. Alison Burford, *Craftsmen in Greek and Roman Society* (London: Thames & London, 1972), 29; and Peter Lampe, "The Corinthian Eucharistic Dinner Party: Exegesis of a Cultural Context (1 Cor. 11:17–34)," *Affirmation* 4 (Fall 1991): 1–15.

3. Jerome Carcopino, *Daily Life in Ancient Rome: The People and the City at the Height of the Empire* (trans. E. O. Lorimer; New Haven, Conn.: Yale University Press, 1940), 23; and Bruce W. Frier, *Landlords and Tenants in Imperial Rome* (Princeton, N.J.: Princeton University Press, 1980), 15, 28.

4. See, for example, Phil 2:25–27 and 2 Cor 1:8; 12:5–10.

5. Paul's subsequent use of body imagery in 1 Cor 12 to discuss spiritual gifts in the *koinonia* confirms the bodily unity Paul is expecting among believers.

6. See, for example, Hans Conzelmann, *Acts of the Apostles* (Philadelphia: Fortress, 1987); Ernst Haenchen, *The Acts of the Apostles: A Commentary* (Philadelphia: Westminster, 1971); and Luke Johnson, *The Acts of the Apostles* (Sacra Pagina 5; Collegeville, Minn.: Michael Glazier, 1992).

7. See, for example, Luke Johnson, *Sharing Possessions: Mandate and Symbol of Faith* (Philadelphia: Fortress, 1981).

8. See, for example, Richard Belward Rackham, *The Acts of the Apostles: An Exposition* (1901; repr., Grand Rapids: Baker, 1964); and G. T. Stokes, *The Acts of the Apostles* (Expositor's Bible; New York: A. C. Armstrong & Son, 1903).

9. Mark McVann, "Family Centeredness," in *Biblical Social Values and Their Meaning: A Handbook* (ed. John J. Pilch and Bruce J. Malina; Peabody, Mass.: Hendrickson, 1993), 70–72; and Paul J. Achtemeier,

Joel B. Green, and Marianne Meye Thompson, *Introducing the New Testament: Its Literature and Theology* (Grand Rapids: Eerdmans, 2001), 47–48.

10. Julian Pitt-Rivers, "Pseudo-Kinship," in *International Encyclopedia of the Social Sciences* (ed. D. L. Sills; New York: Macmillan, 1986), 8:408.

11. I have substituted the words "table service" in verse 1 for the NRSV's "distribution of food," a substitution I will explain more fully below.

12. See, for example, Stokes, *Acts of the Apostles*, 203.

13. See the sources mentioned in n. 6, especially Haenchen, *Acts of the Apostles*, 260–62.

14. Elisabeth Schüssler Fiorenza, *In Memory of Her* (New York: Crossroad, 1983), 44; and S. Safrai, "Home and Family," in *The Jewish People in the First Century: Historical Geography, Political History, Social, Cultural, and Religious Life and Institutions* (ed. S. Safrai and M. Stern; Philadelphia: Fortress, 1976), 1:728–93.

15. John N. Collins, *Diakonia: Re-interpreting the Ancient Sources* (New York: Oxford University Press, 1990).

16. Tal Ilan, *Jewish Women in Greco-Roman Palestine* (Peabody, Mass.: Hendrickson, 1996), 195; and Jill Dubisch, "Culture Enters through the Kitchen: Women, Food, and Social Boundaries in Rural Greece," in *Gender and Power in Rural Greece* (ed. Jill Dubisch; Princeton, N.J.: Princeton University Press, 1986), 195–214.

17. Turid Karlsen Seim even suggests the probability of an established order of widows in Acts 6:1. See *The Double Message: Patterns of Gender in Luke and Acts* (Nashville: Abingdon, 1994), 241.

18. Josephus, *Jewish War* II.viii.3–4; Philo, *Hypothetica* 11.1.

19. Rainier Riesner, "The Essene Quarter of Jerusalem," in *Jesus and the Dead Sea Scrolls* (ed. James Charlesworth; New York: Doubleday, 1992), 209 n. 99.

20. Brian J. Capper, "The Church as the New Covenant of Effective Economics: The Social Origins of Mutually Supportive Christian Community," *International Journal for the Study of the Christian Church* 2 (2002): 86–87.

21. Josephus, *Jewish War* II.viii.13.160–61.

22. Philo, *Apology* 11.10–11.

23. Josephus, *Jewish War* II.viii.2.120.

24. *Damascus Rule* (CD) VI.19.

25. H. J. Klauck, "Gutergemeinschaft in der klassischen Antike, in Qumran und im Neuen Testament," *Revue de Qumran* 11 (1982): 47–79; and Brian Capper, "The Palestinian Context of Community of Goods," in *The Book of Acts in Its Palestinian Setting* (ed. Richard Bauckham; Grand Rapids: Eerdmans, 1995), 323–56.

26. See Bo Reicke, *Diakonie, Festfreude und Zelos in Verbindung mit der Altchristlichen Agapenfeier* (Uppsala Universitets Arsskrift 5; Uppsala: A.-B. Lundequistska Bokhandeln, 1951).

27. Lampe, "Corinthian Eucharistic Dinner Party," 2–3.

28. Jeremy Wind, phone conversation with author, October 28, 2003.

29. Melody Cline, phone conversation with author, October 22, 2003.

30. Sue Gomez, e-mail message to author, October 20, 2003.

31. Miriam Eberly, e-mail message to author, October 20, 2003.

32. Jason Wagner, interview by author, October 31, 2003.

33. Ron Copeland, "Why I Think the Little Grill Collective Will Work," *Our Community Place* 9 (Summer 2002): 24.

34. "OCP Building Renovations," *Our Community Place* 9 (Summer 2002): 4.

35. For a more comprehensive description of Open Door, see http://www.opendoorcommunity.org.

36. Hannah Loring-Davis, phone conversation with author, October 28, 2003.

37. Footwashing is also considered a sacrament and is practiced regularly. See Murphy Davis, "Liturgy and Life, Sacrament and Struggle," in *A Work of Hospitality: The Open Door Reader, 1982–2002* (ed. Peter R. Gathje; Atlanta: Open Door Community, 2002), 205–11.

16

Sabbath-Keeping

CHRISTIAN SABBATH-KEEPING AND THE DESIRE FOR JUSTICE

— *L. Roger Owens* —

Although many can remember a time when stores stayed closed on Sundays, only a few vestiges remain in the United States of the culturally and governmentally imposed observance of the "Lord's Day." This means, among other things, that American Christians can no longer count on governmental regulations or social pressure to help them stay out of liquor stores and malls on Sunday. Now, for better or worse, we are left to our own devices.[1]

Perhaps that is why Sabbath-keeping is making a comeback. We have been free long enough from legalistic restraints and puritanical laws that we are awakening to our need for a break from work, some rest, and a little refreshment. The monotony and stress of our lives cry out to be broken, it seems, by family picnics in the park. Indeed, now that the Sabbath has been divested of its puritanical constraints and connotations, Sabbath-keeping appeals all the more to people whose work and family lives render them frazzled. In the midst of life's rat races, the Sabbath offers itself as an oasis, a needed respite that helps us regroup in time to face Monday's inevitable return.

Unfortunately, much recent writing on Sabbath-keeping stresses the inward, "spiritual" nature of this practice and its beneficial effects on overworked lives. It paints Sabbath-keeping primarily as a balm for the soul-hurts we receive as we relentlessly pursue our desires. In that regard, much of this writing misses the role that Christian Sabbath-keeping plays in God's salvation history: rescuing God's people, body and soul, from "the present evil age" (Gal 1:4). And because these considerations of the Sabbath have been largely severed from the story of God's mighty acts, they ultimately fail to show how Sabbath-keeping can actually reshape our mundane desires.

In this essay I explore how Sabbath-keeping widely construed as a "spiritual" practice unwittingly colludes with an American capitalist economy that seeks to construct our bodies as consumptive entities. Only when Sabbath-keeping is recovered as a counter pedagogy of desire can it play its proper role as a Christian practice that frees our souls and our bodies from the evil age of consumption (and, correspondingly, teaches us to desire justice and peace). Only when we have recovered Sabbath-keeping as a Christian practice integrally related to God's rescue from the powers of sin and death can Sabbath rest become true rest, for when we desire rightly, we rest not in the kingdom of this world but in the kingdom of God.

The Present Evil Age

As is clear from his opening address to the Galatians, Paul preaches a cosmic gospel: "Grace to you and peace from God our Father and the Lord Jesus Christ, *who gave himself for our sins to set us free from the present evil age*, according to the will of our God and Father, to whom be the glory forever and ever" (Gal 1:3–5). Paul preaches an apocalyptic gospel, a clash of ages, and the rescue of those in Christ from the present evil age. It is a gospel that bespeaks our deliverance from the powers that oppress, divide, control, and enslave. In that sense and more, it is a gospel of freedom, both freedom *from* the tyrannical powers of the present evil age and freedom *for* faithful living in the new age inaugurated by the death and resurrection of Jesus Christ. Paul does not want to save our souls. Rather, he wants us "to present [our] bodies as a living sacrifice, holy and acceptable to God" (Rom 12:1). That is, he wants to show us how we have been rescued for a life lived in imitation of Christ.

At least two characteristics of the present evil age deserve our attention, for we will soon see how capitalism exploits these very characteristics and, correspondingly, how Sabbath-keeping can serve as a beacon of freedom and rest. The first characteristic is *social division*, which is the present-age characteristic that Paul addresses most fully in his letter to the Galatians. Human beings, Paul recognizes, are addicted to division. That 50 percent of marriages in the United States end in divorce (as many in the Church as outside the Church) indicates that this addiction to division remains powerful in contemporary American life. The frequently cited but no less significant fact that the Sunday worship hour is the most segregated hour of the week offers further confirmation of this sinful reality.[2] The kinds of divisions that we know all too well—race, class, sex, and age—are, in Paul's view, directly opposed to the gospel of Jesus Christ.

Paul tells the Galatians (and us) that Christ died in order to rescue us from these very divisions, to create a new humanity in which there is "no longer Jew or Greek, . . . no longer slave or free, . . . no longer male and female" (Gal 3:28). Far from being an argument against earning salvation through works, Galatians is a polemical treatise that exposes how certain ways of life and habits of living, because they foster division and dissension, are directly opposed to the new humanity created by Christ. Near the end of his letter, Paul reminds his readers that "the whole law is summed up in a single commandment, 'You shall love your neighbor as yourself'" (Gal 5:14). Then, instead of leaving the Galatians to their own devices to interpret those words, he continues with one last warning against the consuming powers of division: "If, however, you bite and devour one another, take care that you are not consumed by one another" (Gal 5:15).

The second characteristic of the present evil age, Paul suggests, is *insatiable, misdirected desire.* "Live by the Spirit," he writes, "and do not gratify the desires of the flesh" (Gal 5:16). According to Paul, the desires of the flesh are seductive and always turn us away from the appropriate love of God and neighbor. Furthermore, they almost always team up with our tendency toward division, so that misdirected desires destroy the type of human unity that witnesses to the age inaugurated by Christ.

Christians should not misunderstand Paul's language of "spirit" and "flesh" in Gal 5:16 to imply some kind of dualism, thus separating spirituality from our bodily lives.[3] To put matters simply, "flesh" does not mean "body" (and, correspondingly, to abandon the desires of the flesh is not to withdraw from bodily life). Rather, "flesh" refers to the whole way of human life under the condition of sin and enslaved to the present evil age.[4] When we see flesh in this way, we are enabled to recognize that the "desires of the flesh" are not necessarily carnal longings but the disposition of the entire human as bound in the present evil age. In sum, "desires of the flesh" represent the habitual disposition to place oneself in relationship to other people, things, and God in ways that disrupt the possibility of those relationships being characterized by love.

If it is true that the present evil age is characterized by human division and misdirected desire, then it is clear that the present age has our bodies in a kind of bondage. As we shall see, capitalism exploits these characteristics of the present evil age to increase the profit of a very few by enslaving the rest of us along with them.

Capitalism and the Present Evil Age

In order to see how capitalism exploits our divisions and insatiable desire, we must first ask the question: Where do we learn to desire what we desire? This is the very question that theologian Phil Kenneson asks readers to consider in his popular book, *Life on the Vine.* Where did we learn to desire certain things to eat? How did we learn what we should want to wear, or where should want to live? Surely these questions boast no simple answers, but Kenneson helps us see the most obvious ones. "The dominant culture . . . has an enormous power to form our desires and affections," writes Kenneson. "Many cultural practices instill in us the desires that direct and give meaning to our lives."[5] Or, to put it more crassly, we learn to desire certain things from watching television.

The market wants—*needs*, if it is to grow—to construct our bodies as consumptive entities. At this it has done a good job. In listening to discussions of economics it becomes clear that humans are not primarily men, women, children, parents, husbands, and wives. We are consumers. For the economy to get better, consumers need to buy more durable goods. To tell how the economy is doing one looks at the consumer price index. We even fight terrorism (or so we are told) by taking seriously our roles as consumers. In all of this, "the consumer" is ostensibly free, because "the consumer" can pick what "the consumer" wants from any number of items. In fact, the more choices "the consumer" has, the more freedom "the consumer" has. Because human beings are desiring beings (and because, as Christians know, we have a tendency to desire *wrongly*), the market and its advertising gurus can step into the vacuum and train our desires to want insatiably.

Capitalism, then, has a tremendous role in forming our characters by shaping our desires from a very early age. Political theologian Daniel Bell takes this notion even further by suggesting that capitalism's construction of desire is determinative of our humanity. "Capitalism's victory is not merely economic, but ontological," writes Bell. Capitalism "is best understood as an ensemble of technologies that disciplines the constitutive human power, desire."[6] Bell's analysis makes it clear that capitalism is not one among other relatively innocuous influences on our lives. It is a determinative and constitutive power—not unlike the biblical "powers and principalities"—that seeks to constitute our lives in terms of consumption.

Capitalism seeks to construct our desires. Moreover, in light of our earlier description of desire, capitalism seeks to make us want to put ourselves in certain relationships with other people, things, and God for the purpose of satisfying every felt desire. However, since capitalism also constructs those desires as *insatiable*, the very act of putting ourselves into these relationships is always a frenzied movement in and out of relationships with both people and things. And since these desires are so determinative of our humanity, capitalism has us in a kind of bondage. It creates and sustains us in a way of existing at odds with the things of God and those of God's kingdom.

Indeed, capitalism thrives on division and brokenness, capitalizing on social stratification to sell its products. One obvious way the market perpetuates social stratification is by engendering fear and making false promises—for instance, engendering the fear that one will fall out of style and promising a perverse sort of community among people who wear the same brand of clothing (even then the market suggests that everyone in this community all freely chose to shop at the Gap, hiding the fact, of course, that a great deal of the U.S. population cannot afford Gap clothing). As Kenneson writes: "One of the great ironies of consumerism is that it promotes itself as a means to exercise our personal freedom, when in fact it promotes the most insidious forms of homogeneity. We are led to think that we are incredibly free when *we* desire, but it turns out that we end up buying pretty much what everyone else does."[7] So in the end capitalism does produce a sort of solidarity: the solidarity of anxiety. It makes us afraid of being different from other people like us and afraid of being like other people different from us. Thus, it cements the very social division from which Paul said we have been rescued through the death and resurrection of Jesus Christ.

If this is true, then capitalism is a form of bondage. Specifically, it is bondage to the present evil age of misdirected desire and social division. What is worse, as "an ensemble of technologies" that directs our desires, capitalism shapes us and our wishes in perverse ways. Under capitalism's tutelage, we not only relate to others in ways characterized by division, we actually *want* to relate to them in that way. Similarly, we wish to relate to things in ways characterized not by godly use but by endless consumption. Perhaps most disturbing of all, we wish to relate to God in ways characterized not by worship but by utility.

Sabbath-Keeping as Collusion with the Market

Christianity, however, has its own "ensemble of technologies" to help us live lives the way they should be lived, and Sabbath-keeping is one of them. For many Christians, Sabbath-keeping is most immediately associated with ceasing from work and perhaps even from shopping. In these cases, Sabbath-keeping asks Christians to refrain from work one day each week and to step out of relationships determined by the market. This is a marvelous thing.

Unfortunately, much of the recent writing about the Sabbath has resurrected Sabbath-keeping as a practice promising a spiritual balm for our stressed, tired, and wounded lives. This way of keeping Sabbath, rather than challenging capitalism's technologies of desire, joins forces with it. In fact, it is much to the market's advantage for workers and consumers to get a little rest, especially if it is "spiritual" rest, for the market does not care how we *feel*, it just wants our bodies. So it will not object—in fact it will rejoice—if the consumer takes a day to rest and rejuvenate so that the market can have his or her body the rest of the week. In this respect, Sabbath-keeping has been reduced to one more expression of popular, marketable spirituality. The vast majority of spiritualities on the market today collude with capitalism; they are balms the market offers to help us ease our consciences about giving the market our bodies to do with them as it likes. This is not surprising. What is sad and surprising is that so robust and ancient a practice as Sabbath-keeping can be co-opted to help the market keep our lives in bondage.

Donna Schaper's recent book on Sabbath-keeping offers one poignant example of how the Sabbath can be subtly co-opted by the market. Schaper, a contemporary spiritual writer and retreat leader, begins her book on Sabbath-keeping by affirming, "Sabbath is setting aside time for God."[8] But, she suggests, this time for God need not occur on a particular day. Rather, it is a way of looking at all of time spiritually. Seeing all time spiritually is a way of seeing the sacredness of everything at its depth. "Sacred time," Schaper writes, "is not when we get our work done but all the time, which we keep and honor by sabbath living."[9] According to Schaper, whether we are working or playing, we can be keeping Sabbath, because Sabbath-keeping is more an attitude than an activity.

Predictably, Schaper's form of Sabbath-keeping does not call into question how people live in a society enslaved by consumption. In fact, Schaper draws a sharp distinction between "altaring" (the making sacred of any moment) and "altering" (changing one's behavior). According to Schaper, Sabbath-keeping is altaring, which she does by giving her time to God no matter what she is doing with her body. "I 'altar time,'" she writes, "when I carry my basket and my mug even though I am still on the road, still drinking coffee brewed by a multinational corporation. Instead of altering, I altar. I give the time to God."[10] In sum, Schaper has a relationship with things—for instance, with multinational-corporation-brewed coffee—that is not called into question by the way she keeps Sabbath. And thus her desires, what she does with her body, are not redirected. She does not alter. So even though the rest of Schaper's book argues that Sabbath-keeping is a form of countercultural resistance (because when God is with us, life is different, she says), Schaper's way of Sabbath-keeping is both safe for her and profitable for the market. She and Starbucks both win! Divorced from the gospel of Jesus Christ, and disconnected from a kingdom in which enjoying a beverage at the expense of poor coffee farmers actually matters, this Sabbath is a puny replica of the real thing.

Leonard Sweet, another popular Christian writer, offers his readers a Sabbath that is no more robust or life altering than Schaper's. In a recent book delineating the "leadership arts" necessary for postmodernity, Sweet suggests that contemporary church leaders who wish to survive must learn to take breaks.[11] In a chapter entitled "Taking Shore Leave: Sabbath Rest," Sweet writes, "A 24-7-365 lifestyle mandates the art of 24-7-365 sabbaticals," thus dismissing out of hand the possibility that the command to keep the Sabbath might require church leaders to learn how to live 24-6-365 lives.[12] Sweet's notion of Sabbath does not challenge how people work at all; it only offers brief respites "to take mental, spiritual, and emotional shore leaves."[13] For

Sweet, then, Sabbath is only about recharging batteries so that church workers can set sail again with as much vigor as before. There is no sense that keeping Sabbath entails the radical alteration of life's rhythms and activities so that Christians might see more clearly and live more perfectly the freedom they have been granted in Christ. "I declared a sabbatical," Sweet writes, "to loiter through the stacks of a Barnes and Noble while sipping a latte and picking up books and magazines at random."[14] If Schaper and Sweet are right, Sabbath-keeping is good for the soul and very good for the economy—especially, it seems, for coffee corporations.

In these two examples we see quite clearly what I alleged at the beginning of this essay. The authors do not hide the fact that their way of keeping Sabbath gives rest to the wearied soul and inner rejuvenation to the spirit—even while it gives the body to the market to be constructed as a desiring, consumptive entity. Both Schaper and Sweet offer examples of Sabbath-keeping that in no way question whether they should be buying coffee, drinking coffee brewed by multinational corporations, or shopping in elite, chain bookstores in the course of keeping their Sabbaths.

All this should lead us to ponder. Is the world so thoroughly "24-7-365" that there is no hope for rescuing our bodies from capitalism's technologies of desire? Are we fated to spend our sabbaticals sipping lattes and shopping for books? Or does Christianity have its own repertoire of practices that might provide an alternative to capitalism, practices that might shape lives to look more like Jesus' life and reflect more fully the kingdom he proclaimed?

Sabbath-Keeping as a School for Discipleship

We turn, finally, to a consideration of these important questions. What might a robustly Christian Sabbath look like, a Sunday celebration fully informed by the history of God's saving activities—from creation (when God rested on the seventh day) to the resurrection (the day after the Jewish Sabbath when God raised Jesus from the dead) to the Sunday of Pentecost (when God poured out his spirit in an act that defied the divisions of the present evil age)? What might a Sabbath look like that contributes to our rescue from the market's grip, that redirects our desires so that we learn to relate ourselves to others and to God in ways that help us become profoundly human?

Pope John Paul II is instructive in these matters, both theologically and practically. In *Dies Domini: On Keeping the Lord's Day Holy*, an apostolic letter written in 1998, John Paul II begins by reminding his readers that Sunday "is Easter which returns week by week, celebrating Christ's victory over sin and death, the fulfillment in him of the first creation and the dawn of 'the new creation.'"[15] In other words, John Paul II does not suggest that the keeping of Sunday is a spiritual practice independent of the tradition of the Church and the history of God's saving activity. Rather, he shows how the observance of the Lord's Day is a practice wholly informed by God's activity to rescue us by raising Jesus from the dead. From there, the pope offers more specific guidance on how this theological understanding should incarnate itself in the lives of Christians.

Sunday Worship and Eucharistic Celebration

Above all else, the pope's apostolic letter makes clear that the celebration of the Lord's Day is primarily the celebration of Jesus' resurrection from the dead. This stands in sharp contrast to Schaper, who offers the following observation:

> Some of us love both sports and Sunday morning worship. Thus we wonder whether our bodily desire for sports conflicts with our spiritual desire for worship in community. . . . Sports can bring the kind of self-forgetfulness that religion used to bring—a sense of belonging that is ritual in nature. They are more like religious experiences than not. Sabbath is what some people get from soccer and what others get from Sunday services.[16]

To Schaper's observation, Pope John Paul II offers an emphatic "No!" The bodily practicing of sports cannot replace the bodily participation in the new life of Christ offered to us in the sacrament of Holy Communion. "Sunday," John Paul II writes, "is the day above all other days which summons Christians to remember the salvation which was given to them in baptism and which made them new in Christ."[17] Sunday observance is not about self-forgetfulness. It is about training our minds to remember who we are in Christ.

All the things we do in Sunday worship—recite, pray, kneel, sing, eat, laugh, listen, give—constitute bodily activities that help transform our lives in accordance with the new life we have in Christ. They are activities that we do together and that train us to see through the anxiety of difference promulgated by the market that at once breeds an insidious homogeneity and an even more insidious xenophobia. The eucharistic table in particular is where the new humanity comes together to celebrate and live the common life that has been given in Christ.

In this sense Sunday is not only the weekly Easter, it is also the weekly Pentecost, the celebration of the Spirit's making one those in Christ Jesus. The market needs to divide us so it can carry out its technologies of desire on discrete populations, teaching them to desire to be with one another and to despise those who are different. In other words, the market needs us to remain unreconciled—Jews and Greeks, slave and free, male and female—for the unreconciled inevitably buy more. Against this stands the training we receive in the Sunday celebration, which teaches us to live in God's new kingdom where these divisions do not exist. Here we are trained to desire to be with others, to be reconciled even with our enemies (despite the fact that having enemies is good for the economy). Moreover, Sunday worship and eucharistic celebration set the direction for all of our Sunday activities. Pope John Paul II underscores this fact, observing that worship "commits each of Christ's disciples to shape the other moments of the day—those outside the liturgical context: family life, social relationships, moments of relaxation—in such a way that the peace and joy of the Risen Lord will emerge in the ordinary events of life" (52).

Producing and Shopping

If our earlier analysis of the close connection between capitalism and the present evil age is correct, then calling upon us to cease all activities that entail participation in the market (i.e., producing and shopping) is one way the Sabbath offers rest and release from bondage. If this is done well, it will not merely charge us up for another week of production and consumption. Rather, it will begin to teach us that we are not so dependent as we thought on the money we make and the things we buy. Of course, such a suggestion will sound to some people like a reinstitution of Puritanism, but not to John Paul II. "The rest [from work] decreed in order to honor the day dedicated to God is not at all a burden imposed upon man," writes the pope, "but rather an aid to help him to recognize his life-giving and liberating dependence upon the Creator" (61). In the course of observing the Sabbath, our possessions will not possess us and we will walk more easily through the world, a little freer from the market's grasp.

To cease production and consumption on Sunday not only frees our own lives, it also gives us new vision to see the way the market leaves so many enslaved to it, raising coffee to sell in America for practically nothing or, where I live in North Carolina, harvesting cucumbers for the Mount Olive Pickle Company. We become more aware of these conditions and, unlike those who stared at the man with a withered hand (Luke 6:6–11), our hearts become soft. We begin to see with Jesus that it is better to give life than to kill on the Sabbath. Moreover, even as John Paul II insists that people have the right to work, he also reminds us that Sabbath rest from work and consumption gives us "a deep sense of solidarity with the hardship of countless men and women who, because of the lack of jobs, are forced to remain inactive on workdays as well" (66).

Works of Mercy and Charity

"Sunday should also give the faithful an opportunity to devote themselves to works of mercy, charity and apostolate," writes John Paul II. "To experience the joy of the Risen Lord deep within is to share fully the love which pulses in his heart: there is no joy without love!" (69). As we have seen, the day of rest is too often inwardly focused. Jesus, however, showed that the day of rest is a day to give and celebrate life. Creative Christian communities can surely think of ways to attend to the needs of others—needs often left unfilled by the market as we go on filling "needs" that are really only desires—in ways that are joyous and not laborious. In that respect, John Paul II calls the faithful to embrace the desire for solidarity with the poor, oppressed, overworked, lonely, and jobless by relating ourselves to them bodily and attending to their bodily needs. Sunday is a good day, arguably the *best* day, for corporal works of mercy.

Even more, the Sabbath is an alternative pedagogy of desire. The market constructs our desires in such a way that we long for more, better, and newer things, and correspondingly teaches us to overlook the old and the small. Performing corporal works of mercy on Sunday retrains our desire, teaching us to relate ourselves to others in life-giving ways by interrupting our relationships with our tide of possessions. Countering the notion of Sabbath as something inward, John Paul II rightly calls Sunday a "great school of charity, justice and peace" (73). In the course of attending to the Sabbath, "Christians should declare *by their actual behavior* that we cannot be happy 'on our own.' They look around to find people who may need their help" (72; emphasis added).

Conclusion

"Sunday is a true school, an enduring program of Church pedagogy—an irreplaceable pedagogy, especially with social conditions now marked more and more by fragmentation and cultural pluralism which constantly test the faithfulness of individual Christians to the practical demands of their faith" (83). So writes John Paul II in the conclusion of his apostolic letter. The pope thus recognizes what this essay has argued: In the face of capitalism's construction of our desire, Christians desperately need an alternative school, desperately need practices that can help redirect our desires away from division and toward the love of God and neighbor. As we have seen, contemporary North American Sabbath-keeping has, in all too many respects, been co-opted by the market. Rather than challenging the market, it has afforded capitalism's technologies of desire free rein to construct and determine our bodies. In the process of becoming "spiritual," Sabbath-keeping has handed our bodies over to the market.

But that way of keeping the Sabbath forgets the cosmic scope of our salvation. It forgets that Christ has rescued us from the present evil age, from the age characterized by misdirected desire and stratifying social divisions. The Christian Sabbath is about remembering this great salvation and living lives shaped by it. Sabbath robustly kept—by Sunday worship and eucharistic celebration, by ceasing production and consumption, and by performing corporal works of mercy—retrains our lives and schools our desire so that we place our-selves in authentically loving relationships with others. It teaches us that the best picture of right desire is concrete acts of love, mercy, and peace.

Notes

1. For a history of this change, see Alexis McCrossen, *Holy Day, Holiday: The American Sunday* (Ithaca, N.Y: Cornell University Press, 2000).

2. For a sociological and theological exploration of this, see Michael O. Emerson and Christian Smith, *Divided by Faith: Evangelical Religion and the Problem of Race in America* (New York: Oxford University Press, 2000).

3. As Richard B. Hays writes, commenting on Gal 5:16–26, "The whole passage will be badly mis-interpreted if one understands Spirit and Flesh as anthropological terms for a perennial duality within the individual human personality." See *The New Interpreter's Bible* (ed. Leander E. Keck et al.; Nashville: Abingdon, 2000), 11:326.

4. In this regard, liberation theologian Gustavo Gutiérrez argues that "the entire human being is flesh when looked at from a particular point of view." See Gutiérrez, *We Drink from Our Own Wells* (Maryknoll, N.Y.: Orbis, 1983), 56.

5. Phil D. Kenneson, *Life on the Vine: Cultivating the Fruit of the Spirit in Christian Community* (Downers Grove, Ill.: InterVarsity Press, 1999), 65.

6. Daniel M. Bell, *Liberation Theology after the End of History: The Refusal to Cease Suffering* (London: Routledge, 2001), 3.

7. Kenneson, *Life on the Vine*, 70.

8. Donna Schaper, *Sabbath Keeping* (Boston: Cowley Publications, 1999), 1.

9. Ibid., 8.

10. Ibid., 10.

11. Leonard Sweet, *Aqua Church: Essential Leadership Arts for Piloting Your Church in Today's Fluid Culture* (Loveland, Colo.: Group Publishing, 1999).

12. Ibid., 153.

13. Ibid., 157.

14. Ibid., 155.

15. Pope John Paul II, *Dies Domini: On Keeping the Lord's Day Holy* (Boston: Pauline Books, 1998), 1.

16. Schaper, *Sabbath Keeping*, 76.

17. Pope John Paul II, *Dies Domini*, 25. Because the remaining quotations in this essay are from this apostolic letter, subsequent citations are given by page number in parentheses.

Service

CHALLENGING LEGACIES OF ECONOMIC OPPRESSION AND RELIGIOUS NEGLECT: HABITAT FOR HUMANITY IN THE MISSISSIPPI DELTA

— *William R. Sutton* —

In the summer of 2001, *Fortune* magazine introduced a cover article entitled "God and Business" with the assertion, "Bringing spirituality into the workplace violates the old idea that faith and fortune don't mix. But a groundswell of believers is breaching the last taboo in corporate America." Most of the article's examples emphasized spiritual empowerment for business success or relief from stress. One example, however, featured Julius Walls, an African-American Catholic and CEO of Greyston Bakery, a gourmet firm that trumpets the slogan, "Sinful desserts that support saintly causes." Combining "business savvy, Christian faith, and a strong ethic of personal responsibility," Walls has built a company reaching four million dollars in annual sales. To staff the business, Walls adopted an open hiring policy, attracting a number of drug addicts and prison parolees who are given time to prove themselves, are provided with social services, and are paid livable wages. Each day's work begins with a period of silent reflection. Walls describes himself as "spiritual" and his operation as "enlightened capitalism." By including the spiritual in the creation of an economic system, Greyston Bakery has achieved the apparent novelty of acknowledging the presence of God in both the workplace and the wage-profit calculus.[1]

Spirituality—most broadly understood as experiences of the direct, immediate presence of God or the supernatural—promises power, meaningfulness,

212

comfort, and a sense of the right ordering of the universe. Although Christian spirituality has usually been understood through experiences of conversion, sanctification, and various devotional exercises, Julius Walls embodies an equally vital spirituality—that of economic righteousness, where God's presence is evident not only in meaningful, appropriate *attitudes* toward labor but also in the socioeconomic *arrangements* resulting from the profits that labor generates. In the Christian tradition, the spirituality of economic righteousness has typically started with the notion that work is a sacred undertaking. Labor granted opportunities for reflecting God's glory, for pursuing various callings through which God provided individual identity and status, and for relieving the poor through proper stewardship. But the sacramental nature of work transcended the individual; it also posited that God created work as a means for the provision for all humankind, and no one was to monopolize God's gifts to the detriment of others.[2] In a summary statement of this perspective, the renowned eighteenth-century American theologian Jonathan Edwards condemned those who were willing to "grind the faces of the poor and screw their neighbor" to gain "filthy lucre."[3]

At certain junctures in American history, "grinding the face of the poor" (Isa 3:15) was a common idiom implying God's judgment on practices of economic unrighteousness.[4] Those who invoked that phrase could hardly be accused of theological novelty. Traditional Christian economic morality prohibited those in power from taking advantage of the vulnerable as strongly as it required those in subordinate positions to work diligently. The accumulation of wealth as a means to achieve security or access privilege (and thereby to make trust in God unnecessary) was condemned as mammon worship and considered spiritually fatal. Beyond the spiritual mistake of trusting mammon, exploitation and oppression were forbidden, with both practices warranting the judgment of God (as explained, for instance, in Mal 3:5; Jas 5:1–6; and Luke 16:19–31). In place of endless striving and competition for advantage, the spirituality of traditional economic morality espoused an allegiance to the kingdom of God in which all relationships, including work-related ones, were submitted to the rule of Jesus the Messiah.[5]

While this combination of the spiritual with the systemic now seems odd on the American landscape, this has not always been the case; in fact, theologies of economic righteousness have undergirded American reform movements such as trade unionism, abolitionism, populism, Christian socialism, and social gospel progressivism.[6] Kingdom economics required allegiance to the Golden Rule ("Do unto others . . ."), recognition of the godly paradox of the inversion of power ("The last shall be first . . ."), discipline against holding onto resentment ("Forgive us our debts as we forgive . . ."), and acknowledgment of God's preferential option for the poor ("The meek shall inherit the earth"). Weaving these spiritual values into work and socioeconomic

dynamics, in turn, often served the evangelistic purpose of introducing individuals into experiences of Christian salvation. And this peculiarly holistic
expression of the gospel is still manifestly evident not just in the New York
bakeries of Julius Walls but, as we shall see, also in the work of Habitat for
Humanity in the Mississippi Delta. There, traditionally disadvantaged but
spiritually faithful African-Americans have united with socially conscious
but often existentially hungry volunteers to reverse some of the historical
effects of economic unrighteousness as well as to incarnate the gospel realities of love, repentance, forgiveness, and community in life-changing encounters with Jesus.[7]

From Producerism to Capitalism through the Nineteenth Century

Before the Industrial Revolution, the spirituality of work permeated the awareness of American farmers, artisans, and merchants through a precapitalist
ethic known as the small producer tradition, or *producerism*. The small producer tradition valued productive labor for the manual skill, mental intelligence, and general industry necessary for success. Furthermore, the tradition
recognized mutual obligations between producers and consumers (the "just
price" notion), between employers and employees (jointly negotiated wage
scales and work rules), and between individuals and the community (consideration of the common good over individual advancement). The hierarchy
of decision making and profit distribution favored masters, to be sure, but
workers were protected by the widely accepted premise that they deserved a
livable share of the profits their labor generated. Finally, producerism
encouraged individual initiative and forbade labor relationships rooted in
dependency (e.g., slavery). This producerist system, in other words, was as
much moral as economic.[8]

This traditional system, grounded in the medieval Christian ethic of work,
was one of the "unnatural restrictions" challenged by eighteenth-century
liberalism and its economic system of capitalism. Capitalism increased production, expanded markets, augmented entrepreneurial and investment
opportunities, and, in general, generated economic growth by rewarding
ambitious risk taking and increasingly depersonalized and rationalized work
arrangements. Thus, capitalism also subordinated traditional ethics to considerations of profit maximization, destroyed the mutuality of interests between
masters and workers, and privileged the nonproductive phenomenon of
investment over the productive reality of labor. According to economic liberals, these challenges to moral order were of little consequence. If all pursued
self-interest, the liberals optimistically predicted, a balance would be achieved

and, in any case, the discovery of "natural" laws such as supply and demand made medieval moral proscriptions obsolete, or even somehow wrong.[9]

The advantages of capitalism have been well documented, as have the downsides.[10] In fact, much of modern American history can be interpreted as attempts to make capitalism moral. In recent years, however, Americans have tended to assume that capitalism was either inherently moral (because it was opposed to communism) or have accepted the assertion that economics exists outside the moral realm. But economic immorality, including that attached to capitalism and other liberal arrangements, has been the source of all too many sordid tales in American history: land stolen from Indians; national wealth tied directly to slave labor; nondependent skilled artisans reduced to poverty-stricken, dependent machine tenders in factories; postslavery freedmen and poor whites subjected to sharecropping; immigrants factored into business equations as commodified sources of exploitable, controllable labor; and modern-day overseas sweatshops created by multinational corporations. The list is altogether too extensive.

Historically, mainstream American culture made its peace with this process of divorcing morality (and spirituality) from economics for legitimate as well as less than commendable reasons. As noted earlier, Enlightenment liberalism provided the initial "scientific" proof for this separation. At much the same time, religious disestablishment ended the European practice of granting tax revenues to state-supported religion, inadvertently paving the way for ethical accommodation to the exigencies of needing contributions from the well off. (John Wesley proved prophetic in this regard when he warned against Methodist financial decisions that "will make Rich Men necessary to us," thereby making congregations "dependent on them, yea, and governed by them. And then farewell to the Methodist Discipline, if not Doctrine, too."[11]) In addition, racism justified slavery and subsequent oppression of African-Americans, social Darwinism dismissed the victims of economic unrighteousness as unfit, Andrew Carnegie's pernicious perversion of stewardship known as the "gospel of wealth" excused immorally gained wealth if a small part was distributed to good causes, and finally the insidious democratization of aristocratic vices at the heart of consumer culture served to numb people to considerations of the effects of economics freed from moral or spiritual constraints. A faithful remnant contested these cultural developments, to be sure, but those who resisted this discontinuity most vigorously (e.g., the Old Order Amish) have been largely marginalized. Equally important, even within this contrarian tradition an unfortunate bifurcation gradually evolved, as some preferred a spiritual emphasis that encouraged individual salvation, while others stressed systemic change apart from spirituality to bring about "the kingdom of God on earth."

Distortions of Economic Righteousness in
Twentieth-Century America

By the early twentieth century, an increasingly fragmented American religious culture had witnessed tremendous conflict related to the spirituality of work and concerns for economic justice, with the gradual evolution of three distinctive paths as a result. Reflecting confidence in equality of opportunity and enjoying the fruits of the corporate, depersonalized form of capitalism, the broad center of Gilded Age America embraced an emasculated spirituality of sentimentality and respectability, the watered-down social Darwinism of Henry Ward Beecher, and the warped stewardship model of Carnegie's gospel of wealth.[12] Those seeking to hold on to the old Puritan and primitive Methodist traditions maintained the preferential option for the poor and plain, but neglected concerns for systemic change in exchange for concentrating on spiritual consolation and celebrating the inversion of power that located God's presence with the lowly. For Holiness and Pentecostal believers in particular, persons whose spiritual intensity was based as much on their sense of God's presence in breaking down class and racial barriers as it was on the ecstatic evidences of the Holy Spirit, righteous systems would only follow spiritual renewal.[13] Finally, the progressive advocates of social Christianity— the biracial populists, social gospellers, and Christian socialists—gradually abandoned spirituality altogether in their preoccupation with imagining utopian systemic changes to be carried out by a biblically informed but not necessarily spiritually empowered federal government.[14] For social gospel advocates such as Samuel "Golden Rule" Jones, sin was rooted entirely in the environment, making traditional spiritual practices utterly superfluous. If the system were set right, they claimed, spiritual perfection would follow.[15]

With its economic growth rooted in capitalist economics, most twentieth-century Americans were happy to conflate material prosperity and middle-class respectability with the blessings of an America-first God. George Kennan spoke bluntly for the foreign policy makers in the 1950s: "We have about 50% of the world's wealth, but only 6.3% of its population. In this situation we cannot fail to be the object of envy and resentment. Our real task in the coming period is to devise a pattern of relationships which will permit us to maintain this position of disparity. . . . We should cease to talk about vague and . . . unreal objectives such as human rights, the raising of living standards and democratization. . . . The less we are hampered by idealistic slogans the better."[16] This marginalization of concern for economic justice was only magnified by the atheistic communist usurpation of socioeconomic utopianism, creating in the minds of most Americans an insufficiently explanatory but widely held "communism versus capitalism" dualism. *Christianity Today* reflected popular opinion by claiming divine sanction for

U.S. corporate capitalism in the Cold War because American capitalists encouraged global mission work and adhered to Christianity, with no concern whatsoever as to what effect their capitalist practices might have on non-Americans.[17] According to the post–World War II liberal consensus, any critique of capitalism and the materialism it encouraged was considered evidence of communist subversion, just as any overt expression of spirituality came to be seen as pathological. Eventually challenging this unholy alliance of meaning-of-life materialism and self-congratulatory capitalism was the civil rights movement, where the reconnecting of spiritual power and social justice proved culture changing. But even in this process, the FBI consistently and falsely denigrated the movement as communist, and Martin Luther King Jr. himself felt constrained to mute his growing conviction that racial justice could not be reached without also reforming American capitalism.

Now in the twenty-first century, however, we find ourselves in strange and potentially exciting times. Postmodernism has reopened the doors to a smorgasbord of spiritualities, the more exotic the tastier. At the same time, the surrender of communism to global capitalism has freed Americans to consider economic justice without fear of being demonized and, as long as people resist the temptation of replacing the bogeyman of communism with the terrorist axis of evil, possibilities to take seriously the demands of economic righteousness could present themselves. Many such options exist,[18] with a significant example being the Habitat for Humanity affiliates in the Mississippi Delta. The Habitat vision is to unite volunteers with the underprivileged in helping the poor help themselves by constructing affordable housing in Jesus' name. The explicit expectation is that the work will have spiritual dimensions—that is, in the acts of building houses, sharing resources, and encouraging nondependency and dignity, God's presence in Christian community will be manifestly present.[19] In both a personal and a social sense, salvation through Jesus has become a reality for many of the participants in this dynamic of social justice.

The Legacy of Economic Unrighteousness in the Mississippi Delta

The poverty faced by African-Americans in the Delta (the northwestern corner of Mississippi) is the direct result of recognizable historical factors. The Delta county of Coahoma is a fertile area bordering on the Mississippi River and is justly famous for being both the heartland of cotton production and the birthplace of the blues. But Coahoma County has a less savory history as well, marked by violence and socioeconomic injustice. The entire county was part of the larger defrauding of the Chickasaw Indians under the Treaty of Dancing Rabbit Creek in 1832, and a few years later it became a way station for the Cherokee on the infamous Trail of Tears. A new type of exploitation—

African-American slavery—was not far behind. The Civil War in the Delta was largely devoid of the usually celebrated heroics of wartime. Instead, residents reported sporadic depredations perpetrated by both sides as they skirmished over control of the Mississippi River.

The majority of Coahoma County inhabitants received their freedom in 1863 with the Emancipation Proclamation, but the promise of the Reconstruction period for Coahoma freedmen was quickly challenged. Thaddeus Stevens's imaginative program for confiscation of Confederate plantations for redistribution in forty-acre plots to the freedmen died in Congress[20] and, in Coahoma County, a violent political coup led by planter-politician (and later governor) James Alcorn ended biracial Republican rule in 1875, driving well-respected black sheriff John Brown from the county in the process. The coup inspired resistance from Brown's black supporters, who were promptly scattered by a better-armed group of whites. The instructions of one of the white leaders proved most prophetic: "Do not shoot these negroes, boys, we need cotton pickers."[21]

Thus, sharecropping came to the Delta and cotton production soared. White planters owned the land and provided seed and technology, while blacks provided the skill and the hard labor. But the planters controlled the books and made the laws, and croppers became increasingly oppressed—educationally deprived, socially discriminated against, politically disenfranchised, and economically exploited, with no protection from local, state, or federal governments.[22] Horrific examples of injustice abounded over the decades. Around the turn of the twentieth century, outside Duncan in Coahoma County, black farmers formed a community they called New Africa. In 1908, one of these farmers, Samuel Kendrick, welcomed to his farm a sharecropping family from a nearby white-owned plantation. For his effrontery, Kendrick was nearly murdered by a white mob.[23] In 1919, black sharecroppers in Phillips County, Arkansas (across the river from Coahoma County), tired of being cheated out of their profits, formed the Progressive Farmers and Household Union of America. In response, gangs of local whites erupted in a weeklong reign of terror that killed as many as two hundred innocent blacks, but in the subsequent investigation only blacks were arrested and convicted.[24] In the 1930s, the sharecropping family of Euless Carter raised a crop of cotton guaranteed to make them a yearly profit. When Carter's father settled accounts, however, the white plantation owner informed him that he had just broken even for the year. And when the astonished sharecropper protested this blatant transgression, the white man explained that he needed the extra money to send his own son to college.[25] Such were the economic realities of race in the Delta.

To combat these systemic injustices, African-Americans in Coahoma County developed a number of coping strategies. Some, like Samuel Kendrick, overcame the system to become at least qualifiedly independent. Others, especially after the Great Migration began, left for opportunities in the North. For those who stayed, blues artists such as Robert Johnson and Muddy Waters provided musical outlets for their sufferings.[26] Of course, many African-Americans found spiritual consolation and inspiration in the plethora of rural churches that still dot the Delta landscape. There generations of believers internalized the messages of the gospel: the centrality of Jesus' forgiveness of their sins and the sins of others, the availability of the Holy Spirit for both healing and power, and the inevitable correction of systemic injustice in the coming kingdom. Both an immediate empowerment for the present and an ultimate expectation for the future, the African-American experience of worshiping Jesus exploded in the uninhibited ecstasy of authentic spirituality.

This unique expression of the gospel fueled the civil rights movement that swept Mississippi in the 1960s and forever changed Coahoma County.[27] But other changes were equally significant to Coahoma sharecroppers. In 1944, the first mechanical cotton picker was unveiled on the Hopson plantation outside Clarksdale, and pesticides were also eventually introduced, thereby drastically reducing the need for black field labor. By the 1980s, however, the residual effects of oppression and exploitation were still manifest in the poverty-stricken rural communities of Coahoma County. Paying rent to live in shacks, subsisting on occasional employment and welfare, suffering from generations of educational neglect, and still denied opportunities for meaningful, remunerative work, black folks living in hamlets such as Coahoma, Farrell, and Sherard in Coahoma County looked for ways to help themselves. Not a few of them found it in Habitat for Humanity.

Spirituality and Economic Righteousness Reconnected: Habitat for Humanity in the Delta

The Habitat for Humanity story actually began in 1976 when Millard Fuller, as part of his own deliverance from a mammon-induced malaise, decided to devote his life to helping the poor help themselves in gaining access to decent, affordable housing. Fuller, in turn, had drawn his inspiration from Koinonia Farm in Americus, Georgia, and its founder, Clarence Jordan, who had bravely articulated and lived a Christ-centered vision of racial reconciliation before the civil rights revolution.[28] A few years after its founding, the Habitat program came to the Delta, where it encountered ameliorative efforts already underway in the all-black village of Coahoma (350 people with an average annual income of less than $4,000), led by Mayor Washington L. Jones, a Rust College graduate and Korean War veteran. One of the areas of need was the plethora of substandard housing—shacks, really—that characterized Coahoma. In 1984, Mayor Jones connected with Ray Hunt, a white, low-income properties attorney who had been active in creating Habitat affiliates throughout the

South. Together, and with the backing of many Coahoma residents and other long-term volunteers such as Karen Kennedy, they began to build in 1986. In little more than ten years, Habitat had built nearly fifty homes in Coahoma, and all those who could meet the requirements (a hundred dollars a month for mortgage payments and five hundred "sweat equity" hours of construction help) now have homes.[29]

The Habitat experience in Coahoma County, however, ran deeper than home construction alone. From the beginning, Habitat was a partnership between the community's residents and the volunteers who began to trickle into the Delta. This expression of the Golden Rule, moreover, was self-consciously grounded in an ecumenical, biracial Christian spirituality, combining a sacramental understanding of manual labor and an awareness of God's desire to correct systemic injustices with a foundation of love and forgiveness extended unconditionally to the largely white visitors by the local black believers who had little reason to trust or forgive any whites. For the volunteers, this powerful incarnation of racial reconciliation was initially exemplified by indigenous black leaders such as Mayor Jones of Coahoma and Dorothy Jenkins of Farrell, local whites such as Pat Davis and Millsaps and Elaine Dye of Clarksdale, and newcomers such as Hunt and Kennedy in Coahoma.[30]

In 1990, Habitat leaders envisioned Collegiate Challenge, an invitation to college students to spend their spring breaks working for local affiliates. They chose as their initial experiment Coahoma, and they asked Joe Carton, with his wife Eileen, to serve as volunteer coordinator, spiritual director, and construction supervisor. The Cartons had met at Little Portion Hermitage in Arkansas, the monastic motherhouse of the Brothers and Sisters of Charity, a Franciscan order founded by John Michael Talbot.[31] There they discerned a strong leading to work with the poor in Jesus' name, and they approached Habitat officials in Americus, Georgia, who suggested Coahoma as an appropriate site. For a yearly salary of five thousand dollars and family health benefits, and with a strong vision for unifying labor, justice, and love in action, the Cartons came to Coahoma. The system they gradually developed overcame numerous difficulties, and by 1995 they were handling nearly a thousand volunteers a year in as many as thirty-five weeklong blocks.[32] During these weeks, privileged college students saw firsthand the devastating results of economic exploitation. But because they also heard, from Carton and the local residents, a powerful spiritual message that challenged the soulless materialism and apathy of mainstream culture, they encountered not despair but genuine hope.[33] Equally significantly, the Coahoma pilot program proved immensely successful, and was therefore soon exported throughout the country and worldwide. Now thousands of students each year spend their spring breaks meeting the Collegiate Challenge that started in the rural backwaters of the Delta.

By the mid-1990s, homebuilding in Coahoma was nearing completion. But other county affiliates inspired by Coahoma—Clarksdale, Farrell-Sherard, Jonestown—were just beginning their Habitat work, even as volunteers and residents in Coahoma moved on to other community improvement efforts. One such effort was the construction of a hydroponics greenhouse to grow tomatoes for markets in Memphis, a thriving concern bringing employment and training to long-unemployed residents until an ice storm destroyed the building. Another ongoing project was the Coahoma city library, founded by longtime volunteer Olive Jean Bailey and still run by local residents. In both of these cases, the self-improvement work initiated by Habitat inspired economic and educational opportunities long denied to blacks in the Delta, with great promise for the future. Moreover, families in Habitat homes report a new sense of pride contributing to improved academic performance among their children.

Meanwhile, the other Habitat affiliates continued to thrive. Perhaps the most impressive work was being carried on in Farrell-Sherard under the leadership of Dorothy Jenkins, former sharecropper, factory worker, and upholsterer, and the members of her board. Less populated than even Coahoma, Farrell and Sherard were four miles apart just east of the Mississippi River and so small that Habitat International initially refused to grant them affiliate status. But Jenkins persevered, and the Farrell-Sherard affiliate began building in 1990 on land donated by the Sherards and the Crumptons, longtime local planter families. Like Joe Carton, but from an Afro-Baptist rather than a Catholic tradition, Dorothy Jenkins, in worship, prayer, and dedication, reflected the powerful presence of God in the Habitat work.[34]

Two of the volunteers eternally touched by Jenkins's witness were David and Abby Warfel. Initially introduced to the Farrell-Sherard experience as part of a Collegiate Challenge group from Urbana, Illinois, the newly married Warfels came to the Delta in 1997 as volunteer coordinators and construction supervisors for Farrell-Sherard, Jonestown, and Clarksdale. During the two years they spent in Coahoma County, they helped the affiliates stabilize volunteer efforts, created standardized blueprints for the houses, and continued what had become the evangelistic mission of Coahoma County Habitat, particularly through the potluck dinner/worship services put on for the volunteers by community members. These potlucks filled a powerful sacramental role for volunteers in the Habitat program. Indeed, breaking bread with community members became a sacred moment for these privileged but often alienated young people, hungry for an authentic experience of meaningful community. Exposure to Afro-Baptist worship was also a revelation, especially as the volunteers witnessed a spirituality that fully expected God's love and deliverance from material as well as psychic need. Underpinning it all, however, was the sense of acceptance and love at the potlucks. As Dorothy Jenkins put it, "Y'all are family we just didn't know we had." For their part, the Warfels maintained close ties to their Urbana roots, both in their home church and their former high school, resulting in a pipeline of young volunteers to Coahoma County that persists to this day.[35]

In March 2000, Dorothy Jenkins received word from the national Habitat office that Farrell-Sherard had won the coveted Jimmy Carter Award for the most productive affiliate per capita in the country. For an affiliate once considered impractical, this was another manifestation of the last becoming first. Incredibly, Farrell-Sherard won the award for the next two years as well, and their string was only broken in 2003 by nearby Jonestown. But the affiliate was hardly bereft of continued blessings. In 2002, a retired New York City Port Authority policeman and survivor of the September 11 attacks, Carl Fuller, came to Farrell-Sherard as a full-time, permanent building supervisor, thereby solidifying the ongoing work.

So the Habitat work goes on, even as the poverty and racial polarization persists. In a vivid expression of the potential for Christian believers from disparate socioeconomic backgrounds and theological traditions to work together, the Coahoma County affiliates and their volunteer cadres have combined the financial resources of wealthy white planters with the spiritual wisdom of materially and educationally deprived black folks—a most unusual partnership, given Delta history—to incarnate an otherwise unimaginable Jesus-centered community. Visitors with any knowledge of that history often come prepared to be met with despair and hostility, yet the experience of privileged volunteers working with Habitat in the Delta has been overwhelmingly positive. For their part, many local residents express great enthusiasm for Habitat's program, attributing its empowering effects to the work of God's spirit. Without over-romanticizing the dynamic, the obvious connections between this brand of spirituality and economic justice have introduced some unchurched to the life-changing power of the gospel, even as Delta believers have received material blessing and Christian volunteers have discovered further inspiration, sometimes even callings. In the process, the words of Isaiah have been brought to life: "If you do away with the yoke of oppression . . . and satisfy the needs of the oppressed, then your light will rise in the darkness, and your night will become like the noonday" (58:9–10 NIV).

Notes

    1. Marc Gunther, "God and Business," *Fortune*, July 9, 2001, 59, 72–73.
    2. *The National Trades' Union*, January 17, 1835; January 24, 1835. John E. Crowley, *This Sheba, Self: The Conceptualization of Economic Life in Eighteenth-Century America* (Baltimore: Johns Hopkins University Press, 1974), 17–20, 51–62.

3. Quoted in Gerald R. McDermott, *One Holy and Happy Society: The Public Theology of Jonathan Edwards* (University Park, Pa.: Pennsylvania State University Press, 1992), 123.

4. Baltimore coopers protesting unilateral wage cuts contrary to mutually negotiated agreements introduced their strike manifesto with Isa 3:15. *Baltimore Republican and Commercial Advertiser*, January 13, 15, 1834.

5. William R. Sutton, *Journeymen for Jesus: Evangelical Artisans Confront Capitalism in Jacksonian Baltimore* (University Park, Pa.: Pennsylvania State University Press, 1998), 5–7, 31–35, 61–65, 313–14.

6. Perry Bush, "What Would History Look Like if 'Peace and Justice' Mattered?" *Fides et Historia* 34 (2002): 49–56; Peter Linebaugh, "Jubilating; or How the Atlantic Working Class Used the Biblical Jubilee against Capitalism, with Some Success," *Radical History Review* 50 (1991): 143–80.

7. See Stephen E. Berk, *A Time to Heal: John Perkins, Community Development, and Racial Reconciliation* (Grand Rapids: Baker, 1997).

8. Ronald Schultz, "The Small Producer Tradition and the Moral Origins of Artisan Radicalism in Philadelphia, 1720–1810," *Past and Present* 127 (1990): 84–108; Christopher Lasch, *The True and Only Heaven: Progress and Its Critics* (New York: W. W. Norton & Co., 1991), 201–24, 265–70, 302–3, 486.

9. Stephen Innes, *Creating the Commonwealth: The Economic Culture of Puritan New England* (New York: W. W. Norton & Co., 1995), 25–30, 172.

10. See, for example, Paul Gilje, ed., *Wages of Independence: Capitalism in the Early American Republic* (Madison, Wis.: Madison House, 1997).

11. John Wesley, quoted in *Methodist Protestant*, April 25, 1825, 376.

12. George M. Marsden, *Understanding Fundamentalism and Evangelicalism* (Grand Rapids: Eerdmans, 1991), 9–61.

13. Richard C. Goode, "The Godly Insurrection in Limestone County: Social Gospel, Socialism, and Southern Culture in the Late Nineteenth Century," *Religion and American Culture* 3 (1993): 162. See also Randall Stephens, "The Convergence of Populism, Religion, and the Holiness-Pentecostal Movements: A Review of the Historical Literature," *Fides et Historia* 32 (2000): 51–64.

14. See Robert Handy, *The Social Gospel in America, 1870–1920* (New York: Oxford University Press, 1966).

15. See Marnie Jones, *Holy Toledo: Religion and Politics in the Life of "Golden Rule" Jones* (Lexington: University of Kentucky Press, 1998).

16. George Kennan, "Document PPS23, 24th February 1948," in *Foreign Relations of the United States 1948*, vol. 1, no. 2 (Washington, D.C., 1976).

17. David E. Settje, "'Sinister' Communists and Vietnam Quarrels: The *Christian Century* and *Christianity Today* Respond to the Cold and Vietnam Wars," *Fides et Historia* 32 (2000): 86.

18. See, for instance, Francis Wilkinson, "Divine Right," *American Prospect*, August 28, 2003 (available online at http://www.prospect.org/webfeatures/2003/08/wilkinson-f-08-28.html), which describes the unusual attempt by Alabama Governor Bob Riley and the Beeson Divinity School to address inequities in the Alabama tax code from a scriptural perspective.

19. Millard Fuller, *Love in the Mortar Joints: The Story of Habitat for Humanity* (Chicago: Association Press, 1980), 85–99.

20. Eric Foner, *Reconstruction: America's Unfinished Revolution, 1863–1877* (New York: Harper & Row, 1988), 235–37.

21. Testimony from George F. Maynard, "Friars Point Riot," vertical file, Clarksdale (Miss.) Public Library; Nicholas Lemann, *The Promised Land: The Great Black Migration and How It Changed America* (New York: Vintage Books, 1991), 13–14; Foner, *Reconstruction*, 560.

22. See Neil R. McMillen, *Dark Journey: Black Mississippians in the Age of Jim Crow* (Urbana: University of Illinois Press, 1989); and James C. Cobb, *The Most Southern Place on Earth: The Mississippi Delta and the Roots of Southern Identity* (New York: Oxford University Press, 1992).

23. Charles E. Cobb Jr., "Traveling the Blues Highway," *National Geographic*, April 1999, 46.

24. Arthur I. Waskow, *From Race Riot to Sit-In, 1919 and the 1960s* (Garden City N.Y.: Anchor Books, 1967), 121–42. See also John M. Barry, *Rising Tide: The Great Mississippi Flood of 1927 and How It Changed America* (New York: Simon & Schuster, 1997).

25. Lemann, *Promised Land*, 54.

26. The legend of Robert Johnson allegedly selling his soul to the devil in return for the ability to play better blues than any competitor positions him in Coahoma County, and Muddy Waters was born on the Stovall plantation in the northern part of the county. Bill Wyman with Richard Havers, *Bill Wyman's Blues Odyssey: A Journey to Music's Heart and Soul* (London: D. K. Publishers, 2001), 214–17, 272–73, 80–84; see also Robert Palmer, *Deep Blues* (New York: Viking Press, 1981).

27. See Charles Marsh, *God's Long Summer: Stories of Faith and Civil Rights* (Princeton, N.J.: Princeton University Press, 1997); John Dittmer, *Local People: The Struggle for Civil Rights in Mississippi* (Urbana: University of Illinois Press, 1994); and David L. Chappell, *A Stone of Hope: Prophetic Religion and the Death of Jim Crow* (Chapel Hill: University of North Carolina Press, 2004).

28. See Frye Gailliard, *If I Were a Carpenter: Twenty Years of Habitat for Humanity* (Winston-Salem, N.C.: J. F. Blair, 1996); and Tracy Elaine K'Meyer, *Interracialism and Christian Community in the Postwar South: The Story of Koinonia Farm* (Charlottesville: University of Virginia Press, 1997).

29. Olive Jean Bailey, *Coahoma, Mississippi: A Little Town with a Million Friends* (Minneapolis: Farrar & Associates, 2002), xii, 15–21.

30. For the compelling story of a similar biracial effort at reconciliation, see Chris P. Rice, *Grace Matters: A Memoir of Faith, Friendship, and Hope in the Heart of the South* (San Francisco: Jossey-Bass, 2003).

31. Talbot was a seminal figure in the development of Christian rock music during the years of the so-called Jesus Movement. Before his conversion, Talbot helped found Mason Profit, one of the original country-rock bands of the early 1970s.

32. Bailey, *Coahoma, Mississippi*, 32.

33. Lasch, *True and Only Heaven*, 390–93.

34. For a similar story of spiritual power, see Chana Kai Lee, *For Freedom's Sake: The Life of Fannie Lou Hamer* (Urbana: University of Illinois Press, 1999).

35. The terms of service for these thirteen volunteers have run from one to two years. The Urbana connection is only one of a number of volunteer groups dedicated to Farrell-Sherard. Volunteers from Minnesota, Ohio, and New England return every year, and one group, Kairos Carpenters from Indiana, built a Habitat-type house for Dorothy and Walter Jenkins, who by rules (as affiliate board members) were ineligible for the program. The leader, Paul Swenson, supervised the project—literally, from his deathbed, which was located on the front lawn. He died three weeks after its completion.

18

Education

CURA PERSONALIS:
THE MATRIX FOR SOCIAL JUSTICE IN
JESUIT SECONDARY EDUCATION

— Dominic P. Scibilia —
(with excursuses by Roberto Concepcion Jr.,
Michael Monteleone, Drew Sheeran, Robert Simone,
Stephen Spiewak, and Kapil Verma)

During a recent faculty retreat at St. Peter's Preparatory School, Father James Keenan read participants into one of Ignatius' days in Rome. Awaiting the start of a pilgrimage to Jerusalem, Jesuit founder Ignatius of Loyola and his companions found themselves participating in the social vision Jesus announced in Matt 25. Ignatius began his day with mass. On his way to mass, however, he stopped at places where his companions engaged in various forms of ministry to "the least" of their society. Stopping at a hospice, Ignatius found one of his friends offering consolation to persons close to death (including some awaiting execution), counseling them and their families about last things to put in order. At that same location he found a second companion instructing hospice employees on manifesting a spirit of generosity to their coworkers and patients. Even in the sixteenth century, justice in the workplace was a significant issue.[1]

On a typical day, Ignatius might follow a visit to a hospice with a time of preaching and prayer at a house of ministry for prostitutes, for instance, at Casa de Santa Marta. At this confraternity-sponsored Jesuit ministry, women forced into prostitution by economic necessity were enabled to imagine alternatives for themselves: lives of public service, entrance into a contemplative community, or, with confraternity help, the establishment of a modest dowry that would make marriage possible.[2] Upon leaving Casa de Santa Marta,

Ignatius might find his way to a *habitatunicula*, a collection of small shelters situated near a prison for the purpose of caring for sick prisoners. At shelters such as these, Ignatius and his Jesuit companions might share plans for helping debtors (the majority of prisoners there) secure low-interest or interest-free loans from a Franciscan bank.[3]

One last stop during these early mornings in Rome might be a school at which young men, both rich and poor, studied the classics in preparation for lives of public service. From their earliest days, Jesuit educators stressed *pietas*, an ethic of care wherein their students became persons with moral imaginations.[4] For these sixteenth-century Jesuit educators, learning was more than mere intellectual training. It was the formation of character able to see God in all things and able to respond to divine love with a passionate commitment to justice. It remains that way today.

Education for Justice, *Cura Personalis*, and Student Retreats

The second year of religious education at St. Peter's Preparatory School centers on two questions: Who is Jesus of Nazareth, and who do you (students) say that you are? At this Jesuit high school for boys, located in Jersey City, New Jersey, students and teachers not only read themselves via the gospels into the life and times of Jesus, they also read themselves into the times in which they live by way of various social-ethical resources. Sophomore year thus begins an immersion into the Jesuit mission, understood as faith doing justice.[5] As students move through their second, third, and fourth years at St. Peter's, they spend time in prayer, retreat, and study that further read them into the story of Jesus and contemporary social realities. The ultimate educational objective in all of this is to direct students to become men for and with others, men who conceive the act of loving God to be inclusive of loving those considered least in our world.

The grounding of St. Peter's educational mission is the praxis of *cura personalis*, an ethic of care for the whole person that enables students, teachers, administrators, and support staff to find God in all things. Even though one does not find the ethic of care for the whole person explicitly stated in early Jesuit educational directives, this particular ethic infuses Ignatius's *Spiritual Exercises*. The *Exercises*'s prayers, meditations, scriptural readings, and directions are, in their most fundamental sense, resources for one who accompanies another on a spiritual pilgrimage.[6] Indeed, the Jesuit idea of company is more akin to a traveling companion—being good company for another who seeks God—than it is to the idea of a military company. A proper Jesuit secondary education consists of the careful accompaniment of students as they discover who they are and what they have to give to the world wherein they find God in all things.

The praxis of *cura personalis* at St. Peter's involves various steps that assist students in making good on their promise (potential) as children of God. In keeping with the *Exercises*'s invitation to occasionally step away from daily life, a St. Peter's Prep student takes days of retreat at various points during his second, third, and fourth years. These retreats, informed by the *Exercises* and performed in order to heighten students' awareness of God's presence, prepare and dispose "the soul to rid itself of inordinate attachments" and, after their removal, assist participants in "seeking and finding the will of God in the disposition of our life for the salvation of our soul."[7] Campus ministers, a spiritual life committee, faculty members, and students work together to design retreats, operating from the perspective that both teachers and students are in positions to make determinative life choices. Students in particular are deemed to be on extended pilgrimages through which they discover who they are and what they have to offer the world.

Because the *cura personalis* centers on religious experience, retreat leaders (senior students, faculty, and alumni) endeavor to turn students' attention to their encounters with God. Retreatants travel together through the ebb and flow of desolation and consolation that are part and parcel of the high school years. In the course of their retreat days, students deliberate prayerfully on family, friendship, society, and school—the very environments and relationships that inform or deform their understandings of themselves, God, and others.

The goal, of course, is transformation. In Jesuit secondary education, that transformation (what the *Spiritual Exercises* call "conversion") happens in the convergence of seeking God in all things *and* intellectual formation, the anticipated yield of this union being a commitment to social justice. In that regard, it is significant to note that student spiritual retreats are not divorced from the school's classroom curriculum. Teachers at St. Peter's realize that as students advance intellectually through a rigorous academic program, there is something larger underway. Faculty members thus conceive of the intellectual life as graduating young men of faith with something beneficial to give to the world. In sum, the St. Peter's faculty is committed to the belief that knowledge *of* God and the world, as well as knowledge *about* God and the world, work together to transform our students' lives.

Whether the ethic of care is practiced on a retreat or during a course of study, students and teachers engage in a conversion experience. Knowledge changes us, and conversion is the result of both intellectual and moral inventory. An encounter with God's grace in the process of learning about the world's harsh realities creates a space for St. Peter's students to consider their vocations in light of Jesus' life, passion, and resurrection. Correspondingly, the opportunities afforded a given student to make good on his promise (despite his sins of commission or omission) help him to realize and pursue God's love and compassion. At St. Peter's, sophomore retreats and the junior-year Emmaus experience, in particular, help students attend to their life missions.

AN EXCURSUS: THE EMMAUS RETREAT (ROBERT SIMONE)

The Emmaus Retreat during the third year of studies is the definitive student-centered experience at St. Peter's. In the course of this three-day retreat, students and faculty learn about the histories that each brings to school. Much like Richard Rodriguez in his autobiography, *Hunger of Memory*, each participant carries secrets about the restlessness born of our economic, cultural, and religious homelands.[8] The retreat gave me not only an appreciation for my family life, but it also enabled me to grow in admiration for the courage with which my fellow students face life. How family and friends persevere in faith in the midst of social challenges!

Emmaus is an occasion to know the empathy that comes from self-examination. In that respect, it creates a kind of sacramental encounter with others. As participants we considered who we were before God and in relation to one another, and we thereby challenged the various social boundaries that our cultures have raised around young men. The retreat director and team leaders made spaces for us to speak honestly, pray earnestly, and examine our thoughts about God, our families, and our community. There was a liturgical rhythm to the three days, from the baptismal remembrance by the nearby lake to the eucharistic feast on the final evening. In the breaking of the bread, we shared more than our most personal feelings; we were enabled by the Eucharist to see God in each of our peers, whether their stories hailed from Italy, the Philippines, Puerto Rico, India, Pakistan, Nigeria, or Egypt.

In the course of the Emmaus Retreat, we were changed for the better. Like my companions, I discovered that I was not alone—the kind of alone that many young men often know. And it was in our sense of company that we gained insight into the social nature of human beings.

Cura Personalis and Christian Service

The Apostle Paul was "a man filled with the Spirit of Christ, who gave his life for the salvation of the world; the God who, by becoming man, became beyond all others a Man for others."[9] So wrote Pedro Arrupe, who served as superior general of the Society of Jesus during the Thirty-Second Congregation. Drawing upon the example of Jesus, the life of Paul, and the words of Pedro Arrupe, St. Peter's Prep seeks to foster a desire in its students to be men for and with others. This process of forming men who seek to do Christ's work happens most effectively at St. Peter's through a threefold process of doing Christian service. The first step in this process is an orientation to the spiritual center of the experience, the second step is service itself, and the final step is reflection on the service experience.

St. Peter's requires sixty hours of service during a student's junior year. The director of the program coordinates several options for service completion. For example, a student may participate in an immersion trip that takes place during the summer prior to the third academic year, in a local service venue affiliated with St. Peter's (e.g., the Higher Achievement Program, a summer school for urban youth), or in some independent nonprofit agency. Regardless of the setting, the parameters of the program require students to work directly with people who are poor.

Reflection, the evaluation component of a see-judge-act-evaluate pedagogy, is the most crucial element in the service experience. This element often takes place after the service experience has concluded, though depending upon the type of service being performed, it may occur during the actual work. For instance, during immersion trips, mentors conduct reflection each evening. If students select a local summer option, they attend a reflection group meeting at the end of their summer vacation. Those few students who elect to do service during the third academic year participate in a reflection class as part of their regular schedule.

Reflection entails journal writing, prayer, and group discussion. Service mentors provide writing prompts that invite students into reflection. For example, on the first day of service, students respond to relatively specific prompts such as this: "Describe your particular work requirements or the objective for your service time." By the third day, students are responding to larger, more significant issues, for example: "After working with a homeless person, what did you discover about her life story?" or "How does society respond to people with disabilities?" On the final day of an immersion trip, students might deliberate on how they fulfilled Jesus' command to feed the hungry or clothe the naked, or on Jesus' command to be compassionate as God is compassionate. Rituals sometimes enhance the reflection process; music, candles, and the creation of a sacred space for prayer establish the atmosphere wherein students can connect spirituality and service. Finally, prayer grounded in the *Spiritual Exercises* reminds companions in service that "love ought to manifest itself in deed rather than words. . . . That love consists in a mutual sharing of goods, for example, the lover gives and shares with the beloved what he possesses."[10]

AN EXCURSUS: YOUTH SERVICE OPPORTUNITY PROJECT
(ROBERTO CONCEPCION JR.)

I entered the Youth Service Opportunity Project (YSOP) during the summer between my second and third years at St. Peter's. As soon as we arrived at our base in New York City's East Village, we formed teams. My particular group made its way to the neighborhood north of Columbia University, where Annie, the minister and director of the soup kitchen at Broadway Presbyterian Church, gave us glimpses of what it is like to be homeless.

Annie, I soon discovered, sees her vocation as opening the eyes of people like me. My eyes were indeed opened as I learned that many of the people for whom we prepared lunch pick through garbage for plastic soda bottles to redeem for cash. As they rummage through curbside trash, pedestrians treat them with disdain, moving as far away from them as the sidewalk will allow. To better understand their experience, Annie sent us onto Broadway to pick through and collect garbage ourselves. Some passersby made every effort to distance themselves from us (there was the rare individual from the neighborhood who recognized Annie's ministry at work; one woman in particular thanked us for cleaning her streets). During and after lunch, we worked beside volunteers, people who devote large amounts of time to homeless families as they move in and out of complex situations. I was stunned to find that over time the volunteers had actually become friends with homeless people. Suddenly, homeless men and women became human to me.

On the second day of YSOP, I worked with volunteers at a clothing and furnishings warehouse in the Brooklyn Navy Yard. In the not-too-distant past, New York City police would burn all the contraband they confiscated during raids of illegal businesses. Recently, however, the coordinators of the warehouse, all people who were once homeless or substance abusers, negotiated with the city to put the confiscated material to better use. Volunteers coordinate the collection and organization of the resources, and social service agencies direct people in need to the center. The goal of the warehouse is straightforward: to provide people leaving homelessness with the items necessary for starting a home. I learned a great deal at the warehouse about the systemic nature of homelessness, what we would later call in our classroom studies "the cycle of poverty."

The next day I worked in a West Village Lutheran church's summer neighborhood ministry. This ministry is a cooperative venture between public and religious organizations that provides single working parents with day care and meals for their children during the summer months. There I met Mecca, a precocious three-year-old African-American girl. Mecca's smile was a gift. Despite the threat of rain, she insisted on going to the park to play on the swings and slide. As we moved from arts and crafts to play in the park to lunch at a nearby elementary school, I learned about her family, which lives on the edge of a neighborhood known as Hell's Kitchen. The camp volunteer helped us to hear Mecca's story beyond her engaging smile: the melancholy, the disappointment, the danger not from street gangs but from an economic system that defines wages with terms like "minimum" or "subsistence" rather than "living." I saw God in Mecca—God's image, creativity, and style—and through her I began to grasp God's preference for the poor.

But the human face of homelessness startled me most during an evening of socializing with men from Peter's Place, a drop-in center that helps men make the complicated transition from homelessness to having a home. We cooked a meal together, played board games, and talked about world events, sports, and philosophy. We met two men there who had completed doctoral studies at Harvard, and others who were someone's grandfather or brother. Two men in particular, Eugene and Raymond, moved me as no other homeless men had. We spent the evening playing Casino and sharing our life stories. People like Annie, Mecca, Eugene, and Raymond helped me to discover delight in faith doing justice.

The Vocation of Social Justice

A calling is not attending to an external voice. It is discerning God with us. If God is in all things, then an intellectual life that contemplates divine love awakens one's awareness of God within even oneself. Vocation, therefore, is discerning who one is and what grace one brings to the world as a cocreator with God.

Even as Jesus' ministry of intellectual, spiritual, and moral instruction heightened his disciples' consciousness of the divine response to human need—and made them mindful of the poor—so too the pedagogy of *cura personalis* prompts students to develop intellectual virtues that help them see "the burgeoning isolation of rural and urban poor in the midst of an affluent civilization."[11] The Jesuit ethic of care regards the life of the mind as public in orientation. We see this ethic in Central American Jesuits such as Ignacio Ellacuria and Jon Sobrino, who committed their apostolic resources to educating persons who had no access to higher learning. Similarly, intellectual life at St. Peter's reflects a Jesuit spirituality of learning that does more than ensure our students a foothold in the economic order. At St. Peter's, secondary education is the practice of a social and political spirituality in which students' hearts and minds become nonconformed to conventional social wisdom. In other words, we endeavor to create a space wherein God's grace can transform them in surprising ways. This grace, we trust, will make them agents for social change, contributing to a world in which all people have life abundant rather than life subsistent.

Cura personalis values a democratic pedagogy because such pedagogy encourages students to discover their own voices and become participants in learning. Third- and fourth-year courses such as "Social Justice" and "Church in the Modern World" are configured around tables for the benefit of student conversations. In the course of these conversations, students make connections between faith, justice, religion, and society, frequently making references to their summer immersion experiences. Together students and teachers assess economic issues such as property structures, urban gentrification, and environmental racism. Textual companions such as Vatican II Pastoral Constitutions *Dignitatis Humanae* and *Gaudium et spes*, Alex Kotlowitz's *There Are No Children Here*, Coleman McCarthy's *I'd Rather Teach Peace*, and Fred Kammer's *Doing FaithJustice* not only provide social analyses for our students to learn from, but they also offer models of morally engaged scholarship.[12] Students, in turn, become morally engaged scholars. Recently, in a course called "Christian Vocation," fourth-year students composed faith-informed social analyses of their home communities, then added pages to their spiritual autobiographies in which they documented how their future vocations might foster conditions that would help people in those communities to live more abundantly.

What students imagine for their futures, Pax Christi, a student-led human rights organization, gives them the chance to practice in the present. In the past few years, St. Peter's Pax Christi students have participated in voter education programs, conducted voter registration drives, and in the aftermath of September 11, facilitated dialogues with faculty members from a nearby Islamic school. Pax Christi members have also coordinated activities addressing the civil rights of homosexuals on our campus, in the Catholic Church generally, and throughout the New York-New Jersey region. On one recent Good Friday, students and faculty participated in a Stations of the Cross that began at the United Nations and ended in Times Square. That same year, students and faculty made St. Peter's Prep a gathering place for Journey of Hope, a national movement calling for the abolition of the death penalty. In these events and others, one witnesses at St. Peter's the realization of Pedro Arrupe's vision that the traditional Jesuit pedagogical approach ("transmitting packaged learning") is "yielding ground to a pedagogy of dialogue in which the student takes an active part in educating himself."[13]

AN EXCURSUS: CONNECTING SPIRITUALITY AND SOCIAL JUSTICE
(STEPHEN SPIEWAK, MICHAEL MONTELEONE, AND DREW SHEERAN)

The world became smaller on September 11, 2001. St. Peter's sits two Jersey City blocks from Exchange Place. Only a narrow bend in the Hudson River separates our neighborhood from the World Trade Center, which means that St. Peter's students and faculty were able to watch as two jetliners crashed into the towers that rose like twin American stelae—and where many of our friends and family members worked. In the weeks that followed, our varied responses testified to lives marked by grief, gratitude, hope, and commitment to create anew our neighborhood. The 2001–2002 school year became a time (as the *Spiritual Exercises* would have it) for examination, prayer, conversion, contemplation of divine love, and social transformation. On our best days, St. Peter's contributed (and continues to contribute) to reconstructing social conditions in which our friends and neighbors will flourish.

In the immediate aftermath of September 11, the most striking expressions of the Jesuit charism of care were the school's call for prayer, its advocacy work, and various social and political activities aimed at building peace. In early October 2001, the St. Peter's community took some important steps toward realizing this particular charism. The horrific events of September 11 had instigated among students and staff a predictable but regrettable anti-Arab backlash. In the days that followed September 11, the silence we experienced as we waited for news of our loved ones was replaced by argumentation and accusation. Students who "looked Middle Eastern" (whatever that means) disappeared from view as much as possible. During the weeks following September 11, the poster on the gymnasium's doors intentionally expressed the rage that many of us felt: "Show No Mercy."

The members of Pax Christi quickly recognized what was happening, how we were being swept up into the cycle of violence. We listened closely to each other's grief, and we realized that grief needed expression and consciences needed information. Pax Christi thus planned a morning prayer service in the same courtyard where we witnessed the horror. Shortly thereafter, we contacted an Islamic high school, a sister school in Jersey City, inviting a teacher and the principal to speak at a symposium for students, faculty, staff, and parents. They gladly accepted our invitation.

Our Muslim guests spoke with passion and compassion, enabling those in attendance that day to contrast the core beliefs of Islam with the tenets of militant Islamic fundamentalism. Nevertheless, some students found it difficult to accept our guests' condemnation of terrorism and their factual assertions about Muslims who died in the attack. We wish that we could write that we experienced a conversion that day. We did not. The lust for revenge persisted for many of us, yet the wisdom and courage of our guests began for us a long academic year of self-examination. Consequently, a growing number in the St. Peter's Prep community confessed through our grief that there was much about the world we did not know.

In the coming months, St. Peter's sponsored brutally honest forums on the history of the Middle East, Afghanistan, and United States foreign policy, and our liturgical calendar became filled with interfaith prayer services and memorial masses. Pax Christi, along with St. Peter's campus ministry, raised prayers in Arabic, Hebrew, and English. Each time we gathered to break bread or pray together, we formed our consciences and turned hearts hardened by terror into hearts that asked what we might do so that such things would not happen again. Such questions were not easy to ask. We quickly discovered that engaging in dialogue across cultures is hard to do, especially in the face of escalating violence in the Middle East and elsewhere.

A Peace Walk

Since 1982, Pax Christi Metro New York has been carrying a message of peace to the busy streets of Manhattan on the most solemn day of the Christian calendar. Over the last several years, St. Peter's Pax Christi chapter has led the prayers, reading, and reflection at one of the Stations of the Cross during that annual Good Friday march. Facing a crowd of several hundred persons—pilgrims, bystanders, and curious pedestrians—St. Peter's students have addressed social injustices such as the death penalty, militarism, and the objectification of women. The importance of the day stretches beyond the public display of efforts for social justice, for the Peace Walk enables St. Peter's students to make connections with other religious persons and communities in the New York metropolitan area who share common goals of working for peace and justice.

The Peace Walk is set against the backdrop of a fast-paced city. The large, flatbed truck that serves as our stage often blocks motor and pedestrian traffic alike. The marchers carrying crosses and raising hymns collide with holiday shoppers and sidewalk vendors. Our presence is not welcomed. We are clearly seen as an inconvenience, and we draw strange stares. At an adolescent age when anxieties about embarrassment run wild, we confront our involvement in Pax Christi through the eyes of cynical bystanders. At the same time, we wonder if we are living in a culture that claims to be spiritually hungry yet refrains from embracing a socially responsible faith.

The Stations close with a silent protest at the entrance to a military museum near the New York City harbor. New York's finest come and arrest some of our colleagues. (Among them over the years have been well-known figures such as Daniel Berrigan and John Dear). On a Good Friday afternoon, they are carried away for doing what the outsider from Nazareth did.

AN EXCURSUS: *CURA PERSONALIS*—
REFLECTIONS FROM A HINDU PERSPECTIVE (KAPIL VERMA)

What could high school students possibly know about social justice? After all, is not an issue of such profundity reserved for discussions on elite university campuses? My experience at St. Peter's has made it clear to me that this is not the case at all; teenagers do in fact have the capacity to form critical judgments about complex social issues. One need only observe a junior-year religion course to see students debate issues as diverse as homosexual civil rights, urban gentrification, and the Israeli-Palestinian conflict. Moreover, campus organizations such as Pax Christi seek to foster open discussions about issues that hold global significance.

Nonetheless, while members of Pax Christi organize numerous forums and events, they remain a small fraction of the school community. And even though the primary educational objective of St. Peter's is to form men who understand God's love to include the "least" in our world, the curriculum does not always succeed in realizing this goal. During the first semester of my junior year, I learned about social inequality, especially the issue of homelessness. We received pages of statistics to digest and analyze, and were assigned novels to read and be quizzed on. But even though teachers encouraged us to work for social equality, the opportunities to practice what we were taught were insufficient. Teenagers need to see to believe. It is therefore crucial that students be able to see the persons who comprise the statistics, not just read about them. Furthermore, the pursuit of social justice must be made an ongoing process. While immersion trips are useful, service participation rarely continues beyond them. Too often students think their responsibilities have been fulfilled once the required service hours have been completed.

Ideally the St. Peter's faculty would establish programs that provide their students with more opportunities to work directly with the poor on issues such as affordable housing, job training, and neighborhood economic development. Too often students feel that they have nothing in common with their neighbors who are least advantaged. Most of us have been raised with many things simply handed to us. We have therefore misplaced the moral imagination that makes empathy possible. Rather than study homeless people statistically or do social analyses from the distance of the classroom, why not engage us more fully and frequently in work with nongovernmental organizations based in poor communities?

My parents learned Hinduism from their parents and grandparents, and have in turn taught its fundamental tenets to me. I am no expert in it, yet I do have a faith that enables me to form judgments regarding social justice. That faith informs both my appreciation for and frustration with the practice of *cura personalis* at St. Peter's. The Hindu notion of *karma*—the process of actions with ensuing consequences—holds particular relevance for my thinking about social justice. When we as human beings perform deeds that demonstrate respect for all human life, we may receive the ultimate reward of *moksha*, or liberation from the continuous cycle of rebirth. Hinduism further teaches that those who have the means to be heard must use their status to improve the conditions of others. Consequently, Hinduism has taught me that it is the duty—the *dharma*—of the privileged to protect and love all other people.

The pursuit of social justice is indeed active at St. Peter's. However, in order for the school to realize more effectively the spirituality of *cura personalis* (and thus its commitment to form men for and with others), further steps must be taken to locate learning outside the classroom and in the world—the world into which St. Peter's men will eventually be loosed.

The Contemplation of Divine Love: Spirituality and Education for Justice

We return to the questions with which we began: Who is Jesus of Nazareth? Who do you say you are? The formation of young men for and with others through an ethic of care demands that teachers and students engage in a process of conscientization: seeing, judging, acting, and evaluating social realities in light of the gospel of God in Jesus Christ. Secondary education defined by an ethic of care must include direct experiences (seeing) of the poverty and powerlessness of homeless families, slum dwellers, and "downsized" workers. The praxis of *cura personalis* makes the classroom into a space where students deliberate about (judge) social injustice in light of the gospel. Judgment, the contemplation of divine love, charges a student's moral imagination to act in ways that foster just living, not just subsistence living. This same moral imagination allows students to evaluate what they have seen and what they have done, and immerse themselves once again in God's gritty world.

A commitment to this process makes special demands on faculty members, but these demands are not without their reward. Marianne Conway, who teaches at the Fordham University Preparatory School, reminds us that teachers grounded in *cura personalis* will embody the aspirations of the Jesuit *Ratio Studiorum*. These teachers, writes Conway, "are commissioned to pray for each of their students, to be mindful of the different gifts in each of their students, to temper justice with mercy—gentle reminders, each one, that every student in every one of our classrooms deserves to be cared for as an individual with a unique story and unique needs, difficulties, and gifts."[14] When students encounter this sort of divine love around a seminar table or on an extended retreat, they are enabled to contemplate such love given for them. At its best, the consolation consequent to the contemplation of divine love carries them into conversion and disposes their hearts for the praxis of God's preferential option for the poor. In sum, they become evangelical subjects for social transformation. And like Ignatius, they learn to pray:

> Take, Lord, and receive all my liberty,
> my memory, my understanding,
> and my entire will, all that I have and possess.
> You have given all to me. To you, O God,
> now I return it. All is yours, dispose of it
> wholly according to your will. Give me your
> love and your grace, for this is sufficient for me.[15]

Notes

1. John W. O'Malley, *The First Jesuits* (Cambridge, Mass.: Harvard University Press, 1993), 175.
2. Ibid., 182ff.
3. Ibid., 168.
4. Ibid., 212.
5. The contemporary mission of the Jesuits took formal shape in 1974–75 during the Thirty-Second Congregation, a meeting of Jesuit representatives from around the world. The Thirty-Second Congregation defined the modern Jesuit mission as faith in Christ Jesus that moves the Jesuit apostolate to proclaim the gospel, promote justice, and enter into solidarity with people whose voices are discounted.
6. O'Malley, *First Jesuits*, 37.
7. Ignatius of Loyola, *The Spiritual Exercises of St. Ignatius: Based on Studies in the Language of the Autograph* (trans. Louis J. Puhl; Chicago: Loyola University Press, 1951), 1.
8. See Richard Rodriguez, *Hunger of Memory: The Education of Richard Rodriguez: An Autobiography* (New York: Bantam Books, 1983).
9. Pedro Arrupe, *Justice with Faith Today* (St. Louis: Institute of Jesuit Sources, 1980), 137.
10. Ignatius of Loyola, *Spiritual Exercises*, 101.
11. For a consideration of this idea as articulated by Latin American provincials, see Alfred T. Hennelly, *Liberation Theology: A Documentary History* (Maryknoll, N.Y.: Orbis, 1990), 77ff.
12. See Alex Kotlowitz, *There Are No Children Here: The Story of Two Boys Growing Up in the Other America* (New York: Anchor, 1992); Coleman McCarthy, *I'd Rather Teach Peace* (Maryknoll, N.Y.: Orbis, 2002); and Fred Kammer, *Doing FaithJustice: An Introduction to Catholic Social Thought* (New York: Paulist Press, 1991).
13. Arrupe, *Justice with Faith Today*, 166.
14. Marianne Conway, "The Jesuit Ethic of Care," a paper presented in February 2001 at the Conference on Faith and Learning (as part of the Rhodes Consultation, sponsored by the Lilly Endowment), St. Peter's Preparatory School, Jersey City, N.J.
15. Ignatius of Loyola, *Spiritual Exercises*, 102.

CONTRIBUTORS

GERALD J. BIESECKER-MAST is associate professor of communication at Bluffton University in Bluffton, Ohio.

RICHARD D. CRANE is a lecturer in theology at Messiah College in Grantham, Pennsylvania.

LISA D. MAUGANS DRIVER is assistant professor of church history and director of mentoring at the Center for Church Vocations at Valparaiso University in Valparaiso, Indiana.

RETA HALTEMAN FINGER is assistant professor of New Testament at Messiah College in Grantham, Pennsylvania.

KENT IRA GROFF is the founding mentor of Oasis Ministries for Spiritual Development in Camp Hill, Pennsylvania, and adjunct professor of Christian spirituality at Lancaster Theological Seminary in Lancaster, Pennsylvania.

BRAD J. KALLENBERG is associate professor of religious studies at the University of Dayton in Dayton, Ohio.

AARON KERR is an ordained United Methodist elder and a candidate for the Ph.D. in systematic theology at Duquesne University in Pittsburgh, Pennsylvania.

C. NORMAN KRAUS is professor emeritus of religion at Goshen College in Goshen, Indiana.

L. ROGER OWENS is a graduate student in theology at Duke University in Durham, North Carolina.

RAYMOND H. REIMER earned his doctorate in biblical studies from Princeton Theological Seminary and currently teaches at North American

Baptist Seminary in Sioux Falls, South Dakota, and Associated Mennonite Biblical Seminary in Elkhart, Indiana.

DAVID RENSBERGER is professor of New Testament at the Interdenominational Theological Center in Atlanta.

DOMINIC P. SCIBILIA is on the religion faculty at St. Peter's Preparatory School in Jersey City, New Jersey. His essay was coauthored with six St. Peter's students, now graduated: Roberto Concepcion Jr. (Cooper Union, New York City), Michael Monteleone (University of Chicago), Drew Sheeran (Georgetown University), Robert Simone (New York University), Stephen Spiewak (Loyola University, Chicago), and Kapil Verma (Columbia University).

J. ALEXANDER SIDER received his doctorate in theology and ethics in 2004 from Duke University in Durham, North Carolina.

RANDI SIDER-ROSE is a Ph.D. candidate in theology at the University of Chicago Divinity School and paints icons with the Iconography Institute of Mt. Angel Abbey in St. Benedict, Oregon.

WILLIAM R. SUTTON teaches American history at University Laboratory High School in Urbana, Illinois, and with his family spends spring breaks with the Coahoma County Habitat for Humanity affiliates.

J. DENNY WEAVER is professor of religion at Bluffton University in Bluffton, Ohio.

DAVID L. WEAVER-ZERCHER is associate professor of American religious history and chair of the Department of Biblical and Religious Studies at Messiah College in Grantham, Pennsylvania.

WILLIAM H. WILLIMON is bishop of the North Alabama Conference of the United Methodist Church, where he leads the ministry of over eight hundred churches. For twenty years he was dean of the chapel and professor of Christian ministry at Duke University in Durham, North Carolina.

RICK L. WILLIAMSON is professor of religion and chaplain for adult and graduate students at Mount Vernon Nazarene University in Mount Vernon, Ohio.

INDEX

Abraham, 17, 51–52, 120, 150, 159, 171–72

Acts, book of the

        2:42–47   191–92

        6:1–4   193–95

Advent, 175

African-American Christianity, 10 n. 23, 145, 174, 219–22

agape. *See* love

agape meals. *See* communal meals

Al Qaeda, 133

Ambrose, 39

Amos, book of

        5:21–24   1

Anabaptism, viii, 36, 81, 84, 120, 197

Anglicanism, 167, 179–80, 183

        conflict with Methodism, 179–81

Anselm, 55–56, 181

anthropological holism, 73, 84 n. 8

anthropology, theological, 27, 32–33, 73, 79, 103–5

        Hebrew understandings of, 24, 35 n. 32

apartheid, 151, 71 n. 31, 176 n. 18

apocalyptism, 70 n. 6, 92, 96, 99, 100 n. 20

Arendt, Hannah, 86 n. 35

Aristides, 81

Aristotle, 15–17, 130

Arrupe, Pedro, 228, 232

ascesis, 107–8, 110–11

asceticism, 25, 44

Asterius of Amaseia, 102–6, 110–11, 112 n. 4

Athanasius of Alexandria, 107, 112 n. 4, 160

atonement, 49–50

        Christus Victor, 53–57, 58 n. 9

        penal substitutionary, 55

        satisfaction view, 55–56, 58 n. 10

Augustine, 16, 32, 72–74, 79, 86 n. 30

Aulén, Gustaf, 58. n. 9

autobiographies, spiritual, 232

baptism, 64, 69, 82–83, 86 n. 38, 106–10, 208, 228

Babylonain exile, 51

Barth, Karl, 14, 21 n. 4, 141

Basil of Caesarea, 103, 106, 108–12, 112 n. 3, 112 n. 4, 114 n. 43, 114 n. 45

Bass, Dorothy, 6, 10 n. 19

beatitudes, the, 169, 173

beauty, 145, 154–55, 153 n. 21, 160–61, 165

Beecher, Henry Ward, 216

Bell, Daniel, 204

Berger, Peter, 34 n. 18

Bernard of Clairvaux, 49–50

Berrigan, Daniel, 234

Bible reading, 6, 38, 148–49, 182, 184

Boesak, Allan , 176 n. 18

Bonhoeffer, Dietrich, 151

Book of Common Prayer, 180

Borg, Marcus, 46 n. 7

Brevint, Daniel, 179
Buber, Martin, 85 n. 20, 115
Budde, Michael, 68, 71 n. 31
Bush, George W., 22 n. 15, 134

Calvin, John, 29, 151
capital punishment, 54, 232, 234
capitalism, 15, 67, 127, 133–34, 203–5, 207,
    214–17
        divisiveness of, 204–5
        enlightened, 212
Cappadocians, 105–6, 109, 111, 112 n. 4, 116,
    122, 181. *See also* Gregory of Nyssa;
    Gregory of Nazianzus; Basil of Caesarea
care, ethic of. *See* Jesuits, ethic of care
Carnegie, Andrew, 215–16
catechesis, 107–9
Catherine of Genoa, 178
Catholic Workers, 151, 196–98
Catholicism, Roman, 6, 10 n. 26, 178, 225–37.
    See also Jesuits
Chafer, Lewis Sperry, 26–28, 34 n. 10
Chalcedon, Creed of, 60
Chambers, Oswald, 147
charity, 17, 39–40, 75, 134, 183, 209–10
chastity, 72
Chickasaw, Indians, 217
Chittister, Joan, 6
Christ. *See* Jesus Christ.
Christology, 122–24. *See also* Jesus Christ
Christus Victor. *See* atonement, Christus Victor
Church, the, 7, 16, 20, 63–64, 117, 123, 136
        as alternative community, 20, 62, 64–66,
           69, 82–84
        as body of Christ, 4, 37, 64–65, 76–77,
           142, 178, 185, 190, 199 n. 5
        mission of, 23–24, 27–29, 52, 57–59, 62,
           82, 178
        nature of, 59, 62, 71 n. 19
        as temple of Holy Spirit, 76
        witness of, 52–53, 82, 87 n. 46
civil rights movement, 146, 174, 217, 219
Civil War, 26, 133, 149, 218
Clapp, Rodney, vii, 9 n. 6, 67
Clement of Alexandria, 181
communal meals, 190–97, 199 n. 1
communism, 215–17
Constantine, 51

consumerism, 59, 67–68, 102, 112, 204–5, 209,
    214–15
contemplation, 73, 82, 144, 148–52, 154,
    163–65, 225, 233, 236
conversion, 227, 233
Corinthians, first letter to the
        7:17–24   96
        11:17–30   189–91
        11:17–34   177
Corinthians, second letter to the
        5:18–19   93
creation
        care for, 105
        doctrine of, 35 n. 19, 58 n. 4, 106, 117,
           156–57, 159, 164
cura personalis. See Jesuits, ethic of care
Cyril of Jerusalem, 109, 112 n. 4, 113 n. 37

Dallas Theological Seminary, 26
Day, Dorothy, 6, 36, 151, 196
Dead Sea Scrolls, 195
death penalty. *See* capital punishment
deconstruction, 128–32, 136, 137 n. 2
Denys. *See* Pseudo-Dionysius
Derrida, Jacques, 127–32, 136, 137 n. 2, 138 n.
    12
Descartes, René, 86 n. 30, 143
Didache, 195
discipleship, 4–5, 9 n. 16, 16, 49–50, 52–56,
    59–60, 62–63, 124, 178
discipline, vii, 4, 6, 10 n. 23, 22 n. 17
disciplines, spiritual, 40, 42–44, 46 n. 8,
    110–11, 165. *See also* practices, Christian
dispensationalism, 26–27, 35 n. 20
divinization, 109, 164
dualism
        body-soul, 3, 72–73, 77, 79, 86 n. 30, 142
        evangelism-social action, 23–24, 26, 31
        natural-supernatural, 23, 29–31, 34 n. 2
        philosophical (Greek), 24–25
        public-private, 29
        sacred-secular, 26, 30–31
        spirit-flesh, 24–28, 32–33
        spiritual-social, vii, 23, 27, 30
Dunn, James D.G., 4–5, 9 n. 16, 65
Dykstra, Craig, 6, 10 n. 19

Easter, 150, 207–8

Eastern Orthodoxy, 7, 10 n. 26, 71 n. 18,
102–112, 164, 181
ecclesiology. *See* Church, the
Eckhart, Meister, 72, 142, 84 n. 4
education, 107–8, 219–21
Jesuit, 225–37
Edwards, Jonathan, 213
egalitarianism, 69, 94–95
Enlightenment, the, 14, 21 n. 1, 142–43, 215
environmentalism, 145
Ephesians, letter to the
4:25–5:21 78
eschatology, 26–27, 60–61
Esquivel, Julia, 148, 151
Essenes, 61, 195
Eucharist, 83, 106–8, 113 n. 37, 177–87,
188–99, 208–9, 228
as command, 182
early Church practices of, 69, 71 n. 28,
83, 183, 187 n. 27, 189–90, 191–96
frequency of, 179–83
function of, 69, 71 n. 28, 181–85
as mercy, 181
social implications of, 178, 188–89,
196–99
as testimony, 182
Evangelicals for Social Action, 31
evangelism, 27, 29–31, 34 n. 2
examen, daily, 146
Explo '72, 34 n. 10

fall, the, 58 n. 4, 71 n. 26, 87 n. 46, 104–7, 121
fasting, 110–11, 145, 149–50, 154
fertility, 170, 172
flesh, 24–25, 28, 64, 142
as evil, 25, 27, 77, 203, 211 n. 3
renunciation of, 25
footwashing, 200 n. 37
forgiveness, 81–82, 101 n. 34, 131, 185,
219–20
Fosdick, Harry Emerson, 168
Foster, Richard, 10 n. 22
Foucault, Michel, 127
Francis of Assisi, 36, 75–76, 167, 178
Frankl, Victor, 147, 152 n. 15
free will, 54–55, 104–5
friendship, 70 n. 2, 105, 130–31, 138 n. 12, 227
Fuller, Millard, 219

fundamentalism
Christian, 26–31, 34 n. 2, 34 n. 17
Islamic, 134, 233

Galatians, letter to the
1:3–5 202
3:26–28 94–95
3:28 64, 203
6:14–18 76
Gardner, Howard, 144–45
Genesis, book of
1 105
18 159
Gentiles. *See* Jew-Gentile tensions
geometric order, 159–61
globalization, 127, 133–34
Gnosticism, 25, 33
God
as all-seeing Other, 130
as Beauty, 155
domestication of, 121
grace of, 55, 181–83
hiddenness of, 115, 120, 124, 130
immanence of, 32, 122
immortality of, 106
judgment of, 213
kingdom of, 4–5, 9 n. 17, 13, 16, 29, 33,
41, 50, 53–54, 57–62, 126, 165, 208
love of, 38–42, 45, 94, 144, 146
nearness of, 118, 122
transcendence of, 24, 32, 120, 122
violence of, 120–21
Good Friday, 232, 234
grace, responsible, 184
Graham, Billy, 26
Graham, Franklin, 23, 31
greed, 17, 105
Gregory of Nazianzus, 104–5, 111, 112 n. 4
Gregory of Nyssa, 25, 110–11, 112 n. 4, 116,
122–24
Gutiérrez, Gustavo, 6, 211 n. 4

Habitat for Humanity, 214, 217, 219–22
Hall, Tony, 150
Hammarskjöld, Dag, 153 n. 31
Hauerwas, Stanley, 14, 19–20, 21 n. 9, 112 n. 5,
125 n. 28
heaven, 24, 29, 83, 99, 117, 142, 179, 183

Hellenists, 83, 193–94

Henry, Carl F. H., 30–31, 35 n. 23

Heschel, Abraham, 146

hierarchy, 116–19, 121

Hinduism, 234–35

Holland, Scott, 120–22

Holy Face, the (icon), 160–61

Holy Spirit, the

    baptism of, 65

    fruit of, 33

    gifts of, 28, 35 n. 20, 199 n. 5

    healing power of, 93–94, 219

    relational metaphors for, 85 n. 14

    as Third Person of Trinity, 74

    work of, 65, 81

Holy Trinity, the (icon), 150, 158–59

homelessness, 198, 230–31, 235

homosexuality, 232, 234

hospitality, 6, 110, 129, 132, 145, 150–51, 159, 197

human rights, 9 n. 13, 38, 150, 216, 232

humanity. See also anthropology, theological

    fallen nature of, 104–5, 111

    in image of God, 32–34, 103–4, 111, 181, 183

humility, 81, 146, 150, 170–71

hunger, 145, 150, 173

Hunter, James Davison, 31, 35 n. 25

hymnody, 8, 167–68, 170, 174–75, 179–80

iconography, 154–66

icons

    aesthetic characteristics of, 157–65

    as material pointers, 155–57

    as mediating objects, 156

    as transparent windows, 156

    veneration of, 154–57

idolatry, 156–57

Ignatius of Antioch, 117, 195

Ignatius of Loyola, 146, 225–26, 236

image of God. See humanity, in image of God

incarnation. See Jesus Christ, incarnation of

individualism, 68, 73, 79, 142, 192

inerrancy, biblical, 27

intelligences, multiple, 144–45

interfaith dialogue, 233

interiority, 72–73

inverse perspective, 157–59, 163

Iona Community, 175

Irenaeus of Lyons, 107, 119

Isaiah, book of

    58:9–10   222

Islam, 19–20, 22 n. 15, 23–24, 50, 133, 232–33

Israel

    oppression of, 171

    people of , 51–52, 119

James, book of

    2:26   188

James, William, 14

Jenkins, Dorothy, 220–22, 224 n. 35

Jesuits, 225–36, 237 n. 5

    educational practices of, 226–36

    ethic of care, 226–29, 231, 234–36

Jesus Christ

    birth of, 25, 170–73, 175

    communication of, 184

    death of, 53, 55, 63, 70 n. 9, 91, 187 n. 27

    divinity of, 60, 103, 163

    as head of Church

    humanity of, 60, 103, 163

    incarnation of, 76, 104, 106–7, 126, 142, 156, 159–61, 164

    as Messiah, 52, 136

    ministry of, 4–5, 52, 61, 169

    as model, 1, 60, 65–66

    nonviolence of, 19, 50, 53, 120

    parables of, 13, 18, 21, 41, 61–62, 148

    resurrection of, 20, 53, 65, 74, 164, 207

    teaching of, 4–5, 13, 18, 36, 41–42, 50–51, 229

    union with, 63–64, 71 n. 18

    wisdom of, 163–64

Jew-Gentile tensions, 64, 97, 169, 193–95

John, book of

    14:6   151

John Chrysostom, 106

John of Damascus, 156

John Paul II, 161, 164, 207–210

Jordan, Clarence, 219

Josephus, 195

journaling, 148–49, 184, 229

justice

    biblical references to, 18, 38

    as Church's mission, 20, 52–53, 169

    in contrast to love, 15, 26, 33

    definitions of, 4, 9 n. 13, 15–17, 19, 21, 38

of God, 33
    Reinhold Niebuhr's view of, 15, 21 n. 10
justification by faith, 63

Kaiser, Christopher, 28–29, 34 n. 17, 34 n. 18
Kant, Immanuel, 13–14, 17, 21 n. 1
Kennan, George, 216
Kenneson, Phil, 203–5
King Jr., Martin Luther, 36, 217
kingdom of God. *See* God, kingdom of
kin-groups, 192, 195–96
Ku Klux Klan, 133

labor. *See* work
Lacan, Jacques, 127, 132
language, 73–79, 132, 145
    as communal practice, 81, 85 n. 21
    limitations of, 74, 85 n. 10, 116, 118–19
lectio divina, 148
Lent, 149
Levinas, Emmanuel, 128, 132
liberation theology, 231
Lord's Prayer, 142
Lord's Supper. *See* Eucharist, the
love, 5, 23, 82, 97, 105, 135. *See also* God, love of
    in contrast to justice, 15, 26, 33
    for enemies, 41, 43, 86 n. 31, 130
    for God, 38–39, 42–45, 128, 146, 152
    for neighbor, 128, 130, 134–35, 146, 152,
        183, 203
Luckmann, Thomas, 34 n. 18
Luke, book of, 168–75
    1:46–55   170–71
    1:67–79   171–72
    2:13–14   172–73
    2:28–35   173–74
    4   52
    4:18–19   52, 61, 83, 169
    24:30–31   184, 199
Luther, Martin, 16, 63, 70 n. 14, 82, 86 n. 38, 167

MacIntyre, Alasdair, 9 n. 13, 10 n. 19, 17, 68,
    82, 86 n. 38
mammon, 213
Mark, book of
    12:28–31   36
    12:30–31   43
Marx, Karl, 3
Mary, 25, 162–64, 170–75

virginity of, 170
materialism, 16–17, 217
Matthew, book of
    5:8   123
    6:9–13   142
    12:22–29   60
    18:15–20   83
    20   21
    20:8–16   18
    22:37–39   1
    25   111–12, 184, 197, 225
    25:31–46   150–51
    25:40   66–67, 161
Maximus the Confessor, 116, 122
meditation, 38, 226. *See also* contemplation
Mennonites. *See* Anabaptism
Merton, Thomas, 6, 73
messianic age, 61, 129–30
Methodism, 22 n. 15, 167, 179–81, 184, 186 n.
    16, 215–16. *See also* Anglicanism
Micah, book of
    6:6–8   1
    6:8   2, 10 n. 18, 33
Middle East, 19, 233–34
Milbank, John, 64, 71 n. 19, 137 n. 1, 138 n. 12
miracles, 30, 34 n. 17, 35 n. 20
modernity, 67, 78
Moody, D. L., 26
Mosaic Law, 61
Moses, 44, 123, 171, 174
Mother Teresa, 75
Muhammad, 19
Murphy, Nancey, 31–32, 35 n. 32
Murray, Andrew, 27, 34 n. 15
music. *See* hymnody

narcissism, 59, 68
negative theology, 116–122
Neoplatonism, 24–25, 32–33, 79, 86 n. 30, 154,
    165
New Age spirituality. *See* spirituality, New Age
new birth, 30, 35 n. 20
new creation, 62, 65, 76, 85 n. 16, 134, 136, 207
Nicea, 155
Nicholas of Cusa, 159
Niebuhr, Reinhold, 14–15, 21 n. 10, 82
Nikephoros, 156–57, 159
nonviolence, 9 n. 17, 19, 53–54, 96–97, 120–22,
    137

Nouwen, Henri, 6

oppression, 62, 66, 71 n. 31, 213–19, 222
order, divine, 159–60
Origen, 25, 123
Orthodoxy. *See* Eastern Orthodoxy
orthopraxis, 178, 187 n. 36
Osama bin Laden, 133

pacifism. *See* nonviolence
panentheism, 32, 35 n. 28
parables. *See* Jesus Christ, parables of
paradox, 55, 57, 119, 131, 136
Paul, 62–67, 76–77, 91–99, 116, 123, 134–35,
        142, 189–91, 199, 202–3, 228
        conversion of, 97
        as peacemaker, 92, 96–99
        as persecutor of church, 97
Pax Christi, 232–35
peace, 15, 38, 172–73, 175
        through Christ, 93
        definitions of, 96
        Pauline understandings of, 92–96, 99
Pentecost, 78, 171, 207–8
Pentecostalism, 27, 34 n. 10, 35 n. 20, 216
Perfection, 101 n. 36, 104, 110, 123, 216
person, doctrine of. *See* anthropology, theological
Peter, 53, 78, 98, 113 n. 37, 148, 171
Pharisees, 61
Philippians, letter to the
        2:5–11   70 n.13, 101 n. 34
Philo, 195
Plato, 15, 79–80, 82, 128, 154
pleonasm, 118
Plotinus, 154–55, 161, 165
Plymouth Brethren, 26–27
poor, the, 5, 9 n. 16, 17, 39, 66–67, 143, 161,
        168–69, 173, 185, 192
        encountering God in, 184, 196–97
        God's option for, 213
        solidarity wth, 196
postmodernity, 137 n. 1, 144, 206, 217
poverty, 17, 143, 152 n. 3, 169
powers, the, 53, 55, 60, 65–67, 69, 71 n. 26, 136,
        202–4
practices, Christian, 8, 20, 38, 43–44, 67, 69,
        80–84
        characteristics of, 6, 82

definition of, 6
        purpose of, 6, 67
prayer, 28, 40, 141–53, 229, 236
        definition of, 144
        practice of, 145–51
principalities. *See* powers, the
producerism, 214–15
prophetic tradition (Hebrew), 1, 36, 62, 168, 171
Protestantism, 6–7, 10 n. 22, 10 n. 23, 34 n. 2,
        55–56, 63, 68, 70 n. 16, 71 n. 18, 178, 184–85
interest in spirituality, 6, 10 n. 27
Psalms, book of the
        145:8–11   41
Pseudo-Dionysius, 116–23, 125 n. 16
Psychoanalysis, 132
Puritanism, 209, 216

Quakers, 10 n. 22, 145, 148–49, 152, 153 n. 25
Qur'an, 19

racism, 66, 69, 133, 202, 215, 217–19, 232
realism, artistic, 157–59, 163
recapitulation theology, 107
reconciliation, 62–65, 83, 96–97, 121, 131, 151,
        181
        with God, 93–94
        with neighbor, 67, 81, 83, 94–95
        racial, 69, 219–20
Reconstruction, 218
Reformed Christianity, 58 n. 4, 174, 180. *See*
        also Calvin, John
reign of God. *See* God, kingdom of
Reimer, A. James, 120–22
retreats, spiritual, 226–28
rich, the. *See* wealth
righteousness, 33, 63–64, 77–80, 175
        economic, 213–17
        and justice, 18, 29, 93, 95, 168
        of God, 16, 18, 64, 99
Rodriguez, Richard, 228
Roman Catholicism. *See* Catholicism, Roman
Roman Empire, 53, 96, 171, 192
Romans, book to the
        8   93
        8:8–11   77–78
        12   66, 85 n. 18
        12:1   202
        12:14–21   95

Romero, Oscar, 6, 36
Rublev, Andrei, 150, 158–59

Sabbath-keeping, 201–11
    as alternative to market, 209–11
    as break from production, 209
    popular treatments of, 205–8
    as refreshment, 201, 206–7
    as school for discipleship, 207–10
    and solidarity with poor, 209–10
    and works of mercy, 209–10
    and worship, 208–9
sacraments. *See* baptism; Eucharist
Sadducees, 61
saints, transfiguration of, 163–64
salvation, 23–25, 54–57, 60, 62–68, 71 n. 18, 173, 181–82, 187 n. 27, 210
sanctification, 64–67, 168, 181–83
Satan, 53–55, 60–61, 70 n. 6, 96, 109
Scofield, Cyrus I., 26
scripture reading. *See* Bible reading
secularism, 28–30, 34 n. 17, 34 n. 18
secularity, biblical, 28–29, 34 n. 17, 34 n. 18
September 11 (2001), 17, 133–35, 143, 146, 222, 232–33
Seraphin, 73
Sermon on the Mount, 120
Sermon on the Plain, 173
Seventh Ecumenical Council, 155, 164
sexual immorality, 63, 101 n. 31
shalom, 62, 92
Sheldon, Charles, 59
Shema, the, 145–46
Sider, Ronald J., 31
silence, 43, 145–47, 149, 153 n. 25
Simeon, 173–75
simplicity, 102, 110–12, 149–50
sin, 54–56, 64, 126, 187 n. 27, 202–3
singing. *See* hymnody
slavery, 3, 71 n. 31, 83, 92, 149, 153 n. 25, 215, 218
Sobrino, John, 231
social Darwinism, 215–16
social gospel, the, 30, 34 n. 2, 213, 216
Society of Jesus. *See* Jesuits
Socrates, 79–80
Sojourners Community, 31
Sophists, 79

soteriology. *See* salvation; atonement
spirit (the word)
    English uses of, 75–76
    Greek uses of, 76–79
spirit of God. *See* Holy Spirit
spiritual gifts. *See* Holy Spirit, gifts of
spirituality
    as corporate endeavor, 4, 7, 9 n. 12, 37, 43, 57–58, 67–68, 77–79, 84
    as essence of faith, 1, 42
    incarnational, 142–43, 145–46
    as inward reality, 2, 9 n. 6, 72–73, 115
    New Age, 40, 134
    primodern, 142–44, 147–48
    privatization of, vii, 3, 56, 59
    as relational experience, 37–39, 42–45, 49, 56, 212–13
    trivialization of, vii, 14, 59, 68, 115
    understandings of, 2, 4, 8 n. 1, 9 n. 5, 9 n. 12, 27–28, 33, 37–38, 137, 212–13
spirituals, African-American, 145, 174
Stations of the Cross, 232, 234
Stevens, Thaddeus, 218
Stott, John R. W., 31
stylized naturalism, 161–64
suffering, 17, 61–62, 69, 70 n. 13, 105–6, 147, 168, 171, 190

table fellowship, 188–99, 221–22
Talbot, John Michael, 220., 224 n. 31
terrorism, 137, 233
    war on, 20, 22 n. 15, 204
theological anthropology. *See* anthropology, theological
Thurman, Howard, 147
Tillich, Paul, 35 n. 28
Tracy, David, 32
Trinity, the, 14, 38, 74, 107, 120, 150, 158–59
Truth and Reconciliation Committee, 151
Turner, Denys, 119, 124 n. 13
Tutu, Desmond, 36, 151

Underhill, Evelyn, 141–42

Vatican II, 232
veneration. *See* icons, veneration of
violence, 9 n. 17, 38, 51, 53, 58 n. 10, 62, 96–97, 133–34, 217, 233

of God, 120–22
virgin birth, 25, 35 n. 19, 162
Virgin of Vladimir (icon), 162–64
virginity, 25
vocation, 26–27, 58 n. 4, 227, 230–32

Warfield, Benjamin B., 23, 34 n. 1
wealth, 39, 102–3, 105–6, 113 n. 16, 190–92,
    195, 199 n. 2, 213–16
Wesley, Charles, 167–68, 178–186
Wesley, John, 29, 151, 167–68, 178–86, 187 n.
    36, 215
Wesleyan movement, 29, 178–79
Westminster Confession, 16
Williams, Rowan, 122–23
Wink, Walter, 9 n. 17

Wittgenstein, Ludwig, 81, 85 n. 10
women, role of, 50, 92, 169, 193–97
Woolman, John, 149, 153 n. 25
work, 205–10, 212–17, 220. *See also* Sabbath-
    keeping
works righteousness, 6, 10 n. 22, 63, 66, 79
World Vision, 31
worship, corporate, 57, 177, 185, 191, 208–9.
    See also Eucharist; hymnody
Wycliffe, John, 36

Yoder, John Howard, 51, 58 n. 8, 60, 69, 82–84
Youth for Christ, 34 n. 10

Zechariah, 171–72, 175
Žižek, Slavoj, 127, 132–36